INSTRUCTIONS
FROM
THE CENTRE

By Christopher Andrew and Oleg Gordievsky

*KGB: The Inside Story of its Foreign Operations from
Lenin to Gorbachev*
(Hodder & Stoughton, 1990)

By Christopher Andrew
Théophile Delcassé and the Making of the Entente Cordiale
(Macmillan, 1968)

The First World War: Causes and Consequences
(Volume 19 of the *Hamlyn History of the World*, 1970)

*France Overseas: The Great War and the Climax of French
Imperial Expansion*
With A. S. Kanya-Forstner
(Thames & Hudson, 1981)

*The Missing Dimension: Governments and Intelligence Communities in the
Twentieth Century*
With David Dilks (Macmillan, 1984)

Secret Service: The Making of the British Intelligence Community
(Heinemann, 1985)

Codebreaking and Signals Intelligence
(Frank Cass, 1986)

Intelligence and International Relations, 1900–1945
With Jeremy Noakes
(Exeter University Press, 1987)

INSTRUCTIONS FROM THE CENTRE

Top Secret Files on KGB Foreign
Operations 1975–1985

Edited by

CHRISTOPHER ANDREW
and
OLEG GORDIEVSKY

Hodder & Stoughton

LONDON SYDNEY AUCKLAND TORONTO

British Library Cataloguing in Publication Data

Andrew, Christopher
   Instructions from the centre: Top secret files
   from the KGB's foreign operations, 1975–85.
   I. Title II. Gordievsky, Oleg
   327.1247

   ISBN 0-340-56650-7

Published by Hodder and Stoughton,
a division of Hodder and Stoughton Ltd,
Mill Road, Dunton Green, Sevenoaks, Kent TN13 2YA.
Editorial Office: 47 Bedford Square, London WC1B 3DP.

Photoset by Rowland Phototypesetting Ltd,
Bury St Edmunds, Suffolk.

Printed in Great Britain by
St Edmundsbury Press Ltd, Bury St Edmunds, Suffolk

Contents

Illustrations

Abbreviations

A	Active Measures
ANC	African National Congress
CCP	Chinese Communist Party
CEC	Commission of the European Community
Centre	KGB Headquarters
CIA	Central Intelligence Agency
CMEA	Council for Mutual Economic Assistance
COCOM	Coordinating Committee on Multilateral Export Controls
COMECON	Council for Mutual Economic Assistance
COREPER	EC Committee of Permanent Representatives
CSCE	Conference on Security and Cooperation in Europe
DAR	Agent Cultivation File (KGB)
DGI	Cuban Foreign Intelligence Agency
DLB	Dead Letter-Box
DM	Documentary Material (KGB)
DZK	Long-term Posting Abroad (KGB)
EC	European Community
EEC	European Economic Community
EK	Economic Section of FCD Directorate K
EM Line	Emigration Line in KGB Residencies (refounded in early 1980s; until the 1950s EM had been a subsection of the KR Line)
EPC	European Political Cooperation
EURATOM	European Atomic Energy Community
FCD	KGB First Chief Directorate
FRG	Federal Republic of Germany
GRU	Soviet Military Intelligence
Humint	Intelligence derived from human sources
ICBM	Inter-continental Ballistic Missile

ID	International Department of Soviet Communist Party Central Committee
IISS	International Institute of Strategic Studies
K Directorate	FCD Counter-Intelligence Directorate
K Line	Operations against PRC in KGB Residencies
KGB	Committee of State Security
KR Line	Counter-Intelligence Department in KGB Residencies
LLB	Live Letter-Box
MFA	Ministry of Foreign Affairs
N Line	Illegal Support Department in KGB Residencies
NATO	North Atlantic Treaty Organisation
ND	People's Democracies
OT	Operational-Technical
PC	Political Committee of EC Council of Ministers
PLA	PRC People's Liberation Army
PN	Undeveloped Negative (KGB)
POA	Permanent Operational Assignment (KGB)
PR Line	Political Intelligence Department in KGB Residencies
PRC	People's Republic of China
R Directorate	FCD Operational Planning and Analytical Directorate
RT Directorate	FCD Directorate responsible for operations inside USSR
RUSI	Royal United Services Institution
RYAN	Nuclear Missile Attack (KGB Operation)
S	*Spez*/Special
S Directorate	FCD Illegals Directorate
SDI	Strategic Defence Initiative (Star Wars)
SI	Socialist International
Sigint	Intelligence derived from intercepting, decrypting and analysing signals
Sotsintern	Socialist International
SS	Special Secretariat (FCD)
S & T	Scientific and Technical/Technological Intelligence
SW	Secret Writing
SWAPO	South West Africa People's Organisation
T Directorate	FCD Directorate responsible for S & T
tel	telegram
VM	Foreign Currency
X Line	S & T Department in KGB Residencies
Z apparatus	Bugging and surveillance equipment (KGB)

KGB Codenames of Centre Officers and Residents

ALEKSEEV	Viktor Fyodorovich GRUSHKO (as Deputy Head, FCD)
ALYOSHIN	Vladimir Aleksandrovich KRYUCHKOV
ARISTOV	Pseudonym for Secretary of FCD Third Department Communist Party Bureau
BATOV	Pseudonym for Secretary of FCD Communist Party Committee
DAVIDOV	Viktor Nikolayevich LAZIN
GORNOV	Oleg Antonovich GORDIEVSKY
IRTYSHOV	Yevgeni Izotovich SHISHKIN
KIMOV	unidentified
KORABLEV	unidentified
KORIN	Mikhail Petrovich LYUBIMOV
LARIN	Igor Viktorovich TITOV
LAVROV	Leonid Yefremovich NIKITENKO
LEBEDEV	Vadim Vasilyevich KIRPICHENKO (as Head, FCD Directorate S)
LEONOV	Leonid Yefremovich NIKITENKO
PETROV	Pseudonym used by any of the 4 Deputy Heads of Directorate S
SEVEROV	Viktor Fyodorovich GRUSHKO (as Head of FCD Third Department)
SILIN	Gennadi Fyodorovich TITOV
SVETLOV	Nikolai Petrovich GRIBIN (not to be confused with 'Svetlov' at London Residency)
SVIRIDOV	Yuri Vladimirovich ANDROPOV
VADIM	Ivan Ivanovich VIKULOV
VADIMOV	Vadim Vasilyevich KIRPICHENKO (as Deputy Head, FCD)
VLADIMIROV	Anatoli Tikhonovich KIREEV
YERMAKOV	Arkadi Vasilyevich GUK

Note. MS codenames written on documents by the Resident refer to Residency officers on the circulation list.

FORMAT OF KGB COMMUNICATIONS FROM
THE CENTRE TO RESIDENCIES

vn[1]-1[2]

No. 1234[3]/PR[4]   Top Secret

11.12.83   To Residents

We are sending you instructions on the work of sections of the Service and organisations abroad in 1984.

Attachment: As indicated in text, no. 1235/PR[5], Top Secret,
              10 pages, PN[6].
                   SILIN[7]

Manuscript notes: Comr[ade] Gornov[8]
                    Comr[ade] Fred[8]
                    Comr[ade] Brown[8]

                    Yermakov[9]
                    14.12.83

KEY:
1   Initials of typist
2   Copy number (1 in this instance)
3   Number of despatch
4   Residency Line concerned (political intelligence in this instance)
5   Number and Line of enclosure
6   Format of enclosure (undeveloped film negative in this instance)
7   Codename of Centre officer signing despatch (G. F. Titov, head of FCD Third Department)
8   Codenames of Residency officers chosen by Resident to read despatch
9   Codename of Resident (A. V. Guk)

Note on the Documents

One of the purposes of the elaborate security procedures described in the Appendices, which protect KGB files and records, is to make a volume such as this impossible. In this instance the procedures failed. Most of the top secret documents which follow were copied or photocopied by Oleg Gordievsky while serving in the KGB Residencies at Copenhagen and London. The commentary which accompanies these documents, though written by Christopher Andrew, is based on joint analysis by both Editors. We are very grateful to Dr Richard Popplewell for help with the translation of the documents.

This is a companion volume to our *KGB: The Inside Story of Its Foreign Operations from Lenin to Gorbachev*, published by Hodder & Stoughton, which draws on other KGB records to which Gordievsky had access, as well as on the material available in Western libraries and archives. A further selection of KGB documents will be published by Frank Cass in 1992.

CA

OG

Introduction

The Centre and Foreign Intelligence

The top secret documents in this volume cover the main priorities of Soviet foreign intelligence operations during the decade which culminated in the rise to power of Mikhail Sergeevich Gorbachev. The KGB, when Gorbachev became General Secretary in 1985, ran a vast security and intelligence empire with over 400,000 officers inside the Soviet Union, over 200,000 border troops and a huge network of informers. Its most prestigious arm was the First Chief (Foreign Intelligence) Directorate (FCD). Though comparatively small by KGB standards, the FCD had undergone a major expansion during the previous twenty years. In 1985 a twenty-two-storey annexe and a new eleven-storey building were added to its headquarters at Yasenevo, near the outer Moscow ring road. FCD officers multiplied from about 3,000 in the mid-1960s to 12,000 in the mid-1980s.

The fall in oil prices and the growing economic crisis in the Soviet Union denied the KGB the further hard currency it required to continue expanding its foreign operations on more than a modest scale. The prestige of the FCD, however, remained unimpaired. Gorbachev's unprecedented range of foreign policy initiatives made it vital, in his view, to have the fullest possible intelligence on Western responses to them. For the first time in Soviet history, the men who ran foreign intelligence were promoted to run the KGB. In October 1988 General Vladimir Aleksandrovich Kryuchkov, head of the FCD throughout the period covered by these documents, was made KGB Chairman.

Kryuchkov was born in 1924. He remains proud of his humble origins. 'I had nobody to prop me up,' he told an interviewer in 1991. 'My father was an ordinary worker and my mother was a housewife.'[1] Kryuchkov too began his adult life as a factory worker but took correspondence courses in the evening which enabled him to graduate from the USSR Institute of Law. According to a later television profile, 'During the postwar years of rampant crime he was employed in a provincial procurator's office.'[2] Then came what Kryuchkov calls a 'change in life': training at the Foreign Ministry's Higher Diplomatic School, followed by five years at the Soviet Embassy in Budapest (1954–9) where he witnessed the Hungarian Rising and became the protégé of the Ambassador, Yuri Vladimirovich Andropov.[3] From 1959 to 1967 he worked in the Central Committee Department for Relations with Socialist Countries, initially under Andropov. Soon after Andropov became KGB Chairman in 1967, Kryuchkov was appointed head of his secretariat and custodian of some of the KGB's most sensitive secrets. In about 1971 he moved to become deputy head of the FCD.[4] As chief of the FCD from 1974 to 1988 Kryuchkov established a reputation as a workaholic which he retained as Chairman of the KGB. He told an interviewer in 1989 that he worked fourteen to sixteen hours a day, 'And on Sundays I allow myself four to five hours off, and no more.'[5] Some of the most important of the documents which follow bear Kryuchkov's personal codename, Alyoshin.

In February 1991 Kryuchkov carried through what he called a 'somewhat unusual' reshuffle of the KGB leadership. According to *Izvestia*, the reshuffle was 'the most major of recent times'. The most important promotion was that of Viktor Fyodorovich Grushko, Kryuchkov's former deputy in the FCD, who became First Deputy Chairman of the KGB.[6] Born in 1930, Grushko was a career foreign intelligence officer. His first foreign posting was to the large KGB Residency at New Delhi from 1951 to 1954. Thereafter he served two terms in Oslo, from 1954 to 1958 and from 1962 to 1972, becoming Resident (head of station) during his last year in Norway. Soon after returning to the Centre, Grushko became head of the Third Department (responsible for operations in Britain, Ireland, Scandinavia, Australasia and Malta). In 1979 he became Deputy Head, then in 1984 First Deputy Head, of the FCD.[7] From 1990 to 1991 Grushko headed the KGB Second Chief (Counter-Intelligence) Directorate.[8]

A further important promotion in the February 1991 reshuffle of the KGB leadership was the appointment of another career foreign intelligence officer, Gennadi Fyodorovich Titov, to succeed Grushko as Head of the Second Chief Directorate.[9] Titov was a Soviet Karelian born in 1932. When he was about five or six years old, his father was shot during the Great Terror. Despite his family history, Titov was accepted for training in 1955 by the Leningrad Military Institute of the KGB. After his entry into the FCD he followed for some time in Grushko's footsteps, succeeding him first as Resident in Oslo (1972–7), then as Head of the Third Department (1979–84). In the mid-1980s Titov spent several years as Deputy Head of the KGB base at Karlshorst near East Berlin, the largest outside the Soviet Union.[10]

The codenames of Grushko (Severov or Alekseev) and Titov (Silin), like that of Kryuchkov, figure prominently in the pages which follow. This collection of documents thus provides a highly classified insight not merely into Soviet foreign intelligence operations at the dawn of the Gorbachev era but also into the thinking and conspiracy theories of the KGB leadership which set out to bring that era to an end in the attempted coup of August 1991. In March 1985 Kryuchkov had backed Gorbachev during the struggle to succeed Konstantin Chernenko as General Secretary, believing that his personal dynamism would breathe new life into the Soviet system. By the summer of 1991 he had concluded that, on the contrary, the survival of the Soviet Union and Communist rule required Gorbachev's removal from power. The coup ended, however, not in the overthrow of Gorbachev but in the arrest of Kryuchkov, Grushko and the other leading plotters, and in the end of the Communist era.

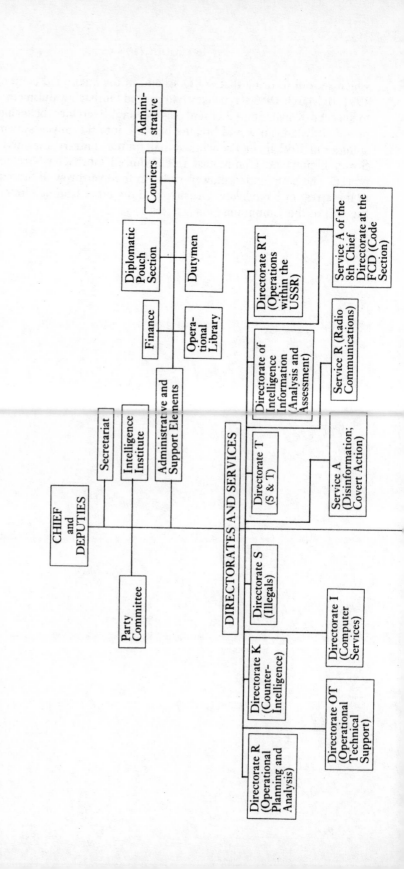

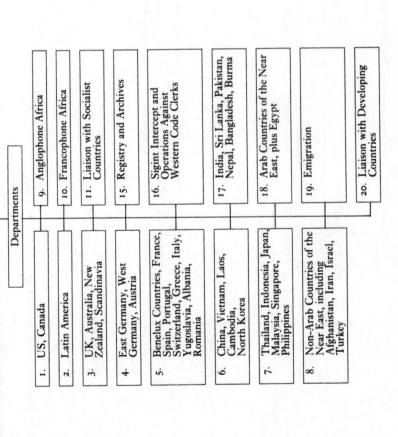

Departments

1. US, Canada

2. Latin America

3. UK, Australia, New Zealand, Scandinavia

4. East Germany, West Germany, Austria

5. Benelux Countries, France, Spain, Portugal, Switzerland, Greece, Italy, Yugoslavia, Albania, Romania

6. China, Vietnam, Laos, Cambodia, North Korea

7. Thailand, Indonesia, Japan, Malaysia, Singapore, Philippines

8. Non-Arab Countries of the Near East, including Afghanistan, Iran, Israel, Turkey

9. Anglophone Africa

10. Francophone Africa

11. Liaison with Socialist Countries

15. Registry and Archives

16. Sigint Intercept and Operations Against Western Code Clerks

17. India, Sri Lanka, Pakistan, Nepal, Bangladesh, Burma

18. Arab Countries of the Near East, plus Egypt

19. Emigration

20. Liaison with Developing Countries

Source: Desmond Ball and Robert Windren, 'Soviet Signals Intelligence (Sigint): Organisation and Management', *Intelligence and National Security*, vol. IV (1989), No 4; and GORDIEVSKY.

The organisation of the KGB First Chief Directorate

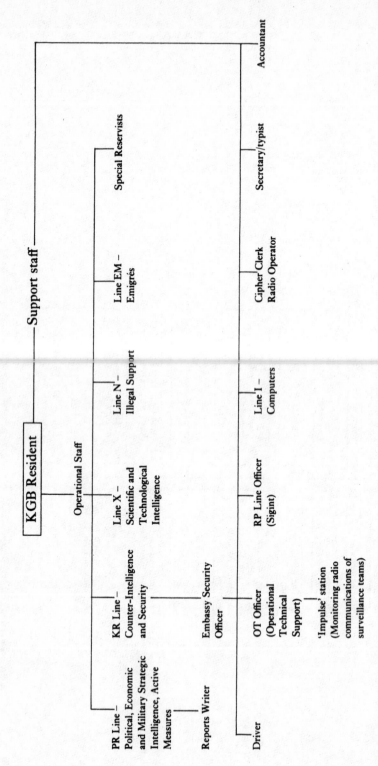

The organisation of a KGB Residency

1

The KGB's Global Priorities

URING Kryuchkov's fourteen years as head of the FCD, conferences of senior officers took place in alternate years, usually in
late January, to review the work of the previous two years. The conferences were opened with an address by Kryuchkov which lasted about
an hour. Only Residents from the more important foreign Residencies
were invited to attend; some spoke during the conference, along with
senior staff from the Centre. In January 1984 the speech of the London
Resident, Arkadi Vasilyevich Guk, was drafted for him by the head of
his PR (political intelligence) line, Oleg Gordievsky. There were also
speeches by visitors from the Communist Party Central Committee
(Administrative Organs Department), the KGB Second Chief
(Counter-Intelligence) Directorate and the KGB Party Committee
(PARTCOM).

The mood of the 1984 conference was more sombre than at the
beginning of the decade. Then there had been optimistic talk of
the new opportunities for expanding KGB operations and exploiting
the weaknesses of the United States in Latin America. The head of
the FCD Service I (reports), Nikolai Sergeevich Leonov, who over
twenty years before had been the first to grasp Fidel Castro's potential
as a revolutionary leader,[1] had emphasised the advantages of supporting
non-Communist liberation movements which, like Castro's, could seize
power in their countries and establish themselves as influential allies of
the Soviet Union. From 1979 to 1982 Castro was Chairman of the
Non-Aligned Movement, still a reliable ally of Moscow and at the peak
of his influence in the Third World. In March 1979 a pro-Cuban
regime had seized power in the Caribbean island of Grenada, led by the
Marxist-Leninist lawyer, Maurice Bishop. Of much greater significance
was the ousting four months later of the brutal and corrupt Somoza
dictatorship in Nicaragua by the Sandinista Liberation Front whose
anthem branded *yanqis* as 'enemies of mankind'.

By 1984 the prospects for superpower rivalry appeared altogether less encouraging. During the 1970s Richard Nixon, whose administration had inaugurated a policy of détente with the Soviet Union, had been followed by two Presidents (Gerald Ford and Jimmy Carter) whom the Centre considered to be weak. By contrast, Ronald Reagan took only a few months after entering the White House in January 1981 to establish himself in Moscow as the most feared and hated US leader since the depths of the Cold War. In October 1983 American troops invaded Grenada and overthrew the Marxist-Leninist regime. The Centre feared that the Reagan administration's covert attempts to undermine the Sandinista regime in Nicaragua might be followed, as in Grenada, by open intervention. Much more seriously, however, the FCD believed that Reagan had embarked on a policy of global confrontation with the Soviet Union which might end in a US nuclear first strike.[2] It took Reagan's 'evil empire' rhetoric with deadly seriousness.

The report on the 1984 conference vividly illustrates the traditional nature of the Centre's priorities. The United States was still described, as it had been throughout the Cold War, as the 'Main Adversary' (*Glavny Protivnik*); it remained the priority target of KGB foreign operations. Kryuchkov interpreted the Reagan administration's 'fantastic idea of world domination' in orthodox Marxist-Leninist terms: 'American monopolies would like to recover the positions they have lost in recent decades and conquer fresh ones.' Though well aware of the economic gulf between the superpowers, the Centre clung to the traditional dogma that capitalism was faced with insoluble internal contradictions. The 'deepening economic and social crisis' which resulted was leading Western imperialists to consider war as a possible way of escape from their increasing difficulties.

After the United States and its NATO allies, the Centre's main preoccupation was the rival Communist regime in the People's Republic of China.[3] 'Peking,' it concluded, 'is counting on deriving political advantages for itself by manoeuvring between the West and the Socialist countries [Soviet Bloc], and trying to blackmail the West with the prospect of an improvement of relations with the Soviet Union.' The FCD saw little prospect of a serious Sino-Soviet rapprochement. A decade earlier there had been prolonged discussion in the Centre as to whether China now qualified for the title 'Main Adversary', hitherto applied exclusively to the United States. In the end it was relegated in official KGB jargon to the status of 'Major Adversary', with America keeping its unique position as 'Main Adversary'.

The conference acknowledged that, despite some improvement over the past two years, the KGB had 'not had great success in operating against the main adversary'. The FCD faced two intractable problems. First, intelligence on some imperialist plots, notably plans for a nuclear first strike, was exceptionally difficult to come by for the simple reason that the plots themselves did not exist. Secondly, there had been few successes in recruiting American agents: 'The position regarding infiltration of agents and confidential contacts into the United States is unsatisfactory.' A major effort was required 'in order to improve performance in recruitment of Americans'.[4]

The FCD conference, however, also heard of some successes. Among them was the collection of scientific and technological intelligence (S & T): 'The amount of material obtained has increased and, what is more important, the quality has improved.'[5] The dynamic and ambitious head of FCD Directorate T (responsible for S & T), Leonid Sergeevich Zaitsev, claimed (though his remarks are not reported in the conference report) that the value of the S & T his directorate obtained covered the entire foreign operating costs of the KGB. Zaitsev campaigned for Directorate T to leave the FCD and become an independent directorate within the KGB. Kryuchkov, however, was determined not to allow such a prestigious part of his empire to escape from his control.

The conference was also told that 'As in previous years, a great deal of attention has been devoted to active measures' (to influence operations directed against foreign public opinion and governments). Though the conference report did not mention it, between the mid-70s and mid-80s, Service A (Active Measures) grew from about fifty to over eighty officers in the FCD Yasenevo headquarters, with a further thirty or forty in the Novosti Press Agency offices at Pushkin Square. PR line officers in Residencies abroad were supposed to spend about 25 per cent of their time on 'active measures'. Kryuchkov himself was an enthusiastic believer in them with, probably, an exaggerated faith in their effectiveness. In the United States and Britain, 'active measures' against Ronald Reagan and Margaret Thatcher (the two main Western targets) had limited success.[6] But in the Third World attempts to exploit anti-Americanism and to blame the problems of developing countries on imperialist exploitation were far more effective. The tendency of the Non-Aligned Movement and much of the Anti-War Movement to see the United States and 'imperialism' as the main source of the world's ills made them, the conference was told, 'our natural allies': 'The essential trend of their activities is anti-imperialist, and on the issues of war and peace they come out on the side of progressive forces.'

No 156/54
01.02.84

Top Secret
Copy No. 1

To Residents and Representatives (as listed)
CONFERENCE ON RESULTS OF WORK IN 1982–1983

A meeting of heads of our service was held in the second half of January this year at which the results of our work in 1982–1983 were discussed and tasks set for the immediate future.

In order to guide you in your work we are sending you a briefing in which the main conclusions and points of view of this meeting are set out. Please acquaint your deputies and assistants with the full text of this briefing and inform operational personnel of the main contents.

Destroy the briefing as is laid down and send the certificate of destruction to the Centre.

Attachment: Guidance on the conference of heads of the Service, 12 pages, No 152/54, Top Secret, 'PN' [on undeveloped film]

VADIMOV
[V V KIRPICHENKO]
[A First Deputy Head, FCD]

[In manuscript:]
  To Comrades Leonov
          Gornov
          Brown
          Yelin
          Svetlov

Signed YERMAKOV   13.03.84

Reference No. 156/54
01.02.84

Top Secret
Copy No. 1

CHIEF CONCLUSIONS AND VIEWS ADOPTED AT THE MEETING OF HEADS OF SERVICE

The results of our work in 1982–83 were discussed at the meeting in January of the heads of our Service and tasks were set out for the coming period.

The head of our Service [Vladimir Kryuchkov] stressed in his report that we are building communism in the Soviet Union in a complex international situation. Reactionary imperialist groups in the USA have openly embarked on a course of confrontation. They are increasing tension in literally all sectors of

Дк. 99

Совершенно секретно
Экз. № I

Резидентам и представителям
(по списку)

О совещании по итогам
работы за 1982-1983 гг.

Во второй половине января с.г. состоялось совещание руководящего состава нашей Службы, на котором были подведены итоги работы за 1982-1983 гг. и определены задачи на ближайший период.

Для руководства в работе Вам направляется ориентировка, в которой излагаются основные выводы и установки данного совещания. С полным текстом ориентировки ознакомьте своих заместителей и помощников, ее основное содержание доведите до сведения оперативного состава.

Ориентировку уничтожьте в установленном порядке и акт об уничтожении вышлите в Центр.

Приложение: ориентировка о совещании руководящего состава Службы
на 10 л., № 152/54, сов.секретно, "ПН".

13.03.84.

the struggle between the two opposed social systems, and in consequence, *the threat of outbreak of a nuclear war has reached dangerous proportions.*

American monopolies would like to recover the positions they have lost in recent decades and conquer fresh ones. The fantastic idea of world domination has become the initial basis of the Pentagon's plans for a preventive, 'limited', 'protracted', 'cosmic' and other conceptions of conducting a nuclear war. The White House is advancing in its propaganda the adventurist and extremely dangerous notion of 'survival' in the fire of a thermonuclear catastrophe. This is nothing else but psychological preparation of the population for nuclear war. There is evidence of this also in the manifest unwillingness of the United States Government to follow the example of the Soviet Union and accept the undertaking not to be the first to use nuclear weapons.

All attempts by the Soviet Union to halt the fatal arms race are meeting with stubborn resistance from the United States. The deployment of American missiles in Europe has shown that Washington used the talks in Geneva as a screen for increasing its military arsenal. To continue the talks would be tantamount to fostering an illusion for the world at large. There were good reasons for our departure from the talks. It was designed to expose the real cause underlying America's militarist foreign policy.

Reagan's last speech on Soviet–American relations did in fact produce nothing new. The same policy from a position of strength, the same demagogy, the same effort to deceive the world community.

What, then, has caused the present volte-face in United States policy, and to some extent also in the capitalist West as a whole? It is the class reaction to consolidation of the socialist position, the successes of the peoples' struggle for national liberation and the growth of democratic and progressive forces in the world.

One of the reasons for the increased aggressiveness of imperialism, especially American imperialism, is the deepening economic and social crisis in the capitalist world. The slowing down in the growth rates for industrial production, together with continuing technological progress, have led to permanent mass unemployment and to exacerbation of other social problems. The prospect of a worsening of these trends is frightening the imperialists. They are seeking an escape from the difficulties they have created in their own ways, including that of war.

The policy of the Chinese government is also complicating the international situation. Some new factors have recently been noted in it and we must analyse them thoroughly and make use of them in the interests of the Soviet Union.

The PRC has recently been devoting increased attention to developing its powers of production and making use of economic levers. Steps have been taken to improve efficiency in the Party and government apparatus. Certain amendments are also in train as regards foreign policy, although Peking is not going further than tactical modifications of its line in the international arena.

The strategic policy of the PRC is based on exploiting and, above all, on intensifying the conflicts between the two world social systems.

Peking is blocking normalisation of Sino–Soviet relations. As before, it is putting forward 'conditions' which are unacceptable to the Soviet Union, affecting our relations with third countries – Vietnam, Afghanistan, Mongolia. This was demonstrated once more in the results of the third round of Soviet–Chinese consultations, held in October 1983. Peking is counting on deriving political advantages for itself by manoeuvring between the West and the socialist countries, and trying to blackmail the West with the prospect of an improvement in relations with the Soviet Union. At the same time the third round showed that the Chinese leaders are ready for a measure of expansion in commercial, economic, scientific, technical and cultural relations with the USSR.

The consistent peace policy pursued by the Soviet Union and other fraternal socialist countries is of decisive importance in the present alarming international situation. The Non-Aligned Movement and the Anti-War Movement are our natural allies. The essential trend of their activities is anti-imperialist, and on the issues of war and peace they come out on the side of the progressive forces. A certain section of social democracy is beginning to grasp the dangers of imperialism's militarist policy. The objective contradictions existing among the imperialists also constitute a factor in our favour. Intelligent and effective exploitation of these in our interests depends on our political perspicacity and skill in operation.

The tension in the international situation is inevitably reflected in the operational situation. The adversary is doing everything possible in capitalist and pro-Western developing countries to paralyse the activity of Soviet intelligence. His operations in this field are of a complex nature, envisaging utilisation of the facilities of the counter-intelligence services, the agencies of the law and the mass information media. The adversary's special services are operating against Soviet intelligence on a broad front, having recourse more and more often to the sharpest methods and means of struggle such as detention and arrest of our officials and attempts to recruit members of our residencies, using special devices against them.

The adversary is undertaking more active study and ideological cultivation of Soviet citizens abroad. There has recently been an increase in the number of provocation approaches made to them, especially by the Americans. Their efforts to persuade Soviet citizens not to return home are becoming more and more extensive and aggressive.

The subversive activity of émigré, nationalist and Zionist organisations and associations abroad has shown a marked increase. At the same time, anti-Soviet pronouncements from reactionary Muslim organisations have intensified.

The rising trend in the number of anti-Soviet diversionary and terrorist operations is giving rise to particular anxiety. Counter-revolutionary organisations of various shades in a number of developing countries are hatching, and attempting to carry out, plans to seize Soviet citizens as hostages in order to put forward their political demands. This type of operation has already taken place in Afghanistan, Mozambique and Angola. At the same time we have also noted energetic attempts by the adversary to penetrate Soviet institutions using technical devices.

Assessment of the operational situation throughout the world shows that the factors affecting its development are predominantly negative. In planning and organising intelligence activity in present conditions, we should start from the assumption that there will be a further deterioration.

The head of the Service [Kryuchkov] underlined the fact that the growing threat of war is creating a new situation in the world. Everything indicates that the threshold for using nuclear weapons is being lowered. The significance of the surprise factor has sharply increased. For the intelligence service this means that it must concentrate its efforts to the maximum extent on the principal task to be pursued – it must not fail to perceive direct preparation by the adversary for a nuclear missile attack against the USSR, nor overlook the real danger of war breaking out. It is important not to allow any alteration in the existing strategic parity or permit the adversary to gain military superiority through any scientific or technical break-through. It is our task to increase the contribution made by intelligence towards strengthening the country's defence capability.

Our starting point must be, that *in spite of the importance of the other problems with which we are engaged, the problem of military strategy establishes itself more and more firmly in the foreground* and its centre of gravity is the USA. This means that each station abroad must organise its work first and foremost round this primary task. It is precisely from this point of view that our successes and failures must be assessed.

In our information-gathering activity the main emphasis was put on obtaining secret documentary information giving us early warning of the main adversary's military policy and strategic plans revealing his preparations for war against the Soviet Union, or any crisis which may be developing. Our efforts have also been directed to supplying our authorities promptly with information about the most immediate political, economic, scientific and technical problems and the domestic and foreign policy of the chief capitalist countries.

It is increasingly important at present to provide our authorities with *political information* about the emergence and development of pre-crisis and crisis situations in strategically significant parts of the world. The number of international and local conflicts may increase in the foreseeable future. Our stations abroad are consequently faced with the necessity of preparing at once to operate in an increasingly complex situation. We must take steps without delay to ensure a smooth flow of information in all circumstances.

International economic problems are becoming increasingly important in the information-gathering field. This is due on the one hand to the need to counteract the adversary's designs to undermine the economy of the countries of the socialist community by means of 'economic warfare', and on the other, the need to make use of the economic facilities of capitalism in the interests of the economy of the Soviet Union.

Notwithstanding certain achievements, the necessary improvement in the quality of our information-gathering is slow in arriving. *The proportion of deeply analytical material with some attempt at forecasting, in the overall volume of documents is still small.* There is, as before, a serious shortage of secret information which would enable us to draw more substantial inferences about the key questions of American, NATO, Japanese and Chinese policy.

On the basis of reliable information, stations abroad must forecast the development of events and make recommendations for possible action on our part. However, certain heads [of stations] and a number of operational personnel are not displaying the necessary political acuteness in assessing the situation and preparing proposals.

Information from the intelligence service must assist our authorities to reach optimum foreign policy decisions.

In regard to *scientific and technical intelligence*, the main effort has been directed towards the task of obtaining information of military strategic and also of economic significance. The amount of material obtained has increased and, what is more important, the quality has improved.

In the last two years the quantity of material and samples handed over to civilian branches of industry has increased by half as much again. This included information which has been used to real economic effect in our own industrial enterprises. Certain results have been obtained from information clarifying problems connected with implementing our Energy and Food Programme.

We cannot however affirm that its work on clearing up the most important questions is wholly satisfactory. As previously, we are experiencing an acute shortage of secret information about new types of weapon and their means of delivery. The percentage of secret documentary information, especially on problems of military strategy, is still small.

Scientific and technical intelligence can only fulfil its mission if it operates with more precision, taking into account future developments in science and technology abroad. The ability to detect new tendencies and indicate the possible consequences of their development has today acquired a particular significance.

The contribution of *counter-intelligence sections abroad* to the work of information-gathering has increased recently. KR-line [counter-intelligence] officers in a number of residencies have acquired important information of a political nature and also valuable data on questions of military strategy and economic matters.

On the whole one can claim that the intelligence service's information-gathering activity has steadily improved over the last two years, but even so it has not had great success in operating against the main adversary. Now is the time for us to anticipate literally every large-scale operation of the United States. To seek to achieve that is our primary task.

As in previous years, a great deal of attention has been devoted to active measures. They have been directed first of all towards promoting successful implementation of Soviet foreign policy.

The range of questions dealt with by means of active measures has been continually widening. A number of large-scale, long-term complex operations designed to safeguard the security and defence capability of our country have been carried out in recent years. Among them was action to expose the United States' plans for aggression in front of the international community and to exert influence promoting our interests on the policy of a number of capitalist countries and deepen the disagreements between the United States and its allies. Considerable work has been done to provide support for unofficial organisations in a number of countries abroad in their struggle against implementation of the American administration's militarist plans. Complex operations to help in concluding commercial and economic agreements with capitalist countries to the Soviet Union's advantage have also proved effective.

In the current situation it is becoming increasingly important to promote efforts to put into practice Soviet initiatives to improve the international climate. *Our chief task is to help to frustrate the aggressive intentions of American imperialism.* It is extremely important that the international community should recognise that the threat to peace comes from the USA. We must work tirelessly at exposing the adversary's weak and vulnerable points.

Really effective active measures can be worked out on the basis of full, especially documentary, intelligence data. Therefore stations abroad must be unremitting in their efforts to acquire fresh, reliable sources of such information and channels for carrying out our operations.

One of our important tasks is constantly to step up the *security of intelligence activity itself.* Certain useful results have been achieved in this direction, including recruitment of members of the adversary's special services.

There are however serious shortcomings in the work of our foreign counter-intelligence service. The agent network in the field is far from fully enabling us to obtain advance information about the subversive plans and intentions of the adversary's special services. Consequently we do not always have specific information about large-scale anti-Soviet operations which they are preparing, or their attempts to direct the activities of terrorist and other extremist elements against Soviet citizens.

New working methods and devices of the hostile special services urgently require us to seek effective and determined measures for protecting residencies and each individual operational officer.

Operational security must be strictly observed when carrying out operational measures. There is already a question-mark over any intelligence officer who forgets it.

Wider use must be made of non-personal means in maintaining communications with reliable agents, including employing more up-to-date technical devices. Especial care must be taken to safeguard the security of valuable agents and work with them must be under the personal control of the head of station abroad.

In no event must it be forgotten that it is of prime importance to carry out comprehensive checking of agents, confidential contacts and persons being studied for recruitment purposes. This expedient has often saved us from serious trouble and, on the other hand, neglecting it has led to exposure for which we have had to pay dearly.

Efforts to safeguard the security of intelligence operations must be based on the fact that the importance of this particularly crucial sector will in future continue to grow. At the same time it must always be remembered that the chief means of ensuring that the security of intelligence operations is protected is, and has always been, agent penetration of the other side's intelligence and counter-intelligence agencies.

The last two years have seen a sharp *deterioration in the general position of Soviet institutions and citizens abroad*, and the situation in this sector is becoming alarming. Our authorities have recently examined more than once aspects of the work and operating conditions of Soviet groups based abroad. We have also given the matter especial consideration. Today it is essential to step up our work substantially in this direction and above all, to improve its efficiency.

It must always be borne in mind that officers of all lines are responsible for the security of Soviet citizens and institutions abroad. This is the duty of every operational officer. Experience has shown that where proper attention is given to provision for security, and where instruction is given a regular place beside Operational work, adversary machinations encounter a repulse and his provocations end in exposure.

It was emphasised in the report that operational work with agents is the foundation stone of all Chekist work. The principle that the agent is and will in the foreseeable future continue to be the main resource for dealing with the tasks confronting the intelligence service remains in full force. *Therefore recruitment of valuable agents from among foreign nationals first and foremost for working against the main adversary, is the keystone of all operational measures involving agents.*

In spite of certain favourable factors, the number of successes in cultivating Americans for recruitment has not been great. It is a matter for disquiet that many residencies do not in fact study American citizens or foreign nationals who are working in local American installations. The position regarding infiltration of agents and confidential contacts into the United States is unsatisfactory.

In order to improve performance in recruitment of Americans, provision must be made for wider use of the most effective forms, methods and devices, such as a 'foreign flag',* agent-recruiters, and auxiliary agents, operational

* The pretence to an agent that he or she is assisting an organisation other than the KGB (such as the peace movement or a Third World liberation movement).

equipment, the facilities of friendly intelligence services and the special services of developing countries. More attention must be devoted to improving the professional skills of intelligence officers and deepening their feeling of responsibility for the work entrusted to them.

The head of our Service drew attention to the fact that in working against NATO, some stations abroad have continued as before the practice of unwarranted direct approaches to targets of study, which for the most part leads to sheer waste of time, 'blowing' our intelligence officers, and exposures. In cases like this we are also coming across 'plants'. *When organising agent penetration into NATO, one must start from the premise that one of the promising methods is infiltration of foreign nationals already working for Soviet intelligence.* In this context, greater care must be taken over work among diplomatic personnel of countries belonging to the bloc, MFA officials and those of other state institutions from which personnel are selected for the central and peripheral departments of NATO.

The intelligence service has achieved some useful results over the past two years in its work against China, but the successes obtained have been in general in the nature of isolated episodes. Many residencies are still slow in dealing with the specific tasks posed by recruitment. Insufficient attention is being given to promising categories of Chinese nationals abroad such as specialists, students and trainees. Small effort is being made to select agents for prolonged periods in the PRC or in Hong Kong or Taiwan.

Residencies must step up their endeavour to achieve solid results in recruiting Chinese nationals. The most highly trained officers and experienced agents must be directed into this work. We must not let slip the opportunities created by the changeover in personnel in the Chinese state administration, the process of discrediting Maoist ideology and the purge carried out in the Party.

Nowhere more than in working against China do we require circumspection, patience, endurance and accurate appreciation of the particular characteristics of the Chinese. All these qualities must be continually fostered in operational personnel.

In speaking of operational work with agents as a whole, one must underline once more the *need to pay strict observance to the targeting principle.* This enables the effort of the intelligence service to be concentrated on its main tasks and the highest possible success to be achieved in its recruiting activity. We must, as previously, continue to rely on exploiting ideology and politics as a basic motive. At the same time we must be bolder in making use of the material factor as well.

Further improvement in operational work with agents calls for fuller and wider utilisation of confidential and special unofficial contacts. These should be acquired chiefly among prominent figures in politics and society, and important representatives of business interests and science, who are capable not only of supplying valuable information, but also of actively influencing the foreign and domestic policy of target-countries in a direction of advantage to the USSR.

Well-qualified agents must be widely co-opted from among Soviet nationals to deal with these tasks.

Positive improvements have taken place in the last two years in *utilisation of technical resources by residencies abroad*, and the number of technical operations employed to obtain intelligence information and protect the security of intelligence work has increased. The geographical range of residencies using technical devices has expanded. At the same time there are also stations abroad where poor use is being made of technical operations. Apparently those in charge of them have not yet reached the stage of understanding the importance of this sector of their work.

One of the important aspects of our work is to enhance the *preparedness of our stations abroad for mobilisation*. A plan of action must be prepared well in advance for the event of emergencies. The chief part of it must be concerned with ensuring the uninterrupted operation of the agent apparatus. No turn of events must take us unawares.

The report pointed out the growing importance of cooperation with the security agencies of fraternal socialist and some developing countries in almost all sectors and directions of our operational activity. Our cooperation with friendly intelligence services has on the whole expanded at a good tempo in the last two years at a fairly high operational and organisational level.

The most serious attention was given to the further reorientation of friendly intelligence services to operating first and foremost against the USA, NATO and China.

The head of our Service drew particular attention to one aspect of our cooperation with friends. In dealing with any work problems we must use political tact, set an example of good organisation and precision, listen to our friends' views and pay attention to their worries and problems. All this forms an important part of political work with them.

The last two years have seen further expansion of cooperation with the *special services of some developing countries*. On the political plane this has been directed to rendering all possible assistance to seeing that the Soviet Union's foreign policy is implemented in relation to the developing countries, and consolidating liberated countries on the road to progressive development. On the operational plane, cooperation enables us to deal with a large number of specific intelligence and counter-intelligence problems.

Today the main problem in this field is to achieve more active participation by our partners in the struggle against the main adversary. Great tact must be displayed here. We must recognise that their interests do not always coincide with ours. Therefore in cooperation it is above all essential to define the range of common interests, and to be purposeful and tactful in making the heads of the security agencies understand how vitally important it is for them to combat the subversive activities of the American special [intelligence] services.

Cooperation with security agencies must be orientated more and more to our mutual advantage. The scale of our aid must be in conformity with the extent of our political task in this or that country, and the readiness of the local special services to cooperate with us in the fight against our main adversary. There must be increased coordination with the security agencies of the fraternal socialist countries in aiding the special services of developing states.

The report pointed to the great importance of personnel work with intelligence officers abroad. Each operational officer belonging to any station abroad must be an active combatant bending all his efforts to carrying out his complex and responsible tasks. If everyone in our apparatus abroad worked at full capacity and maximum efficiency, we could deal with a wider range of tasks successfully with our present resources.

The measures we have taken to conceal our operational personnel have not yet produced the desired effect. One of the reasons is insufficient attention given to this by stations abroad. Senior officials of all ranks are required to pay due attention to the problems of concealment in order to preserve the operational longevity of intelligence personnel. The leadership keeps this matter constantly in view and will hold strictly accountable anyone who fails to appreciate fully the importance of concealment as a key aspect of safeguarding the security of intelligence activity and the professional personnel of stations abroad.

In concluding his report, the head of our Service expressed his confidence that our organisation will make every effort honourably to fulfil the assignments with which it is faced and made a worthy contribution to the task of safeguarding the security and protecting the interests of the Soviet state.

No. 152/54

T HE main concerns of the FCD review of its foreign operations during 1982–3 were reflected in its Work Plan for 1984. The ultimate responsibility for determining the KGB's main priorities in the field of political intelligence rested with the Secretariat of the Communist Party Central Committee as the interpreter of the policies formulated by the Politburo. In practice, these priorities were formulated chiefly by the International Department (ID) of the Central Committee. The ID itself directly supervised 'grey' (semi-covert) active measures conducted through front organisations and other channels with a partly visible Soviet presence, leaving the FCD to implement 'black' (covert) active measures whose Soviet origin was concealed.

The ID head from 1948 to 1986, Boris Nikolayevich Ponomarev, who became a candidate (non-voting) Politburo member in 1972, was a true believer in the Marxist-Leninist gospel. Khrushchev had nicknamed him 'Ponomar' (sacristan in the Orthodox Church). 'Ponomar,' he said, 'is a valuable Party official but as orthodox as a Catholic priest.'[7]

'For Marxist-Leninists,' Ponomarev insisted, 'it is axiomatic that theory is the key to the correct solution of practical problems ... It is safe to say in the light of past experience that the valuations and forecasts based on Marxist-Leninist analysis have proved entirely correct.'[8] The work of the ID was overseen until his death in 1982 by the Party patriarch and chief ideologist, Mikhail Andreevich Suslov, a full Politburo member for thirty years. 'Cloaked in the robe of doctrinal infallibility,' wrote one Soviet diplomat, '[Suslov] regularly issued reminders of what he saw as the correct Marxist-Leninist policy.'[9]

At the beginning of the 1980s Ponomarev, like Suslov, was still claiming that the Soviet system made economic crisis impossible. The internal contradictions of capitalism, by contrast, were becoming steadily worse: 'The scientific-technical revolution not only aggravates the old social antagonisms, but also creates new ones.' It was these internal contradictions which were driving the West to confrontation with the Soviet Union.[10]

Ponomarev and the ID laid down the FCD's priorities only in outline. These were then handed to a group of senior KGB officers, officially known as 'Consultants to the Chairman', who translated them into operational requirements which were transmitted to Kryuchkov. Though the Plan for 1984 is described in a covering letter to Residents as 'Comrade Alyoshin's [Kryuchkov's] instructions', it is clearly based on Party policy. It begins by quoting the moribund General Secretary, Yuri Vladimirovich Andropov, formerly a long-serving KGB Chairman (1967–82), who died in February 1984. The Plan also claims to be 'in strict accord' with Party Congress and Central Committee decisions.

At the root of the Plan is a vast conspiracy theory (set out in detail in Chapter 4): that the United States has plans 'for launching a surprise nuclear attack on the USSR', and 'is involving its NATO allies and Japan in pursuing its aggressive designs'. These designs were to be countered not merely by intelligence collection in order to gain prior warning of them but also by a wide variety of active measures aimed at, *inter alia*, 'exacerbating conflicts between the USA, Western Europe and Japan', 'stepping up the activity of anti-imperialist forces in Asian, African and Latin American countries, and deepening the antipathy of these countries towards development by capitalist states', and 'counteracting the rapprochement in military policy between China and the USA and other imperialist countries on an anti-Soviet basis'.

But for these aims to be achieved, the KGB needed more and better agents. Existing recruitment methods were too stereotyped and the results unsatisfactory. Greater imagination was needed to devise recruiting 'ploys', and there should be 'bolder use of material incentives'.

In short, 'The main effort must be concentrated on acquiring valuable agents.'[11]

[ms notes:]   Incoming No 471/ref 180 Gornov
Comr[ade] Gornov
Comr[ade] Brown, Comr[ade] Yelin
Comr[ade] Artyom
Comr[ade] Svetlov
Comr[ade] Fred and Comr[ade] Evans

Study the paper carefully with operational staff of all lines.
YERMAKOV 16.11.83

No 2126/PR   Top Secret
02.11.83   Copy No 1
[To Residents]

We are sending you Comrade Alyoshin's [Kryuchkov's] instructions on planning and organising the work of sections of the Service and organisations abroad in 1984.

Attachment: As indicated in text, No 26ss, Top Secret, 10 pages, PN [on undeveloped film]

SILIN
[G. F. TITOV]
[Head of Third Department, FCD]

[ms notes:]   Leonov 10.1.84
Brown 21.11.83
Fred 21.11.83

Top Secret
Attachment to No 2126/PR   Copy No 16

Planning and organisation of the work of sections of the Service and organisations abroad in 1984.
The present international situation is characterised by an increase in tension. Above all, the militarist attitude adopted by the present American administration represents a serious threat to peace. As the General Secretary of the

CPSU Central Committee, Comr Yu. V Andropov, said in a recent speech: 'Its essential aim is to attempt to secure a dominant position in the world for the United States, regardless of the interests of other states and nations.' The threat of an outbreak of nuclear war is reaching an extremely dangerous point.

The United States is involving its NATO allies and Japan in pursuing its aggressive designs. Consolidation of right-wing pro-Atlantic forces in the Leadership of the principal capitalist countries has brought about greater coordination of subversive action by the West against the USSR, the socialist community as a whole and the national liberation movements.

The imperialist states are pursuing their intrigues over Poland and Afghanistan and exacerbating the situation still more in a number of strategically important regions – in the Near and Middle East, in Central America, South-East Asia and Africa. The existing correlation of forces may be radically altered by deployment of new American medium-range missiles in Western Europe.

In these circumstances, the task of not overlooking immediate preparations by the adversary for launching a surprise nuclear missile attack on the USSR or local wars and armed conflicts threatening the security of the Soviet Union and countries friendly to it, has acquired even greater urgency and immediacy.

In order to discredit the policy of American imperialism and weaken its position, it is essential to exploit systematically the growing resistance of influential political and social groups in the West to the adventurist line of the United States and to intensify the contradictions between capitalist countries in the financial and economic field and on certain political issues.

The policy of China is having a marked influence on the development of the world situation, above all in Asia, and some new factors requiring all-round study and sober assessment have recently been seen in that policy.

Successful achievement of the tasks facing the intelligence service will depend to a considerable degree on how ably and flexibly it is able to organise its work in the complex political and operational situation in the majority of countries under observation. It is important to ensure that the security of organisations abroad is safeguarded in all possible situations.

It is essential to use every means of heightening the processing and implementation of urgent and specific action to improve the quality and efficiency of intelligence activity in every direction, with a fresh approach to questions of planning and organisation.

Taking this into account, IT IS PROPOSED:

The work of stations abroad must be planned and organised in 1984 in strict accord with the decisions of the 26th Party Congress, the November (1982) and June (1983) plenary sessions of the CPSU Central Committee, and the programme directives and fundamental conclusions contained in the speeches of the Secretary General of the CPSU Central Committee, Comrade Yu. V Andropov, as well as the requirements of the May (1981) All-Union Conference of the Heads of the Service.

The principal intelligence capabilities and resources must be concentrated on carrying out the assignments against the main adversary, and taking measures envisaged by the decrees of the higher authorities and the directives from our leaders on external intelligence work, especially in the fields of military strategy and the national economy, and also on major international problems involving the vital interests of the Soviet Union. We must seek close cooperation between sections and an improvement in control of the operational activity of stations abroad.

In doing this, the following is essential:

Information-gathering and analysis

The highest importance must be attached to intelligence processing of priority questions. Especial emphasis must be placed on obtaining reliable, and, above all, documentary information in advance about the USA's and NATO's plans and preparations in the field of military strategy. We must assume that it is essential to obtain intelligence data regularly on the following topical questions:

Political intelligence

– The effect of foreign policy steps taken by the USSR and other countries of the socialist community to strengthen peace and international security, especially in the matter of limitation and reduction of nuclear missiles and other weapons of mass destruction, on government and influential political and social groups in other countries;

– preparation by the USA and its allies of a surprise nuclear attack on the Soviet Union; plans and actions by the main adversary to increase its strategic military potential and to step up the American military presence in Western Europe and other strategically important areas of the world;

– the principal aspects of the strategy of the USA, the countries of Western Europe and Japan in regard to the USSR; the position they adopt on the most important political, strategic, military, economic, financial and currency questions, where Soviet interests are affected; coordination of foreign policy action and any contradictions existing among these countries;

– plans and subversive actions by the main adversary directed towards weakening the unity of the countries of the socialist community [Soviet Bloc], to destabilise the situation in individual socialist countries (especially in Poland), and in particular, the use of economic levers and ideological diversion;

– the development of events in areas where crisis situations exist, primarily in the Near and Middle East; processes in train around Afghanistan;

– the internal political situation in the USA; the possible effect of the electoral campaign and the outcome of the presidential election in 1984 on the formulation of the USA's foreign policy;

– China's foreign policy and its approach to the development of relations with the USSR; tendencies in the pattern of internal political forces in the PRC;

– activities of the Non-Aligned Movement, the Sotsintern [Socialist International], the Vatican, the 'Islamic factor';

Scientific and technical intelligence
– military technology measures taken by the main adversary to build up first-strike weapons: the quantitative increase in nuclear munitions and means of delivery (MX missile complexes, 'Trident', 'Pershing-2', cruise missiles, strategic bombers); replacement of one generation of nuclear missiles by another ('Midgetman', 'Trident-2'), the development of qualitatively new types of weapons (space devices for multiple use for military purposes, laser and pencil beam weapons, non-acoustic anti-submarine defence weapons, electronic warfare weapons, etc);

– information and specimens of significant interest for civilian branches of the USSR's economy, especially in the matter of the Food Programme, industrial exploitation of the Pacific Ocean, the Arctic and Antarctic, and the Soviet Union's energy programme;

– operational equipment of the intelligence and counter-intelligence services of the main capitalist countries; material and samples of interest to our sections;

Counter-intelligence abroad
– plans for subversive action and secret operations by the adversary's special services, and by centres for ideological diversion and nationalists, especially Zionists and other anti-Soviet organisations, against the USSR and other countries of the socialist community;

– activities of terrorist organisations and groups abroad, and the adversary's attempts to make use of international terrorism for anti-Soviet purposes.

Stations abroad must consolidate their intelligence access and improve the quality of the information obtained; they must arrange for analytical processing of priority questions on the spot using agent material and material from open sources;

– when assessing the information-gathering activity of stations abroad evaluation must be based primarily on the results of their coverage of priority problems.

Active measures
The main effort is to be concentrated on developing and carrying out large-scale comprehensive operations using the capabilities of various lines of intelligence in the following key sectors:

– counteracting attempts by the USA and NATO to destroy the existing military strategic equilibrium and to acquire military superiority over the USSR; compromising the aggressive efforts of imperialist groups and their plans for preparing a nuclear missile war, and provoking local conflicts and crisis situations capable of damaging the foreign policy interests and security of the Soviet Union;

– deepening disagreements inside NATO over its approach to implementing specific aspects of the bloc's military policy; exacerbating contradictions between the USA, Western Europe and Japan on other matters of principle;

– exposing before the international community the plans made by the USA to launch a war, its refusal to negotiate in good faith with the USSR on limiting armaments; stimulating further development of the anti-war and anti-missile movements in the West, involving in them influential political and public figures and broad strata of the population, and encouraging these movements to take more decisive and coordinated action;

– assisting in consolidating and stepping up the activity of anti-imperialist forces in Asian, African and Latin American countries, and deepening contradictions between these countries and the developed capitalist states;

– exposing and neutralising the subversive operations of Western special [intelligence] services and the adversary's centres for ideological sabotage, nationalists, Zionists and other anti-Soviet organisations abroad;

– countering the USA's attempts to curtail commercial, economic and scientific contacts between developed capitalist countries and the Soviet Union, and helping to create favourable conditions for concluding treaties and agreements in the USSR's favour in the field of foreign trade, international economic cooperation, currency and credit relations and scientific and technical exchange, and also for acquiring the latest foreign equipment and technology;

– countering the military and political rapprochement between the PRC and the USA and other imperialist countries on an anti-Soviet basis; prompting the Chinese leadership to improve Sino–Soviet relations;

– further consolidation of the anti-imperialist stance of the Non-Aligned Movement; exerting influence in our favour on the activity of the Sotsintern [Socialist International] and clerical organisations on the questions of war and peace and other key contemporary problems.

Attention must be given especially to making more thorough use of existing channels and to acquiring additional ones for carrying out influence operations.

There must be a continual improvement in the forms and methods of working on active measures. Cooperation and mutual assistance must be consolidated and expanded in this field with other sections, ministries and departments, and the security agencies of the socialist countries and some liberated countries.

Operational work with agents

When making plans for operational work with agents, we must proceed from the idea that they must be specific, envisaging concrete and purposeful action to ensure that the agent network is improved and consolidated, above all by recruiting valuable sources capable of coping with the tasks confronting the intelligence service.

The targeting principle must be strictly adhered to in operational work.

There must be careful preparation and consistent implementation of measures for agent penetration of the main targets, of the USA, its NATO allies, the PRC and Japan – national targets, in the first place in the offices of heads of state and government, foreign policy and military departments, and the special services, where the important intelligence information is concentrated. There must be intensive study of targets, efforts to discover possibilities of planting existing agents on their officials and carrying out complex penetration operations with agents.

Taking into account the additional measures adopted by the adversary, in the first place the USA, to reinforce control over observance of secrecy and the embargo on export of commodities, scientific and technical intelligence, we must analyse the existing situation in greater depth and discover fresh resources for dealing with Line X assignments [scientific and technological intelligence].

One must envisage more active personal involvement of all senior officers and operational personnel in recruitment work.

The main effort must be concentrated on acquiring valuable agents. There must be no relaxation of attention in working on confidential and special unofficial contacts among major state and political personalities. Ploys must be devised to create situations for recruitment, including the use of technical devices.

In the interests of improving efficiency and security in recruitment work, steps must be taken to create a network of agents for cultivation and recruitment purposes. While selecting for preference persons who are ideologically close to us for this role, one should make bolder use of material incentives. Leads must be more widely exploited in recruitment work.

A more thoughtful approach should be adopted to assessing the possibilities of foreigners who are being cultivated, especially among young people with prospects for penetrating into targets of interest to us and for infiltration into the main adversary countries.

More systematic use must be envisaged, in recruitment work on foreigners, of agents and reliable persons among our Soviet nationals, even going as far as coopting them for specific recruitment operations, and also for studying targets, obtaining leads, and so on.

The starting point for organising operational activity is the need further to expand and deepen cooperation among all branches of the foreign intelligence service, both at Centre and in stations abroad. In particular, there must be closer coordination of efforts between 'legal'* and 'illegal'† lines and also between operational and technical sections.

Safeguarding the security of the intelligence service in Soviet establishments abroad

More attention must be paid to the security of intelligence activity, vigilance, secrecy, operational security and cover for personnel.

---

* KGB officers abroad, identified as Soviet citizens, usually working under diplomatic or other official cover.

† Officers working abroad under false nationality and identity.

The matter of safeguarding the security of Soviet institutions and citizens abroad must be kept under constant control. Every effort must be made to promote greater political vigilance in Soviet colonies and provide reliable protection for Soviet people against provocation attempts by the adversary. Their efforts to persuade Soviet citizens to betray their homeland must be exposed and stopped, and more active preventive work undertaken in this direction. All the efforts and resources of the intelligence service abroad must be utilised to prevent penetration by the enemy's special services, using agents or technical devices, into Soviet embassies abroad, and to improve measures for their physical and technical protection.

A more energetic and aggressive approach must be adopted in measures designed for intelligence infiltration into the adversary's special services, especially into those sections which are directly concerned with working against the USSR, and its institutions and citizens abroad.

The assignments of safeguarding the security of intelligence activity and protecting Soviet institutions abroad, and of infiltration into the special services must be undertaken in close cooperation with our distant neighbours* and, in cases of necessity, by using the facilities of our friends and special contacts† (where these exist). Work relating to the Soviet colony must be carried out in contact with Soviet ambassadors and heads of Party organisations.

Cooperation with the intelligence services of countries of the socialist community and the special services of some liberated countries

Develop, and give more specific expression to cooperation with friends, in accordance with agreements.

Paramount attention must be given to working against the main adversary. There must be improved coordination of action to deal with priority assignments and to safeguard the security of intelligence operations.

Management

Enhance the organising role played by planning in the intelligence service. Include in your plans only measures which are realistic and well-founded, provide for rational deployment and utilisation of operational efforts and resources and make sure that there is continuity in planning. Step up control and checking of what has been done, and improve reporting and analytical work.

No. 26ss

---

* Distant neighbours – GRU (Soviet military intelligence service).
† Special contacts – KGB agents in the security and intelligence services of friendly countries.

2

Agent Recruitment

'C OMRADE KRYUCHKOV'S instructions' for 1984 decreed that
'The main effort must be concentrated on acquiring valuable
agents.'[1] There is little doubt that, as Chairman of the KGB from 1988
to 1991, he continued to regard that as the first priority of foreign
intelligence. But Kryuchkov's priorities had once been rather different.
When he became head of the FCD in 1974 he had no practical experience of work in a foreign Residency. The rapid expansion of contacts
with the West during the détente of the early 1970s initially persuaded
him that new methods of intelligence collection should be employed
against the Main Adversary. The haemorrhage of American official
secrets and the sensational revelations of investigative journalists as the
Watergate scandal developed, convinced him that the traditional tradecraft of agent recruitment was becoming outmoded. Many secrets
seemed to be there for the taking. In 1974, to the horror of Centre
veterans, Kryuchkov instructed Residencies to concentrate on building
up large numbers of contacts willing to talk openly about official secrets,
rather than engage in the much slower and more labour-intensive
methods of cultivating and recruiting secret agents. A few disastrous
experiences in Western restaurants with KGB officers under diplomatic
cover abandoning their traditional tradecraft and trying to imitate Bob
Woodward and Carl Bernstein of the *Washington Post* quickly persuaded
Kryuchkov to abandon the experiment. He subsequently laid even
greater emphasis than many of his department heads on the need to
recruit a new generation of penetration agents in the West.

Except in the case of 'walk-ins' such as Geoffrey Prime and John
Walker (probably the KGB's most valuable agents during the 1970s in,
respectively, Britain and the United States),[2] agent recruitment is a long
and painstaking process, which requires even longer training. In addition
to undergoing elaborate theoretical courses in agent recruitment at the
KGB's Andropov Institute, young FCD officers are put through a long
series of practical exercises in recruiting techniques, making rendezvous
with agents, checking for surveillance, filling and emptying dead letter-
boxes (DLBs) at a special training school in Moscow known as 'The

Villa', where retired officers play the part of foreign agents and targets for recruitment. Before going on their first foreign postings, officers take further refresher courses. From the mid-70s to the mid-80s Kim Philby ran an annual seminar from October to April for young officers of the FCD Third Department (responsible for operations in Britain, Ireland, Scandinavia, Australasia and Malta). In the course of these seminars, conducted in a KGB safe flat in Gorky Street, Moscow, Philby adopted successively the roles of foreign politician, civil servant, intelligence officer, businessman and journalist, and told his students to try to recruit him. At the end of each course Philby wrote individual reports on each of his students. In a number of cases known personally to Gordievsky, his comments were borne out by the students' future careers.

Once an FCD officer is stationed in a Residency abroad, his first step in agent recruitment is to make a contact with access to information of value to the KGB. Without knowing it, the target then becomes, in KGB jargon, 'an official contact under study by an intelligence officer'. The case officer cultivates the target by invitations to lunch, other forms of social contact, and presents on special occasions. If the target appears responsive to these attentions, he (or, less commonly, she) is promoted to the rank of 'a subject of deep study' (*obyekt razrabotki*). An elaborate file is opened, his (or her) background is researched from a variety of sources, the case officer intensifies the process of cultivation and may initiate technical surveillance of the target by using eavesdropping devices.

Traditionally the most sought after agents have been those with ideological sympathies for the Soviet Union or the 'socialist system'. One variant of the traditional formula introduced in the late 1980s was to exploit sympathy for perestroika and Gorbachev's attempt to lead the USSR into a new era. Ideological sympathy, however, is not enough. Agents are, almost invariably, persuaded to accept money in order to strengthen the KGB's hold over them. Those who are reluctant to take what they are offered are told that it is simply to cover their expenses. As ideological agents have become progressively rarer in the West, money has become increasingly important. In 1984 Kryuchkov ordered agent-recruiters to 'make bolder use of material incentives'. Particularly if he finds it difficult to exert an ideological or financial hold over the target, the recruiter will seek to establish a bond of personal friendship. Frequently, flattery is his most important tool. Gennadi Titov, head of the Third Department from 1979 to 1984, had a reputation as the most accomplished flatterer in the FCD. It was largely through flattery that he maintained his hold over the most important of his agents, the Norwegian Arne Treholt.[3]

In 1976 the Centre sought to systematise agent recruitment by introducing a personality questionnaire for all *razrabotka* targets, requiring information on a great variety of personal traits ranging from self-discipline to sexual perversion. Gordievsky obtained the following example in 1978 while stationed in the Copenhagen Residency.

No 6637/X
24 May 1978

TOP SECRET
Copy No 1

COPENHAGEN

To Comrade KORIN [M. P. LYUBIMOV]
In order to arrive at better operational studies of the professional and personal qualities of foreigners under deep study, and also bearing in mind the necessity to systematise the reporting of the residency's Line X [scientific and technological intelligence] case officers concerning the results of the studies which they have carried out, we are forwarding herewith a model framework on how a psychological personality portrait should be prepared and compiled.

The present psychological personality portrait outline is identical to that incorporated in the questionnaire (form No 6) which was forwarded to you under cover of letter No 690/154 of 26.10.76.

Attachment: 3 pages, secret, No 151/2 6651 DM. [Documentary material.]

KIMOV [unidentified]

I request all the operational staff to familiarise themselves with this. All comrades will make the necessary notes.

KORIN
6.6.78

Ref No 6637/X
24 May 1978

SECRET
Copy No 1

Psychological Personality Portrait

1. Personal qualities which illustrate attitude to operational work:

a) positive qualities – industrious, conscientious, disciplined, carries out instructions, prepared to take initiative, active, punctilious, adheres to

№ 66 37 /Х
от "24" мая 1978 года

ПСИХОЛОГИЧЕСКИЙ ПОРТРЕТ ЛИЧНОСТИ

1. Личные качества, характеризующие отношение к оперативной работе:

а) положительные - трудолюбив, добросовестен, дисциплинирован, исполнителен, инициативен, активен, аккуратен, принципиален, ответственно относится к порученному делу, бдителен, конспиративен;

б) отрицательные - ленив, недобросовестен, недисциплинирован, неисполнителен, неаккуратен, безынициативен, пассивен, небрежен, беспринципен, безответственно и формально относится к порученному делу, не обладает должной бдительностью, неконспиративен, болтлив.

2. Интеллектуальные качества:

а) положительные - сообразителен, находчив, мыслит глубоко, проницателен; умеет анализировать и делать обобщения, ясно и лаконично излагать свои мысли, выделять главное; наблюдателен, умеет дать объективную оценку поведению людей; практичен, имеет хорошую память, обладает организаторскими способностями;

б) отрицательные - замедленно мыслит, легкомыслен, поверхностен; не умеет анализировать и делать обобщения, ясно и лаконично излагать свои мысли, выделять главное, давать объективную оценку поведению людей; ненаблюдателен, непрактичен; обладает слабой памятью, не имеет организаторских способностей.

3. Эмоционально-волевые качества:

а) положительные - смел, решителен, готов пойти на риск; целеустремлен, настойчив в достижении цели, самостоятелен, умеет владеть собой, энергичен; терпелив, жизнерадостен;

б) отрицательные - труслив, нерешителен, избегает риска, перестраховщик, нецелеустремлен, ненастойчив в достижении цели; упрям, несамостоятелен, не умеет владеть собой, пассивен, вспыльчив; вял, пессимистичен.

principles, adopts a responsible attitude to the task in hand, vigilant, security-minded.

b) negative qualities – lazy, not conscientious, ill disciplined, does not heed instructions, slovenly, unwilling to take the initiative, passive, slipshod unprincipled, adopts an irresponsible and uncommitted attitude to the task in hand, does not possess the necessary vigilance, disinterested in security, indiscreet.

2. Intellectual qualities:

a) positive – quick-witted, resourceful, thinks deeply about a problem, penetrating, able to analyse and make generalisations, able to express his thoughts clearly and concisely, able to distinguish between the important and the trivial, observant, able to assess people's behaviour objectively; practical, has a good memory, possesses organising ability.

b) negative – thinks slowly, frivolous, superficial, unable to analyse and make generalizations, or to express himself clearly and briefly, unable to distinguish between the important and the unimportant or to assess people's behaviour objectively; unobservant, unpractical; has a weak memory, does not possess organising ability.

3. Emotional-volitional qualities:

a) positive – bold, decisive, ready to take risks, purposeful, persistent in getting what is required, self-reliant, self-controlled, energetic, has stamina, cheerful.

b) negative – timid, indecisive, avoids risks, plays safe, insufficiently purposeful and not persistent in getting what is required, obstinate, not self-reliant, lacks self-control, passive, irascible, slack, pessimistic.

4. Attitude to other people:

a) positive – well disposed, sociable, sympathetic, polite, tactful, fair, thoughtful, sincere, exacting.

b) negative – ill-disposed, reserved, mistrustful, indifferent, rude, abrupt, unfair, thoughtless, insincere, unexacting, argumentative.

5. Self-appraisal:

a) positive qualities – modest, self-demanding and self-critical, confident of his powers and objective in assessing his own potential, realistic in assessing his successes, possesses self-respect.

b) negative qualities – arrogant, does not demand much of himself, tends to be conceited, not confident of his power, not objective in appraising his own potential, inclined to overrate his successes, adventuristic, does not have self-respect, selfish, ambitious, vain.

6. His attitude and reactions to his Case Officer's comments.

7. Other personal qualities of operational significance:

a) positive – able to adapt quickly to new circumstances, switches easily from one job to another, has experience of life, possesses deep learning, enjoys authority and respect within his own milieu as an expert in his job, an interesting conversationalist, charming, able to draw people to him and influence them.

b) negative – slow to adapt to new conditions, has difficulty in switching from one task to another, has insufficient experience of life, possesses a narrow range of interests, lacks authority and respect in his circle; is a negative character, chases women and cannot hold his liquor, gambles, drinks to excess, is addicted to narcotics and sexual perversions.

8. Personal habits (the degree to which he takes alcoholic drinks, smokes, enjoys eating and dressing well etc).

9. Recreations (kinds of sport, hunting, fishing, collecting things, artistic tendencies etc) and to what degree.

10. Are there any inherent difficulties regarding the ability of the foreigner and the case officer to adapt to each other and if so, for what reasons (differences in age, education, position in the service, peculiarities of character etc)?

I N April 1985 a much more elaborate questionnaire was introduced for politicians and other 'prominent figures in the West' designated as *obyekti razrabotki*. Among the topics whose importance is stressed is that of obtaining 'compromising information'.

[ms note:]
Comrade Gornov and all
PR-Line operational
personnel
LAVROV [L. Y. NIKITENKO] 17.iv.85

No 20-4836/PR/83

5th April 1985   To Residents

Among the various tasks dealt with by our Service an important place is occupied by work on prominent figures in the West who are of interest to us from an operational or information-gathering perspective. Study of such persons requires a further improvement in the efficiency of our methods.

With this in mind we are sending you a model for a report on a state, political, or public leader of a capitalist country. It is intended to help stations and personnel abroad to organise the more thorough, comprehensive and purposeful study of such a figure, in order to obtain, where possible, a fuller description of his public and political personality, and social and psychological character, to avoid missing essential factors, and to organise work on him in a more professional and productive way.

The need for the careful study of this or that personage, and for preparing a report on him, may arise from factors such as: drawing him into some form of collaboration with us (as an agent, or confidential or special unofficial contact), providing the authorities and the departments concerned with information about him when he takes up an important post, and in connection with forthcoming high-level meetings and talks with representatives of the USSR.

In using the model, account must be taken of: the region and country to which the leader belongs, the position he occupies in the state apparatus, party or social organisation; his age and the duration of his activity; the reason for compiling the report; resources of the station concerned, including number of staff, and other factors.

Depending on the purpose of compiling the report, some sections or points may provide more, and others less detailed information and some points may be omitted altogether. The model makes it possible to compile a report of any length, depending on the reason for preparing the document and the quantity of data (ranging roughly from 1.5 to 5–6 pages).

Please be guided by the model in drawing up the report.

Inform those officers who are concerned with this category of foreigner about this letter and the model for the report.

The letter and model should be retained on developed film.

Attachment: as indicated in text, No. 20-4644/PR/83   10 pages secret PN

SVETLOV

[N. P. GRIBIN]

[Head of Third Department FCD]

Gordon 19/4   Simon 15/4

Oliver 18/4

Model layout for a report on a   Secret
prominent figure of a capitalist
country in government or political   Copy No 1
or public life

Attachment to No. 20-4836/PR/83

[MS comment:]

Text is hard to read.

REPORT

on: _____

     full name

_____

post   *country*

1. *Identifying details of person concerned, social origin, material circumstances and education*

1.1 Full name. How otherwise known. Date and place of birth. Citizenship, nationality. Party membership, knowledge of foreign languages.

1.2 Profession, specialisation. Place of work and post occupied. Home address and address at work and telephone numbers.

1.3 Family situation. Full name, date and place of birth and place of work or study of wife and children. Close relatives of subject and wife and their occupation.

     Subject's relations with his wife: does he trust her, does he allow her to make decisions about public, Party or other matters; does she play any part in decision-making or not.

     If this is subject's second marriage, information should be given about his first family, where it is operationally necessary.

1.4 Social origins: to what class, social stratum, etc do the families of subject and wife belong; in which did they grow up and have their education in child-hood and youth. Parents' social position.

1.5 Material circumstances of parents and other close relatives of subject and wife, and of subject himself: Property, capital, income. Annual income of subject's family and what it comprises, including supplementary income. Where does the subject invest his capital; with which firms, companies etc is he connected, what position does he occupy in them, how many shares does he hold. Information about any dissatisfaction on subject's part with his level of material security. Any evidence of material incentives where he is concerned.

Depending on subject's position and on operational necessity, state whether he has a car (cars) and the make, colour and registration number.

1.6 Military service and attitude towards it, stages, involvement in wars.

1.7 Education. Where, when and which secondary school, university or other educational establishment (including military) did he attend, with what degree of success, what abilities did he show, what was he keen on during his years of study. What means did he have for his education. Academic degree and subject.

Membership and work for political parties and other organisations during student years, involvement in student movement.

If subject comes from a capitalist country other than the United States and he studied and at the same time worked in the USA, this must be explained, indicating which American professors he studied with, where and what kind of job he had and whom he knew at work, whether he might have been recruited by the CIA or have come to their notice.

If subject studied in his own country, make this clear and make a note of whether he came in contact with American professors and teachers, diplomats, businessmen or other US citizens working there. Might he have been recruited by the CIA or come to their notice.

A note must also be made of any evidence of interest shown when a student by a person from any capitalist country in Marxism, Marxism literature or ideological closeness to the local communist party, or a sympathetic attitude towards the USSR and its policies, or with revolutionary national liberation and other movements of a progressive nature.

2. Basic elements of subject's political career, whose interests he expresses, the groups with which he is connected, his immediate circle, mode of operation, firmness of conviction

2.1 When and in what circumstances did subject first appear on the political scene of the country and in what capacity. What part did his social origin and position, property, and also his personal qualities, play in this respect.

Subject could come to power (occupy the post of president or prime minister), become leader of a political party or social organisation, or hold another important post as a result of elections, coup d'état, appointment or formation of a grouping (alliance, coalition) of political forces, or manoeuvring, or through succession to the throne, as a compromise candidate, or in some other way.

2.2 What motives, interests and aims prompted subject to engage in state, political or public activity.

Motives, interests and aims may specifically include, in particular, the following: strengthening the position and defending the interests of a class or social stratum for which subject is working; strengthening the position of a government, party or organisation; desire to become a state, political or public figure; drive to power as an end in itself or as a means of solving class, national or other problems; material interest, ambition for wealth or profit; desire to become an historical figure, or go down in history (by which historical figure and by which of his principles and ideas is he guided as a model for imitation); ambition (pretentions to the role of 'liberator and leader', 'father of the nation', 'saviour' etc), of what sort of character and tendency; vanity, ambition; conflict with political opponents; fighting against oligarchy and social injustice, nationalist views; aspiration to liberate his country from the domination of foreign capital; allegiance to national liberation ideas, etc.

2.3 Which are the principal posts occupied by subject from the beginning of his career up to the present. In what circumstances did he take up this or that post. What personal qualities and other factors played a role in this.

Where necessary, make a note of in what connection a change took place in the subject's situation, to what did he owe the fact that he got these posts, what played the decisive role in his appointment, advancement, access etc. How did he attract attention to himself, and in what does his principal merit consist, etc.

2.4 Who promoted, supports and protects subject. Whose interests does he profess and represent, whom does he serve, who supplies him and his activity with financial support.

With what political, public, business, military, religious, tribal and other groups and organisations is he connected in his own and other countries, to what extent is he dependent on these. With which representatives of these groups and organisations, by what means and through whom does he maintain contact. With which state, political and public figures does he have close relations. Role of his family connections.

In particular subject's contacts with financial, commercial, industrial or land-owning circles (banks, monopolies, companies, firms, the military-industrial complex, major Zionist, Arab and other kinds of big business, trading organisations, are of interest. Possible contacts subject has with the Zionist Universal Jewish Congress, the World Zionist Organisation, the Vatican and with lobbyist and other influential organisations. Involvement and contacts of subject in closed, privileged clubs, Masonic lodges and other analogous organisations and societies, and their influence on the individual's position and activity.

For a number of countries, the fact of belonging to and having contacts with castes, with Islam, with this or that tendency, with other religious organisations and sects, communities and so on, is also of interest.

In regard to certain other persons, a note should be made where there is a basis for this, of when, and in what way they achieved recognition by these influential forces, exponents, and supporters of the interests which they have embraced.

2.5 On what political, military or other forces, propaganda organisation (news-papers, radio and television station, individual publications etc) does subject rely in his state, political or public activity, and in pursuing his own political line. His attitude to the existence and activity of political parties and organisations, trade unions and other public organisations in his country.

2.6 In what other affairs is subject engaged simultaneously at this time (business, medical or legal practice, scientific research, teaching work etc).

2.7 Has he been involved in forming an opposition or opposition activities. Has he been subjected to persecution, arrest, imprisonment – and for what reason. Has subject been an émigré.

2.8 Subject's immediate circle, his assistants and advisers, which of them is the most influential. Who has good personal relations with subject and his family.

On whose recommendations and advice does subject rely in questions of selecting members of the government, senior officials in the state administration, of a political party or public organisation.

2.9 Where does subject see his principal task in the post he occupies in the field of domestic and of foreign policy. How far is he informed of and how deep is his understanding of domestic and foreign policy matters. The degree of influence he has on determining and implementing the policy line adopted in this area, or his attitude towards it.

2.10 Characteristic traits of subject's style and methods of work and conduct in the post he occupies. The most important features of the national character which he possesses and their influence on his style of work and conduct.

His experience of working out and adopting very important decisions. Who regularly gives subject recommendations and advice in matters of domestic and foreign policy. Whom does he consult on the most acute problems, especially in crisis situations. Who exerts a decisive influence on shaping the domestic and foreign policy line (attitude) of a prominent figure in the country, government, party or organisation. Is this person a puppet in anyone's hands. Inclination and ability to find compromise solutions. How is the organisational side of subject's work arranged?

2.11 Subject's inclination and ability to manoeuvre. On whom does he rely or who supports him in this respect. Kinds of manoeuvre he employs, frequent changes of attitude on important questions and other methods and devices as means of achieving this or that aim or task.

Level of subject's truthfulness and sincerity. Is he hypocritical or double-dealing? Is he an adroit and unprincipled politician, an adventurer, does he have a penchant for political intrigue?

2.12 How firm is subject's position in the post he occupies?

To what extent is he authoritative, influential, and popular? What degree of recognition has he in the country, in public and political circles as an authoritative state figure, member of parliament, party leader or head of a public organisation, or occupant of some other important post?

What attention is paid to his statements and speeches.

> When assessing how firm subject's position is, it is useful, should this be necessary, to clarify the factors which help to strengthen his position and power of action and those which weaken them.

> Among the first may figure: a favourable positioning of forces in the country, parliament, government, party or organisation; the existence of political alliances and agreements to support him, a constructive or loyal attitude in the principal opposition forces; development of good relations with the trade unions, armed forces, special services, judicial authorities, etc.

> The second type of factor may be: energetic opposition activity in the country, parliament, government, party or organisation; difficulties in, or severance of relations with parliament, the trade unions, the armed forces, the church, the judicial authorities or the special services; the threat of a coup d'état; a partisan movement; activity of extremist organisations and terrorist groups etc. Who is supporting or financing these tendencies.

2.13 Subject's experience. In which matters is he the most competent man? Assessment by those around him of his personality in professional terms.

2.14 How has he shown himself at various stages of his professional activity. Has he any big successes in this field, which have been distinguished by awards, or, on the other hand, any serious failures.

2.15 Compromising information about subject, including illegal acts in financial and commercial affairs, intrigues, speculation, bribes, graft, trading in narcotics, and exploitation of his position to enrich himself. Any other information compromising subject in the eyes of the country's authorities and general public, disclosure of which could have a negative effect on his life and career.

2.16 Prospects of retaining or changing his official or social position, and also his political attitudes, in the future.

2.17 Has subject any connection with CIA or other Western special services or police forces, or has he come to their notice.

> Take into account the possibility of a leader from some other Western country

belonging to the CIA, since he might be recruited there by the CIA or come to their notice.

3. *Subject's political views*

3.1 Subject's political outlook, when it was formed, how firm are his views. What social, economic, political, military, philosophical, religious and other teaching and doctrine have been influential in forming subject's views. What influence was exerted on the formation of his political opinions in childhood and youth by his family upbringing, instruction and training in educational establishments, and his circle of friends and acquaintances at this time. Possible development of subject's views.

A bourgeois personality's views and convictions may be radical, liberal, conservative, right-wing, nationalist, left-wing nationalist, right-wing nationalist, social reformist, fascist etc. He may adopt a progressive, reactionary, centrist, left-of-centre, right-of-centre or other position.

3.2 How firm and consistent is subject in defending the interests of the class or social stratum to which he belongs or which he serves? Is there any deviation from these positions, and does he take up a particular stance on any matters which differs from the views and interests of that class or social stratum?

3.3 Attitude to Marxism, socialism and the communist party of the country concerned and its programme and activity, and to other left-wing forces.

3.4 Subject's attitude to religion (believer or not), how far does he practise it; his religious and other moral and ethical standards and principles; to what extent does he observe them and is he guided by them in his life and work.*

If subject is a believer what religion does he profess and does he go to church? If he is a Catholic, is he a militant one or not; if he is a Muslim, is he a fanatic or not, and so on.

3.5 Subject's views on the world historical process and the driving forces behind it, and on development trends in the modern world. His estimate of his country's place and role in the world.

What ideas does subject hold on internal and external policy matters. His point of view on the principal problems of the present day.

With regard to the country in question and what position subject occupies, it is useful, if need arises, when clarifying his ideas on domestic policy questions, to note his views on his country's social and political system in general and what path of social development he considers would be most suited to it; what kind of economic development does he advocate for it, and with what resources; his attitude to the development of the state sector of the economy; what role does he assign to

---

* This information about subject must take into account the special features existing in the region and country concerned in regard to these matters.

national private capital; his views on restricting the economic and political position of land-owning, financial, commercial and industrial oligarchies and also on instituting other more far-reaching social and economic reforms; his position in regard to restricting the activity of the military-industrial complex, big business, transnational companies and foreign capital in the country; his views and attitude on the question of fighting to achieve independence and national sovereignty.

3.6 Subject's assessment of the place and role of the USSR in international affairs, his attitude towards Soviet foreign policy and peace proposals and initiatives; has he been in the USSR; subject's views and attitude to the question of developing relations with the Soviet Union.

Here, any views (positive or negative) genuinely held by subject and not revealed to those around him, in this respect, regarding Soviet foreign policy and internal structure, are of interest, as are also any possible coincidences of views (due to existence of common interests or for some other motive) with the opinions and attitudes of the Soviet Union on the principal problems of the present day.

3.7 Attitude on the question of developing relations with other socialist countries; with countries with progressive regimes, attitude to the revolutionary national liberation movement; to the non-aligned movement, to the developing countries, to the peace movement and anti-war movement and pacifist views.

3.8 Any action, statements, speeches etc on subject's part directed against or in favour of the USSR and the other socialist countries, and their allies and friends, and also for or against the communist, revolutionary, national-liberation and other progressive movements and forces.

In this context there is particular interest in the adoption, at the subject's initiative or with his participation, of important legislation, amendments, agreements concluded, development and promotion of programmes, reports, initiatives, slogans, and so on, on political questions or foreign or military policy, or economic or other matters. This also relates to any action on subject's part to organise some kind of provocation against Soviet establishments and nationals abroad, attacks on Soviet shipping and other operations and also repressive legislation and persecution of progressive forces and leaders.

In working on which key questions of this kind did subject play a decisive or major role?

3.9 Evaluation by an American of the place and role of the USA in the world. His attitude on American relations with other Western countries, especially members of NATO, the EEC and other groupings.

3.10 Evaluation by a personality from another Western country of the USA's place and role in the world, and opinions and attitude towards developing relations with the USA.

3.11 Subject's attitude towards American foreign policy.

Show, in particular, subject's attitude towards the arms race pursued by the USA, its efforts to achieve military supremacy over the USSR, deployment of various types of weapons of mass destruction in other countries, militarisation of space, exacerbation of international tension, provocation of crisis situations, interference in the internal affairs of other countries, overthrowing legal regimes, creating aggressive blocs etc. Subject's stance regarding American action in choosing the countries to support the US in specific regions (Israel, Pakistan, Saudi Arabia, Japan, Taiwan, Thailand etc), the American position on the major international issues (the Arctic, and Antarctic, the Law of the Sea, the activities of the UN, human rights, etc), and exploitation by the West, especially the USA, of the 'Islamic factor' for their own ends. Of which aspects and measures of the imperialist policy of the USA and its NATO allies, and also Israel and South Africa does subject disapprove publicly or secretly.

Subject's attitude to the new international economic and information order.

3.12 Subject's attitude to racial discrimination in the USA, South Africa and other Western countries; has he open or secret anti-racist inclinations.

3.13 Subject's assessment of the place and role of the PRC in international affairs, attitude towards her foreign policy; has he been in the PRC; views and attitude to the question of developing relations with her.

4. *Personal qualities and psychological traits of subject**

4.1 How honest is subject (honourable, decent), true to his word, or promise, full of initiative, active, punctilious, high-principled, security conscious.

4.2 Subject's qualities as strategist and tactician (very briefly in relation to the post he occupies and in cases where this is necessary).

4.3 Subject's intellectual level: mind, ability to think, quick wittedness, powers of observation, resourcefulness, insight; range of interests, erudition; what kind of knowledge he possesses and in what field; ability to analyse and generalise, express his ideas, and pick out the main point; memory, organising ability, powers of oratory.

Has he produced scientific work or publications, and on what subjects. Inclination and endeavour to achieve self-improvement, acquire knowledge, undertake scientific research, get his work published, etc. Through what sources of information (newspapers, periodicals, films, etc) does he supplement his knowledge and widen his interests.

4.4 Subject's ability to convey to public opinion or other spheres, a required

---

* If subject is not under operational cultivation, this information should be included in the report to the extent that it can be collected through agents, from official sources, taking into account possible contact or acquaintance with him on the part of some member of the station or other officials of the Soviet establishment in the country.

point of view or essential material in a locally acceptable form, style and wording, and also address an audience convincingly.

4.5 Subject's capacity and taste for work. Does he himself work or do others work for him.

4.6 Does he possess will power, courage, resolution, ability and readiness to run risks, persistence and firmness in achieving his aims; how energetic and enterprising is he, can he organise and draw the masses; is he self-disciplined and self-controlled.

4.7 Are pride, arrogance, egoism, ambition or vanity among subject's natural characteristics. How are they expressed.

4.8 To what extent is subject independent and self-reliant, is he capable of taking big military and political decisions on his own, does he consider the views of those around him.

4.9 Manner of behaviour in public, relations with other people: to what extent is he sociable (or reserved, reticent), communicative, loquacious, talkative; benevolent, tactful, polite, sensitive, fair, considerate, sincere, demanding.

4.10 Ability to judge and understand people, to establish contacts with strangers, find a common language when talking to others. Skill as an expert in his line, as an interesting conversationalist, and as a charming man to win over and influence people.

4.11 Are patriotic feelings, national pride, loyalty to authority and a sense of duty among subject's characteristics.

4.12 Are efficiency, pragmatism and realism natural to him.

4.13 Subject's attitude to smoking and alcohol. If he smokes and drinks, what are his preferences and does he over-indulge in alcohol.
    Deviations from the norm in other aspects of life: drug abuse, homosexuality, illegal gambling and other tastes which are reprehensible in the eyes of the public.

4.14 Life style: hobbies, enjoyments, tastes; books – what writers does he prefer; theatre, music, painting, and what he particularly likes; collecting, attitude to sport (riding, hunting, fishing, swimming, chess, football, games, motoring, sailing etc), prizes won; hiking; with what kind of environment and what kind of people does he prefer to associate; what kind of cuisine does he prefer, and so on.

Depending on what kind of persons is concerned and for what reasons we are interested in him, the following qualities and special features might also be of interest:

– is he irascible, irritable, emotional, expansive, or quiet, well-balanced;

– is he naturally inclined to miserliness and acquisitiveness;

— *state of health and its effect on his work; ability to accept emotional and nervous strain;*

— *presence of traits such as cowardice, caution, modesty, endeavour not to hurry into or avoid expressing his opinion, concealing it or, on the other hand, to express it directly and freely; endeavour not to disclose his political convictions and so on;*

— *subject's attitude and sensitivity to assessment of his activity, susceptibility to flattery and praise. Inclination [illeg] [illeg] receiving [illeg] invitations [illeg] souvenir;*

— *how much experience has he of holding talks on international political questions, is one of his characteristics a refined, acute political flair;*

— *style of conducting discussions and behaving during talks; is he more inclined to talk himself or to listen to the other party; does he stick to a prepared text or give a free exposition; what kind of talks does he prefer to hold, short or long; tendency to [illeg words – ? digress to ?side] issues, not directly concerned with the subject of the talk; if so, what does he prefer to talk about (music, painting, theatre, sport, etc); is he in the habit of using [? jokes] and witticisms in his talks? Has he a sense of humour?*

— *attitude towards entering into sharp debate over difficult questions; is it natural to him to avoid sharp questions and awkward situations? How does he behave when he finds himself in a [illeg] position, could be [illeg] at that moment a rigid, uncompromising position [illeg] hard decisions, without reckoning with [illeg words]*

— *is it natural to subject to keep to his word with mutual relations with allies and opponents; can be [illeg – ? change point of view . . . how to [illeg] his partner's inclinations for talks and compromise what position to occupy in connection with [illeg – these relations]*

— *how does he [illeg] and feel in an unofficial situation; attitude to [illeg words]*

— *subject's [illeg . . . ? observance] of diplomatic protocol when visiting other countries, is he fond of trips abroad;*

— *attitude towards public opinion and to journalists, and meetings with them, and to radio and television;*

— *subject's characteristics as a family man;*

— *for purposes of working with subject either directly or through his circle, his attitude towards women is also of interest, is he secretly fascinated by them, is he in the habit of having affairs with women on the side?*

5. *Subject's intelligence access*

5.1 To what kind of secret information, especially about the Main Adversary, has subject access; his ability to acquire and pass it on.

5.2 Which political, military, diplomatic, consular and other establishments and organisations belonging to the USA and other NATO countries does subject visit (or have access to) by virtue of the post he occupies or other circumstances.

5.3 Any links and contacts of subject in government, political, public, business, military-industrial, scientific research, church and other circles who are of intelligence or operational interest; also in international organisations, diplomatic and military missions, in closed and privileged clubs, masonic lodges, sports clubs and so on, both in subject's own country and in other countries, especially the USA, FRG, France, Italy, Japan. Brief description of the most valuable contacts (including unofficial ones) with whom subject maintains the closest personal relations of a confidential nature.

5.4 Description of subject's opportunities and capabilities in regard to carrying out influence operations.

5.5 Potential basis for drawing him into one or other form of cooperation with us.

Signatures and stamps in accordance with the form laid down.

No 20-4644/PR/83

I N order to qualify as a full KGB agent, the 'subject of deep study' has to fulfil two main conditions. First he (or she) has to agree to secret, 'conspiratorial' collaboration. Second, he (or she) must be willing to accept instructions from the KGB. Targets who fail to meet with either of these conditions are classed only as 'confidential contacts' (*doveritelnaya svyaz*); their chances of subsequent promotion to full agent status are slim. As agent recruitment in the West became more difficult with the declining ideological appeal of the Soviet Union during, and after, the Brezhnev era, the Centre became increasingly preoccupied by the problem of 'paper agents': targets recruited by Residencies to keep their agent numbers but who had no access to intelligence of any importance. There were several such agents on the books of the London Residency.

The Centre's concern with the declining numbers and quality of agents in the West led it to call a conference of senior FCD staff in June 1984 with the aim of 'improving recruitment work'. The conclusions of the meeting, together with a directive from Kryuchkov, were circulated to Residencies in the following month. The FCD frankly admitted that 'in recent years' high-level agent recruitment had been 'poor', and denounced the passivity of some Residencies: 'It is particularly difficult to tolerate the fact that some intelligence officers do not even have any prospective cases to develop.' By implication, the practises of recruiting 'paper agents' was also condemned: 'Recruitment must not be pursued in order to obtain some merely abstract result . . .' Residencies were urged to abandon their old, increasingly unsuccessful 'stereotyped methods', become more 'creative' in finding recruitment opportunities (through sports clubs, for example), and if necessary get their wives to help.

The Centre was particularly concerned about its declining success in recruiting American agents. Wherever they were stationed, PR line officers were ordered to find US 'targets to cultivate, or, at the very least, official contacts'. They were told they would be judged first and foremost by their agent recruitment and handling.

[ms notes:] Comr Gornov
Comr Brown
Comr Artyom and all operational staff of the Residency

Lavrov [L. Y. Nikitenko], 9.VIII.84

No 439
Top Secret
Copy No 1

No 1243/PR
13.07.84

Conference held in the department about improving recruitment work.

In accordance with Comrade Alyoshin's [Kryuchkov's] instructions, an operational conference of senior staff was held in the department in June this year to discuss the question of improving the recruitment work of our stations abroad.

It was noted at the conference that the exacerbation of the international situation for which aggressive imperialist groups are responsible and which has given greater prominence to questions of military strategy and economic matters in the category of priority problems requiring intelligence investigation, has given rise to new and greater demands on the operational staff of our stations abroad. These demands have been freshly interpreted in Comrade Alyoshin's latest directions regarding 'Measures to promote greater efficiency in future in recruitment work and to reinforce the residencies' agent network' (the residency has been informed).

The main points of the questions considered at the meeting are set out below.

1. The existing agent organisation and newly acquired sources enable us in the main to cope with current tasks in the field of information gathering, carrying out influence operations and providing operational support for intelli-

gence activities. However, the agents and confidential contacts acquired in recent years have only in small measure furthered our efforts to deal with the principal tasks facing our Service. Achievements continue to be poor in acquiring agents to provide documents, recruiting agents, talent spotters and agents for cultivation purposes. Not all operational staff are putting their best efforts into obtaining concrete results. It is particularly difficult to tolerate the fact that some Chekist intelligence officers do not even have any prospective cases to develop. The quality of recruitment work continues to suffer because operational staff only have available a restricted group of permanent contacts. It was also remarked at the meeting that the considerable number of tasks set for residencies must not push into second place the effort to deal with the main task – acquiring agents and confidential contacts.

2. In spite of the fact that the Centre is constantly bringing to the attention of residencies the need to keep targeting constantly in mind, this important requirement is frequently not being fulfilled. In a number of cases our stations abroad select an unjustifiably large number of targets for study and cultivation, and this leads in practice to a dissipation of operational resources. Main attention is to be focused on the most important targets of the main adversary* and of your country of residence. There must also be a more systematic effort to discover and develop intermediate targets of interest to us, where penetration can be held to achieve priority intelligence tasks.

3. The targeting principle†, as applied to the work of recruitment, must entail a decisive refusal to pursue the study and cultivation of contacts which show no future promise. Recruitment must not be pursued in order to obtain some merely abstract result, but must be the logical consequence of studying a target for penetration which is of interest to us. The Centre wishes to draw the attention of heads of residencies and their officers to the fact that some operational staff are merely trying to acquire confidential contacts, to the detriment of efforts to create an agent network capable of more effectively achieving the tasks confronting us. Nor is there any justification for the self-satisfaction of some officers after they have attained a definite result of some kind. Moreover, the experience obtained by an officer in the process of actively cultivating a foreigner should be utilised effectively and purposefully.

4. The endeavour to improve the work of recruitment calls for the use of a greater variety of forms of intelligence activity, abandoning stereotyped methods of establishing and developing contacts, and adopting a creative approach towards utilising the individual characteristics of operational staff and the facilities of cover

---

* i.e. the US Embassy.

† The 'targeting principle' means looking purposefully for potential agent recruits in countries where the KGB station is located. Such recruits are primarily those with access to the main penetration targets of the KGB; for example, the Cabinet Office, the Foreign Office, the Ministry of Defence, and the intelligence community.

establishments in the process of cultivation and recruitment. In order to solve operational problems, it is essential to co-opt the wives of our officials to a wider extent for this work, and to increase the exploitation of official occasions and participation in the activities of various clubs, including sport, etc.

5. Following the directives from the heads of our Department, each residency must ensure that in its work conducted against the USA, the position is such that all 'PR' line officers should have American targets to cultivate, or at the very least, official contacts among the Americans. Work against the USA must be subject to special control by the heads of the residency and the 'main adversary' group.

6. The Centre draws your attention once again to the matter of maintaining security when cultivating contacts and in recruitment work as a whole. This applies to every stage of working with a contact: from the stage of initial acquaintance to the completion of the cultivation process with the obligatory comprehensive recruitment test before he is included in the agent network. It is only by adopting a creative approach towards organising and carrying out verification procedures, keeping a strict watch on performance, and a constant improvement in the means and methods of testing adopted, combined with a high professional standard among operational staff, that we shall be able to ensure the efficiency and reliability of the agent network and in consequence, guarantee a successful solution of the problems facing the intelligence service.

We remind you that the chief criterion of operational efficiency of any officer of the residency is still his work with contacts, and no other area of intelligence (information-gathering, active measures, etc) can be considered as 'compensation' for recruitment work.

Please inform all operational staff of the residency about this letter.

SVETLOV
[N. P. GRIBIN]

THIS exhortation produced no significant improvement during the remainder of 1984. The problem was considered afresh by the FCD Party Committee at a meeting on 14 February 1985. Nikolai Petrovich Gribin, head of the Third Department, reported that the problems of recruiting new agents had been compounded by the expulsion of experienced KGB officers from Britain and elsewhere, leading to 'the replenishment of operational staff of Residencies to an overwhelming extent by beginners'. These difficulties, however, were no excuse for inertia:

№ 513 /ПР
от 5 апреля 1985 г.

Секретно
Экз.№I

Р е з и д е н т а м

О задачах коммунистов
в свете решений Парткома Службы

     14 февраля в Парткоме нашей Службы состоялось заслушивание под-
разделения по вопросу " О работе коммунистов и партбюро отдела по
мобилизации сотрудников загранаппаратов на повышение результатив-
ности служебной деятельности".

     С докладом на заседании Парткома выступил тов. Светлов.

     В своем выступлении он подробно информировал членов Парткома о
работе проделанной руководством отдела и партийным бюро в плане решения поставленного вопроса, дал характеристику агентурно-оператив-
ной обстановки в странах, курируемых отделом, подробно остановился
на проблемах воспитательной работы.

     Тов.Светлов подчеркнул, что реализованные противником в послед-
ние годы острые акции в ряде стран против наших резидентур привели
к некоторой утрате важных разведывательных возможностей, частично
нейтрализовали деятельность многих опытных и результативных работни-
ков. Это привело также к тому, что подавляющее большинство оперсостава резидентур укомплектовано в основном начинающими работниками.

     В этой связи важно не допустить такого положения, когда осложне-
ние обстановки и ужесточение контрразведывательного режима стано-
вятся оправданием инертности оперсостава, топтания на месте. Сейчас
необходимо глубокое понимание той очевидной истины, что создаваемые
противником трудности должны стимулировать поиск новых, оригинальных
путей решения стоящих задач, повышать роль личного вклада каждого
сотрудника в дела резидентуры.

     Анализ работы за прошедший год показывает, что достигнутые ре-
зультаты могли бы быть весомее при более четком определении возможностей каждого оперработника, более требовательном спросе за итоги
работы, правильной расстановке кадров, повышении в целом организацион-
ной стороны дела, росте сознательной дисциплины оперсостава.

[F]or beginners, as also for experienced officers, the main requirement is to get results in recruitment. It is essential not only that the
full meaning of this requirement should be appreciated by every
intelligence officer, but that it should become his raison d'être and a
matter of Party and Chekist conscience.*

On 5 April 1985 Gribin sent out fresh exhortations to Residencies in
Britain and other Third Department countries.

[ms note] *Comr Gornov*
    for action (meeting)

No 233
Secret

LAVROV [L. Y. NIKITENKO] 17.IV.85

Copy No 1

No 813/PR
5 April 1985

To Residents

Communists' tasks – in the light of decisions of the Party Committee of the
Service†

A session took place on 14th February in the Party Committee of our Service
on the subject of 'Work done by senior communists and the departmental Party
Bureau to mobilise officials at posts abroad to improve the results of their
activity'.

Comrade Svetlov [Gribin] read a paper at the Party Committee meeting.

In his speech he gave members of the Party Committee detailed information
about the work done by the heads of department and of the Party Bureau to
deal with the matter to be decided, gave an account of the operational situation
in the countries looked after by the department and also dwelt in detail on the
problems of educational work.

Comrade Svetlov [Gribin] emphasised that the severe measures implemented by the adversary in recent years in a number of countries against our
Residencies have led to some loss of important intelligence access and have
partly neutralised the activity of many experienced and productive officers. It
has also led to the replenishment of operational staff of Residencies to an
overwhelming extent by beginners.

In this context it is important not to allow a situation to develop where the
difficulties of the position and the severity of the counter-intelligence system
become justification for inertia on the part of the operational staff and marking
time on the spot. We must now have a profound appreciation of that obvious truth
that the difficulties created by the adversary should stimulate us to search out new

* No. 813/PR of 5 April 1985; see p. 46.
† The FCD.

and original ways of dealing with our permanent assignments and enhancing the role of the personal contribution of each officer to the work of the Residency.

Examination of our work over the past year has shown that the results achieved could have been more solid if the possibilities of each member of the operational personnel had been more precisely defined, more exacting demands had been made for results from work, if there had been proper placing of personnel, improvement of the organisational side of the work as a whole, and more conscious discipline among operational staff.

Moreover, success was not achieved everywhere in getting every member of the Residency to work to full capacity, showing creative initiative and being not only the executor but also the skilled organiser of his work in the sector entrusted to him. We must therefore make the situation intolerable for those who are acting as parasites on the self-sacrificing work of their comrades and who are adopting a consumer role towards the rest of the community. For instance, in spite of the constant efforts of the Centre and the heads of the Residency, No 1 and No 2 are in fact inactive. A harsher kind of persuasion should be used on those who are acting in this way and if there is no subsequent change for the better in operational activity, then the question of sending them home before their time is up should be raised in a more decisive manner.

As regards aspects of recruitment work, Comrade Svetlov [Gribin] stressed the fact that for beginners, as also for experienced officers, the main requirement is to get results in recruitment. It is essential not only that the full meaning of this requirement should be appreciated by every intelligence officer, but that it should become his raison d'être and a matter of Party and Chekist conscience.

In a situation where the staff of Residencies have not been brought up to strength and the majority of operational personnel have not yet acquired enough experience of work in countries with a rigorous counter-intelligence system, then the part played by the personal example of heads of stations is greatly enhanced and we regard them not only as the organisers of intelligence activity, but also as the most experienced operatives. No 3 and No 4 have been named as leaders who meet these requirements and are capable by their example of inspiring a creative mood in their team and inculcating enthusiasm for recruitment work in their staff. At the same time, it has been noted that at other stations, sufficient attention is not yet being given to this side of operations. Such occurrences are particularly inadmissable where the Residency consists of only two or three people.

Comrade Svetlov [Gribin] emphasised in his concluding words that communists in the department regard the section Party Committee session as an opportunity to make a critical examination of their work and of the Residencies under their care, to apply the necessary remedies based on the Party Committee's recommendations and conclusions, to suggest measures to remove the shortcomings and also to mark the 27th CPSU Congress and the 40th anniversary of the Great Victory by producing some significant results.

Comrade Alekseev [Grushko] also spoke during the discussion on the paper, drawing attention to the need to improve Residencies' recruitment work, especially in regard to representatives of the main adversary and its allies, and to step up their productivity. He remarked that success in this field is the main criterion for assessing the results of Residencies' intelligence activity and that of individual officers. He had a number of comments to make in this connection on the fact that, at present, no serious work had been done to study this category of persons in the Residencies under the care of our Department and this did not provide proper foundations for the hope that priority tasks would be dealt with successfully.

One of the reasons for this situation, in Comrade Alekseev's [Grushko's] estimation, is that the department and heads of stations have not entirely managed to arrange for effective control to be exercised over the work of each individual officer, or to see that Residencies are strict in carrying out both prospective plans for cultivation of targets, and current instructions from the Centre.

Comrade Alekseev [Grushko] appealed once more for a more decisive effort to get rid of those officials whose attitude is one of dependence and timorousness, endeavouring to substitute analysis of the local press and meetings with official contacts for actual operational work with agents.

The Party organisation has an important role to play in this process; it must make a more detailed study of the personal and professional qualities of communist personnel and the standard of political and professional training of officials sent to the DZK [long-term posting abroad], reinforce Party influence on communists in Residencies, and be more consistent in requiring that decisions taken on findings at hearings held on individual officials are carried out.

In this context, Comrade Alekseev [Grushko] underlined particularly the need to improve the quality and objectivity of personal reports, both for operational personnel being trained for DZK and for those completing their tour abroad.

Following an all-round discussion of the work of senior communists and the Party Bureau in our section, to which the secretary of the departmental Party Bureau, Comrade Aristov, the Secretary of the Service's Party Committee, Comrade Batov, and the heads of a number of other sections of the Centre contributed, the Party Committee noted that the senior communists and the Party Bureau were performing a useful function in mobilising officials in our organisation abroad to improve the effectiveness and quality of professional and operational activity and to increase the degree of personal responsibility of communists for the work entrusted to them. A sound moral and psychological atmosphere had been created in the department. Discussion of professional and Party matters proceeds in a comradely atmosphere and the heads of the department rely on the Party Bureau when dealing with personnel, educational and other tasks. Stations are being run in a style which is both business-like and benevolent.

On the other hand, full use is not yet being made of all the ways of exerting professional and Party influence on communists in the department in order to enhance productivity, above all in recruitment work, and to make educational measures more effective.

Party influence is not yet being exerted sufficiently on communists in the matter of improving work against our main adversary. Most stations are showing no recruitment achievements in this direction and the level of recruitment 'work in hand' is poor. Effort has not been fully deployed on questions of military strategy. Not all senior communists in posts abroad are showing a personal example in carrying out these tasks.

Hearings on reports on communists at stations by the Party Bureau and the recommendations given to them have, in individual cases, not been sufficiently specific. These hearings do not always achieve the desired end. For instance, no practical results ensued in regard to comrades No 1 and No 2 when they returned to the station after their work had been examined by the Centre.

Effectiveness in educational work is also reduced by the fact that not all those who are in charge of work teams abroad show initiative in making suggestions where this kind of work needs to be done with one or other of their members. The personal reports sent in from stations are often of a formal nature. Organisations abroad do not always respond promptly to letters from the Party Bureau.

Senior Communists and the departmental Party Bureau have not got heads of stations to make comprehensive studies of the wives of officials and to compile detailed personal reports on them.

Our Service Party Committee has resolved as follows: to take steps to eliminate the shortcomings noted, to improve results in the professional operational activity of members of stations abroad which are looked after by our section, in the first place regarding military strategy and economic questions, and in recruitment work against targets representing the main adversary and its allies.

To step up the effectiveness of Party influence on communists in posts abroad, and of all the measures undertaken.

When examining reports from heads of stations, an assessment must be given of their personal contribution to carrying out the set tasks. The Party Bureau is recommended to hold discussions of the points mentioned with representatives present from the sections concerned.

Bolder action should be taken to propose that officers whose work is not producing results, should be sent home before their time. Communists who are sent back from postings because they show poor results must be held more strictly to account.

Senior officials and the Party Bureau must see that the instructions from the heads of the Centre about compiling personal reports of members and their wives, reflecting objectively both positive and negative aspects, are precisely complied with, for the record and for use of this information in subsequent educational work.

In line with our Service Party Committee's decision, the Party organisation will carefully study the recommendations and proposals issued and will embody the necessary amendments in plans for Party organisation and political education work: communists in stations abroad will be informed of these.

I hope that all 'PR'-line members will carefully acquaint themselves with the document and will draw the necessary conclusions in regard to an improvement in the quality of their work.

Please hold a 'PR'-line meeting on the matter concerned and inform the Centre of the results, in the prescribed manner, by 5 May.

SVETLOV
[GRIBIN]

No 2 – Patrick
No 4 – Gornov

A GENT recruitment of foreigners takes place inside as well as outside the Soviet Union. Responsibility is divided between the First and Second Chief Directorates. In theory the First is responsible for 'offensive operations' against foreigners, while the Second limits itself to counter-intelligence. In practice the Second Chief Directorate's responsibility for embassy surveillance has led it to mount a series of operations, many involving sexual seduction, designed to recruit or suborn foreign diplomats and embassy staff. The first head of the CIA station in Moscow, Edward Ellis Smith, was seduced in 1953 by a maid working for the Second Chief Directorate. In 1955 John Vassall, a clerk in the office of the British Naval Attaché at the Moscow Embassy, was blackmailed into working for the KGB after, in his own words, being photographed engaging in 'a complicated array of sexual activities with a number of different men'. During Maurice Dejean's term as French Ambassador from 1956 to 1964, both he and his Air Attaché were seduced by Second Chief Directorate 'swallows'. Such episodes continued into the Gorbachev era. In 1987 Clayton J. Lonetree, a US marine guard who had given Second Chief Directorate officers access to the Embassy after an affair with a 'swallow', was sentenced to thirty years imprisonment.[4]

In about 1975 the FCD Twelfth Department, which was responsible for 'offensive operations' against foreigners in the Soviet Union, was upgraded to become Directorate RT. It quickly began demanding more intelligence from Residencies on foreign visitors. Lists of visitors based on their visa applications had traditionally been circulated to both the First and Second Chief Directorates. Directorate RT wanted more detailed information on the most promising targets in advance of their visits. In June 1976 the Centre berated Residencies for their lack of zeal in meeting this requirement.

2565/67
of 28 June 1976

TOP SECRET
Copy 1

To all Residents

Operational experience in recent years has shown that many intelligence tasks related to capitalist and developing countries can be successfully covered from the territory of the USSR by close cooperation between Residencies and the appropriate components of the central apparatus of the Service.

Having at their disposal the necessary agent resources of Soviet nationals, as well as a variety of operational-technical facilities, the components of the central apparatus are in a position to carry out a study on Soviet territory of foreigners who are of intelligence interest, and are able to exert on them influence which will work in our favour; they can also carry out complex checking measures, and obtain operational information on the targets through the deployment of agents. Moreover the components of the Centre can despatch to foreign countries officers and agents to carry out intelligence tasks, and to extend help to Residencies for the realisation of their specific operational agent requirements.

However, the possibilities mentioned above are at present insufficiently used. This is illustrated in particular by the fact that Residencies seldom treat as meriting operational attention information regarding foreigners visiting the USSR as members of various delegations, on courses, for study, or as tourists etc.

There are cases where questions from the Centre to the relevant Residency for information about foreigners taking part in various international events in the USSR – congresses, conferences, symposia, discussions etc – are answered purely formally, sometimes without even giving the personal details which could be obtained through official channels.

In order to make more effective use of the potential for intelligence tasks on and from USSR territory, the following action is essential:

1. When drawing up operational plans, you should take more fully into consideration the potential of the central apparatus to give help from Soviet territory to Residencies in the solution of their intelligence problems. Include in the special sections of the annual plan of work those agent-operational measures which Residencies regard as suitable for execution on USSR territory, either with their own resources or with those of the central apparatus.

2. Warn the Centre in good time about foreign visitors to the USSR who are regarded as suitable subjects for some kind of operational action, and give such essential identification and personal detail as are known to the Residency.

3. Carry out a preliminary study of foreigners travelling to the USSR for study purposes, either as students, as trainees, on courses, or attending military training institutions (from developing countries) with the object of pin-pointing

in good time persons of operational interest. Submit to the Centre in good time all operationally relevant information about these people.

4. Make suggestions to the Centre for the issue of suitable invitations to the USSR to foreigners, especially governmental and party personalities, representatives of the business world, academics, journalists etc, with the purpose of studying and checking them, and of exerting on them an influence favourable to us. For this it is essential to indicate the institutions in whose name the invitations are to be sent, and the most acceptable pretexts for the invitations.

5. Where it is necessary to send out to the country abroad staff from the central apparatus, and co-opted Soviet citizens to carry out specific operational tasks, you should indicate in your requests the most appropriate cover function for the visiting case officer or official function for a co-opted helper.

6. Residencies in countries with harsh counter-intelligence regimes should prepare and send to the Centre suggestions for the participation of departments of the central apparatus in the cultivation of individual intelligence targets to whom it is difficult for members of Soviet cover establishments in their country of residence to gain access for the purpose of study.

7. In the solution of intelligence reporting, recruiting and other intelligence problems, make fuller use of the operational potential of officers from the Centre, and of agents and trusted contacts among Soviet citizens who are sent to capitalist and developing countries as members of various delegations, for scientific and student exchanges etc.

Report on your own channels any political and operational information obtained from them, marking such reports with the suffix 'RT'.

When officers from the Centre, or agents or confidential contacts of the central apparatus or of the regional organisations of the KGB, have been overseas on temporary missions, you should report the results promptly to the Centre together with all the agents' written reports.

8. In the Residency's annual reports, agent-operational measures on or from territory of the USSR should be put in a separate section, giving the Residency's opinion of their effectiveness and about ways of improving intelligence work from USSR territory.

To ensure the more effective use of the potential for the solution of the intelligence tasks from the territory of the USSR, it is essential to entrust this sector of work to the Resident's PR Line Deputy or to one of the experienced operational officers who, when he is visiting the Centre, must be briefed in the appropriate department of our Service.

KORABLEV

3

Illegals

ALONGSIDE the foreign intelligence operations by 'legal' KGB officers working under diplomatic or other official cover, the FCD runs a parallel network using 'illegal' officers operating abroad under assumed names and false nationalities. For most of the 1930s illegals played as large a part in foreign intelligence as legal Residencies. The best of them were cosmopolitan, multilingual Central Europeans, inspired by visionary faith in the Communist millenium. Many had unconventional backgrounds of a kind which would be unthinkable in today's KGB. The recruiters and first controllers of the Cambridge Five, the Austrians Teodor Maly and Arnold Deutsch, were, respectively, a defrocked Catholic priest and a lapsed orthodox Jew with a serious interest in sexology as well as Marxism.[1] Since a majority of the illegals of the 1930s were non-Russians, some used identity papers and travel documents in their own names and nationalities. The golden age of the cosmopolitan illegals, however, was cut short by the xenophobic paranoia of the Great Terror in the Soviet Union. Most were liquidated in 1937–8.

The bulk of post-war Soviet foreign intelligence operations were conducted by legal Residencies. Illegals remained, none the less, an important subsidiary arm of the FCD. But they were men of a different breed from Maly and Deutsch. Though they assumed foreign nationalities and frequently recruited foreign agents, the illegal officers themselves were almost always Soviet citizens. The cosmopolitan, unconventional flair of the 1930s was replaced by bureaucratic thoroughness rigidly controlled by FCD Directorate S (S for *Spez*, Special).

When Gordievsky joined Directorate S in 1963 at the beginning of his career as a KGB officer, he found its largest department (the Second) solely occupied with fabricating false identities and cover stories ('legends') for illegals. Each legend was worked out in exhaustive detail and backed up by an elaborate set of false or doctored documents prepared with the help of the highly skilled forgers and laboratory technicians of KGB Directorate OTU (Operational-Technical). The Third

Department (Recruitment and Training) provided each illegal with elaborate tuition in ciphers, radio communications, photography, LLBs and DLBs ('Live' and 'Dead Letter-Boxes'), agent recruitment, surveillance techniques and other varieties of tradecraft. A large staff of expert linguists perfected the illegals' language skills.

Even after the laborious preparation of his legend and immensely thorough training, the illegal usually had to spend a further period abroad before he was ready to begin operating in earnest. Before beginning work as an illegal in the United States in 1952, Reino Hayhanen lived for three years in Finland establishing a false identity as Eugene Maki, son of a deceased Finnish father who had become a naturalised US citizen.[2] The increasingly complex bureaucracy of Directorate S had a growing tendency to over-elaboration. The most celebrated postwar KGB illegal, Konon Trofimovich Molody, later recalled how, before leaving for Canada to assume the identity of the deceased Gordon Lonsdale, a KGB dentist drilled several holes in his teeth. Once in Vancouver, he was instructed to contact a dentist who would be expecting him, identify himself by reciting a celebrated line from Heinrich Heine, 'Ich weiss nicht, was soll es bedeuten', then open his mouth and display the 'Moscow holes'. Thus reassured that Molody was not an *agent provocateur*, the dentist filled the holes and helped him file an application for a Canadian passport in the name of Gordon Lonsdale.[3]

Though directly controlled by, and reporting to, Directorate S at the Centre, illegals are assisted by Line N (illegal support) officers at major Residencies abroad. Line N officers help to establish illegals' identities and legends, recruit local agents who, after training in Moscow, can be run by illegals, assist communications between illegals and the Centre, and provide help in emergencies.

Despite the enormous time and resources required to train and support illegals, Directorate S continued to expand its operations. In 1974 it acquired a new empire-building chief, Vadim Vasilyevich Kirpichenko, Resident in Cairo for the past four years, who had a reputation as one of the FCD's leading agent-runners. Over a decade earlier he had recruited President Nasser's intelligence chief, Sami Sharaf.[4] The difficulties encountered by legal Residencies in operations against their main targets – the United States, NATO and the PRC – strengthened Kirpichenko's arguments for increasing the number of illegals. Tighter surveillance by Western counter-intelligence services, combined – especially in Britain – with expulsions of KGB officers, required, in the Centre's view, 'an increase in clandestinity'. Operating difficulties in China were more difficult still.[5] 'In the circumstances thus created,' wrote General Kryuchkov, 'illegal espionage assumes great importance.'

ks1
Outgoing letter No 3661/N
6 April 1978

To: Residents

A typical feature of the present international situation is an increase in activity on the part of the enemies of détente. This is aimed towards weakening the foreign-political stance of the Soviet Union, undermining the unity of the socialist bloc and splitting the ranks of the international communist, the workers' and national-liberation movements.

A special part in these hostile acts is played by the 'special services' of the adversary which strive to exploit any errors by Soviet intelligence officers in order to unleash an anti-Soviet campaign, initiating acts of provocation against Soviet representatives abroad, and creating circumstances prejudicial to the smooth running of Soviet institutions abroad. Side by side with the growing arsenal of counter-intelligence facilities the adversary is making use of mass propaganda on a vast scale to discredit both our intelligence service and also Soviet institutions and citizens abroad. Frequently Soviet intelligence officers are simply seized with a view to forcing them to collaborate with the adversary or be expelled from their countries of residence.

All this hinders in a very real way the activities of our 'legal' residencies.

In the circumstances thus created, illegal espionage assumes great importance.

Experience shows that success in illegal espionage depends to a great extent on the level of cooperation with 'legal' residencies, on a skilful combination of the 'legal' and the illegal forms of work. Lately, in the light of instructions Nos 3994/N of 28 March 1975 and 7059/N of 17 June 1976, Residencies have carried out some work to reinforce the position of illegal espionage in a number of target countries. Illegal espionage carried out in conjunction with 'legal' residencies has enabled us to carry out agent-operational measures resulting in the penetration of some intelligence targets and affording access to secret intelligence of interest to us, including some intelligence of a documentary character; it has provided the way to undertake some cases of 'false flag'* recruitment, and it has enabled us successfully to implement combination operations to provide documentation for illegals, as well as for active measures purposes.

Nevertheless the results achieved leave no room for complacency. In a number of residencies Line N work has only been half-heartedly pursued on the part of the Residents, the deep study of those who could be utilised for illegal espionage, especially as special agents has not been conducted sufficiently purposefully; work relating to the study of the legalisation problem is

---

* Operations in which the KGB recruiter poses as a representative of some other organisation (representing the interests of, e.g., the Peace Movement or a Third World country).

proceeding in an unsatisfactory manner, while favourable possibilities for the documentation of illegals are not being exploited.

Serious attention must be paid to work to guarantee the security of Line N operations implemented by residencies, bearing in mind that the adversary's special services, especially in NATO countries with their use of the very latest technical aides, have systematically mounted special search operations to expose illegal espionage on the part of the socialist countries. This requires an increase in clandestinity, a raising of the level of responsibility among those concerned in mounting operations connected with the work of Line N – in fact a general tightening of operational security.

Of paramount importance is the organisation of work in preparing the ground for increasing illegal espionage in the USA and other NATO countries, the Chinese People's Republic, capitalist countries contiguous with the USSR and also in those countries where espionage from a 'legal' base is difficult or impossible. The organisation of work using third countries as a base assumes an important role in the implementation of these measures; it is essential under present circumstances to consider these countries as the main base for an illegal penetration of the USA, the Chinese People's Republic and countries which do not maintain official relations with the Soviet Union.

The following measures are proposed as the necessary steps to secure an increase and improvement in illegal espionage activities:

1. To analyse thoroughly the agent and operational possibilities available to your Residency and to submit to Comrade LEBEDEV's service* by 1 August 1978 proposals on the utilisation of these possibilities for the purpose of illegal espionage work.

2. To regard continual, purposeful efforts to acquire candidates for the role of special agent and auxiliary agents as one of the basic Line N tasks of Residencies. The deep study of suitable candidates should be conducted under conditions of the strictest observance of security procedures. Special agents and auxiliary agents must also be selected from among those trustworthy agents of the Residencies where there is absolute conviction that they are not within the field of vision of the adversary's special services. It is desirable to select as special agents candidates able to travel for long or short periods to the USA, Chinese People's Republic, the Federal Republic of West Germany, Israel, Iran, Turkey, Saudi Arabia and Brazil.

In as far as auxiliary agents are concerned, the most suitable persons are those who can be utilised as employers, guarantors, providers of cover or of clandestine addresses;

3. In order to utilise more effectively officers from the illegal apparatus for Residencies' recruitment operations using 'false flag' tactics, it is necessary to

* FCD Directorate S, headed by General Vadim Vasilyevich Kirpichenko ('Comrade Lebedev').

approach with great care the selection of appropriate candidates for recruitment, the conduct of their deep study, and also the preparation of ways and means for introducing the recruiting officer to the target.

4. In view of the serious complications in the procedural and documentary fields in the main capitalist countries, increased effort should be paid to studying the Consular Corps and institutions concerned with registering the population and the issuing of passports, bearing in mind that we are aiming to recruit agents who are capable of solving problems relating to the documentation of illegals and the acquisition of intelligence on procedural and documentational conditions.

5. To increase the study of the conditions for legalisation abroad (the possibilities for the employment of foreigners, the pursuit of courses of study, the launching of a business, questions related to currency-financial matters, taxation, residence and so on) and to ensure the regular transmission of such information to the Centre.

6. Against the possibility that the situation in the country might worsen and that serious complications might arise concerning the maintenance of contacts with agents, alternative contacting arrangements should be made with the most valuable and trustworthy sources with a view to enabling contact to be maintained with them from an illegal standpoint in case of necessity.

7. To explore continually new openings to acquire cover-slots for Line N officers, making it possible for them to fulfil their tasks in a more effective manner. Apart from Soviet institutions one should also study the possibility of using some international organisations for this purpose and also joint Soviet foreign commercial and other undertakings.

8. Effective help in their work must be given to Line N officers. At the same time they should be instilled with a sense of drive, and of responsibility for results, of the need for care in their preparatory work and for precision in carrying out operational measures.

9. In cases where there are no specialist Line N officers available in a Residency the implementation of the present instructions is to be carried out by the Resident. The requirements and scale of the work on this line is to be agreed with Comrade LEBEDEV's service, when necessary special courses in this field may be organised, to which the most experienced officers of the Residency may be attached.

10. There must be a tightening of security in the implementation of all Line N measures. The Resident bears personal responsibility for the state of affairs in this field.

[Signed]
ALYOSHIN
[KRYUCHKOV]

K GB illegals fell into three distinct groups. 'Strategic' illegals lived as 'sleepers' in the West, usually running small businesses or following a profession but doing little or no operational work. They were intended to become active only in time of East–West conflict. The second group were active illegals living abroad, recruiting and running agents, gathering political and/or scientific and technological intelligence. A third group of illegals was based in Moscow and made shorter-term trips abroad (usually between one and ten months) to perform specific operational tasks such as meeting an agent or carrying out a 'false flag' recruitment.

The Centre usually sends instructions to all three types of illegal by one-way coded radio transmissions which can be picked up on an ordinary commercial radio receiver whose outward appearance, despite some internal modifications, does not attract suspicion. To send reports back to the Centre, the illegal normally employs either LLBs or DLBs ('Live' or 'Dead' Letter Boxes). LLBs are cover addresses with which the illegal communicates through the post, using secret writing or, less commonly, microdots; Line N officers then arrange onward transmission to the Centre. DLBs, also serviced by Line N officers, were to be found in a great variety of locations – including, as the following example shows, churches. Simple messages between illegals and Line N officers (to indicate, for example, the filling and emptying of DLBs) were passed via chalk marks or chewing gum affixed to pre-arranged 'signal sites'.

es-1

No 331
Top Secret
Copy No 1

No 7180/KR
29.4.85

London
Comrade Lavrov [Nikitenko]

We are sending you a description of DLBs and signal sites in Central London, prepared by our source.

Please give us your views on the possibility of using these sites for carrying out DLB operations, from the point of view of safeguarding their security and having regard to the operational situation in the city.

Please exercise particular caution when visiting the area of these sites.

Приложение к №7180/кр

Агентурное сообщение.

Я предлагаю следующее место для тайника в *Лондоне* .
Собственно, там два места в нескольких метрах друг от друга:

Адрес: *Knightsbridge* на *Brompton Road* , ниже магазина *"Harrod"* .

Место № I - внутри Брамптонской часовни (*Brompton Ora-tory*) - это большой католический собор сразу за музеем (*Victoria and Albert Museum"*). Если с улицы стать лицом к собору, вход будет с правой стороны. Войдите в собор. Сразу при входе , справа расположен алтарь. Алтарь является мемориалом англичан, погибших во время войны и имеет копию знаменитой статуи Микельанжело "Пиета" (*"Pieta"*) - мертвый Христос на руках матери. На полу перед статуей слово "*Consummatum Est* ". Сразу слева от алтаря, если стоять к нему лицом , две большие мраморные колонны, которые являются частью архитектуры собора. Обе колонны расположены очень близко от стены.

Attachments: 1) Description of DLBs, 5 pages, No 7318/KR Secret, PN
            s) Packet containing 8 photographs, Secret, DM, No 365/ KR. Please return.

VLADIMIROV
[KIREEV]
[Head of Directorate K, FCD]

nt-2
                                                    Secret
                                                 Copy No 1

Attachment to No 7180/KR

Agent report

I suggest the following site for a DLB in *London*. There are in fact two sites a few metres away from one another:

Address: *Knightsbridge*, on *Brompton Road*, below '*Harrods*' store. Site No 1 – inside *Brompton Oratory* – this is a large Catholic church just behind the *Victoria and Albert Museum*. As you face the church from the street the entrance will be on the right hand side. Go into the church. Just to the right of the entrance is an altar. It is a memorial to Englishmen who were killed in the war and has a copy of Michelangelo's famous statue 'Pieta' – the dead Christ in his Mother's arms. On the floor below the statue are the words '*Consummatum est*'. Just to the left of the altar as you face it, are two large marble columns which are part of the architecture of the church. Both are very close to the wall. The DLB site is behind the column nearest to the wall (if you are facing them, it is the right-hand column), in a little space between the actual column and the wall.

This part of the church is very poorly lit. It is dark there even in the daytime. The impression gained was that no one stops there. Everyone goes into the central part of the church, from which the spot I mentioned is not overlooked. I would suggest leaving a 35 mm film suitably sealed in this place.

As a test, I left a film in a cassette wrapped up in newspaper. I left it in this spot at 11.00. I returned at 18.00, i.e. after seven hours, and the film was still in place. I took it out and I do not think that anyone had noticed this film during the day. When carrying out an operation it would remain there for about 15 minutes.

I chose Brompton Oratory because it is a suitable place in Central *London*. People go in and out of it all day and no one pays any attention to them. The church is not 'state property' so there are no people keeping a round-the-clock watch on it. The area inside the church just to the right of the door is perhaps the least frequented in the church. I would be inclined to think that there is no safer place in Central *London*.

Alternative site in the street behind Brompton Oratory. As you face the church there is a little alley called '*Cottage Place*' immediately to the right. Go along the footpath alongside the Oratory and you will see behind it a small church called '*Holy Trinity Church*'. In front of it is a small paved precinct for pedestrians and exactly opposite this area is a statue of *Saint Francis of Assisi*. The statue is surrounded by a small fence to protect the flowers planted round it. If you stand facing the statue, there is a large tree growing just to the left. The fence passes close to the tree.

The site for the DLB is on the ground at the base of the tree, between the tree and the fence. There is a spot here which is fairly inconspicuous to passers-by.

I also tested this spot, placing here an empty film cassette, which remained there all day. It was exactly in place when I returned.

I should like to repeat that this is a good place since it is away from the main road. Pedestrians used it but not many. It is quite easy to take the container out of, or put it into the DLB, choosing a moment when no one is near. Since this is Central *London* it attracts less attention than anywhere on the edge of a wood.

In addition, those going there do not return the same way. Traffic goes through the area straight to the next street, so when passing through, it is possible to lay or clear the DLB in a few seconds.

Signals:

There are two suitable places for placing signals: one of these is on *South Audley Street*, and the other in the part just behind the street. They are not far from the south section of the American Embassy if you go down *South Audley Street* in the direction of *Curzon Street*.

1. Go down *South Audley Street* and about 5–6 blocks below *Grosvenor Square* you will reach *Tilney Street*. Stop on the west side of *South Audley Street*, facing the east side. You will see a small square called *Audley Square* with a garage for motor vehicles. On the right-hand (south) side of this little square there is a prominent lamp post. A white figure '8' is painted at the base of the lamp post on the road side, about a metre from the pavement. The lamp post is easily seen from a car passing slowly by (and if one judges from the usual traffic in this street, it is impossible to drive fast there). I would put a light blue chalk mark below the figure '8', which would mean that I was filling the DLB the same day at a certain time (let us say 1600). I will place signals only on certain days selected in advance (say every Thursday up to 1200). Having placed the signal on the lamp post, I shall then have to make sure that the signal has been read before going to the DLB in *Brompton Oratory* (a little more than 1 km from the spot).

2. About 200 m from the lamp post, also south along *South Audley Street* on the Grosvenor Square side, there is a church on the right hand (east) side. A notice on the front of the church states that the church was built by the Americans in honour of the victory over Germany in the Second World War.

A short path (about 50 m) leads along the north side of the church to an iron gate into the square. Go through the gate and along the metalled path for a few metres. You will see a group of wooden garden benches placed in a circle. Go to the second bench on the right side of the path. The back part of the bench will be towards you as you approach it. *The majority* of the benches have small tablets on them dedicated to someone. The second bench is dedicated to the Americans, so there can be no mistake. Put a chalk mark signal in the middle on the upper part of the horizontal wooden (back) slat, on the rear side of this slat. This will mean that you have read my signal on the lamp post. I will then go to the DLB site and lay the container within exactly 15 minutes of your planned arrival. After depositing it, I shall return and wipe my signal off the lamp post. When you have taken the material out, you will go back and wipe your signal off the back of the bench.

This will mean that the DLB has been successfully cleared. If I find that the signal has not been removed at the time arranged, I shall go back to the DLB and take out what I left, if it is still there.

No 7318/KR

T HE last illegal operation with which Gordievsky was directly concerned during his career in the KGB was Operation 'Ground' in the spring of 1985 in London, where he had recently been reappointed Resident-designate. In March the London Residency was sent a packet containing £8,000 from the Centre to be passed to an illegal codenamed 'Dario', due to arrive in London two months later. 'Dario' was to signal his arrival and readiness to collect the £8,000 at two pre-arranged signal sites. A Residency technician was ordered to construct a hollow artificial brick in which to stuff four hundred £20 notes. Because of the difficulty of making a cavity large enough for £8,000, he had to make the imitation brick somewhat oversize.

No 7733/N-11
[?] 03.85

No 203
Top Secret

Copy No 1
Personal

London
Comrade Lavrov [Nikitenko]

Carrying out the 'Ground' DLB Operation with 'Dario'

The Centre is planning to carry out on No 1,* DLB operation 'Ground' with 'Dario' to hand over money to him. DLB operation 'Ground' is carried out according to the following plan: On No 2† – in the evening, 'Dario' will inform [us] with the signal 'arrived in the country' at the 'State' permanent signal site that he is ready for the DLB operation. The Residency will check the signal before 11 in the morning on No 1 and will fill the DLB at 19.45, but only after receiving the signal. 'Dario' will do the clearing at 20.00 and will place the confirmation signal (piece of chewing gum) at the 'Koran' permanent signal site‡ at 20.40. (Your No. 300 of 26.2.85.)

Please give local instructions for preparing the container (piece of brick) and put the money in it.

Please telegraph the Residency's agreement to the proposed plan for the 'Ground' operation.

Attachment: £8,000 (eight thousand pounds) in one packet, secret VM

REBROV
[pseudonym used by the deputy heads of Directorate S]
Comrade Gornov
Comrade Svetlov

LAVROV 3.IV.85

T HE over-elaboration of Operation 'Ground' was one further piece of evidence that Directorate S had unconsciously adopted the maxim, 'Never do anything simply if a complicated way can be devised'. Because of problems in radio communication with 'Dario', the Centre changed the signal site on which he was instructed to acknowledge

---

* Saturday 18 May.
† Friday 17 May.
‡ A post at the intersection of Guilford Street and Gray's Inn Road.

receipt of the £8,000. Instead of affixing a piece of chewing gum to a post ('Koran') at the intersection of Guilford Street and Gray's Inn Road, he was told to place it on another post ('Box') near the Ballotbox public house.

On Saturday 18 May 1985, in the absence of the Line N officer who should have left 'Dario' his money, Gordievsky took his two small daughters to play in Coram's Fields in Bloomsbury. Before leaving he deposited the artificial brick containing £8,000, which he had brought with him in a plastic bag, on a grassy verge between a path and a fence on the northern edge of the park (the 'Ground' site).

Top Secret
Copy No 1
Personal

No 10437/N-11
23.04.85

London
Comrade Lavrov

Ref No 7733/N-11
Carrying out DLB Operation 'Ground' with 'Dario'

Because of the poor conditions for radio communications, we have been unable to give 'Dario' a description of the new signal site 'Koran' (Your No 300 of 26.2.85) where, according to the 'Ground' arrangements, he must place the clearing signal. He will place this signal at the 'Box' site before 21.00 and we are repeating the description of this site.

If you go along street No 1 from the intersection with No 2 southwards, passing Pub No 3, 3 metres from the south exit of the Pub, there is a metal lamppost on the pavement along the road and a wooden post with 2 metres between the two. Between these two posts there is a little concrete post 50 cm high. The signal will be a piece of chewing gum at the top of the concrete post. The rest of the arrangements for the DLB operation 'Ground' will remain as before.

We will confirm by telegraph whether to proceed with the operation on the appointed day.

We are sending you a photograph of 'Ground'.

Attachment: Top Secret, 'DM', photograph enclosed.

REBROV

No 1 – Horsenden Lane
No 2 – Robin Hood Way
No 3 – The Ballotbox

On 19 May, the day after carrying out Operation 'Ground', Gordievsky left for Moscow, whither he had been summoned, ostensibly for discussions, in reality for interrogation. A few weeks later, while planning his successful escape from the Soviet Union, he was asked by a surprised former colleague from Directorate S, Boris Bocharov, unaware that Gordievsky had been accused of working for SIS: 'What happened in London, old chap? We had to recall all the illegals. Our operations are ruined.' It is reasonable to conclude that in the summer of 1985 the KGB, for the first time in over sixty years, may not have had a single illegal left in Britain.

Elsewhere there were probably approximately 200 KGB illegal officers. About half were stationed abroad; the remainder were either being trained or waiting in Moscow for a new assignment. Directorate S, about 300 strong when Gordievsky joined in 1963, had increased in complexity and doubled in size. The GRU ran its own illegal network, probably about 70 per cent the size of that of the KGB. Other Soviet Bloc intelligence services also employed illegals. Some former East German illegals seem to have been taken over by the KGB after the disintegration of the Soviet Bloc in 1989.[6]

(*above*) S. A. Vaupshasov, I. D. Kudrya, K. T. Molody; (*below*) R.I. Abel, Kim Philby.

At the beginning of the 1990s the Centre was engaged, as part of an ambitious public relations campaign, in an attempt to glamorise the careers of some of its leading past illegals. The campaign extended even to philately. In 1990 the Soviet Union issued a set of postage stamps to commemorate five of its intelligence heroes. Among them were Rudolf Abel and Konon Molody, the leading KGB illegals in, respectively, the United States and Great Britain, as well as Kim Philby, possibly the ablest foreign agent ever recruited by an illegal. The other two faces on the postage stamps were those of two less well known partisan leaders behind German lines in the Second World War, S. A. Vaupshasov and I. D. Kudrya, included in the series at least partly to imply that Abel, Molody and Philby had a similar status as war heroes.

The reality is rather different. The post-war Soviet illegals in the West seem never to have equalled the great cosmopolitan Central European illegals liquidated during the Great Terror. Even the achievements of Abel and Molody, awarded pride of place in the seclusion of the FCD Memory Room as well as on millions of postage stamps, appear to have fallen well short of the spectacular. The probability is that Directorate S, for all its cumbersome bureaucracy and elaborate tradecraft, has failed to justify the vast resources lavished on it.

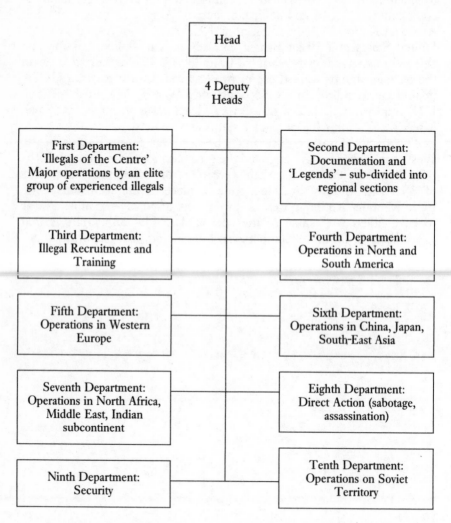

First Department: 'Illegals of the Centre' Major operations by an elite group of experienced illegals	**Second Department:** Documentation and 'Legends' – sub-divided into regional sections
Third Department: Illegal Recruitment and Training	**Fourth Department:** Operations in North and South America
Fifth Department: Operations in Western Europe	**Sixth Department:** Operations in China, Japan, South-East Asia
Seventh Department: Operations in North Africa, Middle East, Indian subcontinent	**Eighth Department:** Direct Action (sabotage, assassination)
Ninth Department: Security	**Tenth Department:** Operations on Soviet Territory

Head

4 Deputy Heads

Source: Vladimir Kuzichkin, *Inside the KGB* (London: André Deutsch, 1990), pp. 78ff; and Gordievsky.

FCD Directorate S (Illegals)

4

Operation RYAN

OPERATION RYAN, a newly devised acronym for *Raketno-Yadernoye Napadenie* ('Nuclear Missile Attack'), was the largest peacetime intelligence operation in Soviet history. Its purpose was to collect military strategic intelligence on the presumed (but non-existent) plans by the United States and NATO between 1981 and 1984 to launch a surprise nuclear first strike against the Soviet Union. The origins of RYAN lay in a potentially lethal combination of Reaganite rhetoric and Soviet paranoia. During the American presidential election campaign in 1980, Moscow had expected the anti-Soviet rhetoric of the victorious Republican candidate, Ronald Reagan, to mellow once he had been elected. It did not do so. In May 1981 the ageing Soviet leader Leonid Brezhnev denounced Reagan's policies in a secret address to a major KGB conference in Moscow. The most dramatic speech, however, was given by Yuri Andropov, the Chairman of the KGB, who was to succeed Brezhnev as General Secretary eighteen months later. The new American administration, he declared, was actively preparing for nuclear war. To the astonishment of most of his audience, Andropov then announced that, by a decision of the Politburo, the KGB and GRU (Soviet military intelligence) were for the first time to cooperate in a worldwide intelligence operation codenamed RYAN. Though the main American experts in the Centre did not doubt Andropov's genuine alarm at Reagan's policies, they believed that pressure for Operation RYAN originated within the high command. Its leading advocate in the Politburo was probably the Minister of Defence, Marshal Dmitri Fyodorovich Ustinov, who had been Stalin's Armaments Commissar as far back as 1941. He would also prove to be one of Andropov's key supporters in the struggle to succeed Brezhnev.[1] During 1981 the former Soviet spy in the Foreign Office, Donald Maclean, who had defected to Moscow thirty years before, became aware of a dangerous change of mood among the Soviet leadership. He wrote a secret memorandum expressing alarm at the way the Soviet Union appeared 'hypnotised by the size and variety of American nuclear forces', and at the influence on the Kremlin of the high command.[2]

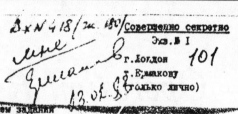

№ 373/ПР/52
17.02.83 г.

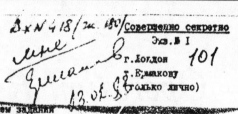

Вх.№ 418/ви. 480/ Совершенно секретно
Экз.№ I
г.Лондон 101
т.Ермакову
(только лично)

О постоянно действующем задании
по выявлению подготовки НАТО к
ракетно-ядерному нападению на СССР

В связи с возрастанием важности решения задачи своевременного выявления подготовки противника к ракетно-ядерному нападению (РЯН) на СССР Вам направляются постоянно действующее задание (ПДЗ) и ориентировка по этой проблеме.

Цель ПДЗ - обеспечить систематическую работу резидентуры по вскрытию планов подготовки главного противника к РЯН и организацию постоянного слежения за признаками принятия им решения о применении ядерного оружия против СССР и осуществления непосредственной подготовки к ракетно-ядерному удару. Выполнение ПДЗ является лишь одним, хотя и крайне важным, аспектом деятельности резидентуры по военно-стратегической проблематике. Работа в этом направлении должна вестись наряду с решением других, ранее поставленных задач по добыванию военно-стратегической информации.

По мере поступления сведений по проблеме РЯН Центр предполагает вносить в данное ПДЗ соответствующие дополнения и уточнения.

Информацию, добытую резидентурой в соответствии с заданиями разделов I и П (ближайшие и перспективные задачи), направлять в Центр с индексом "И-ВН", который предусматривает рассылку телеграфной информации по разметке: руководство службы, подразделения, информационная служба и обязательную передачу почтовой информации в информационную службу.   Для уточнения линии, работником которой добыта информация, можно указывать после индекса "И-ВН" дополнительный индекс (ПР, КР, Х и т.д.).

ПДЗ (приложение № I) должно быть проработано всем оперативным составом резидентуры. Конкретные предложения и соображения резидентуры, направленные на максимально эффективное выполнение ПДЗ, доложить в Центр до 31 марта 1983 года.

Хранить ПДЗ в резидентуре постоянно в особой папке резидента.

Приложение: I) № 374/ПР/52, на 4 листах, сов.секретно, ПН. 102
2) № 6282/ПР/52, на 9 листах, сов.секретно, ПН. 103

While the GRU was made responsible for detailed monitoring of the (non-existent) military preparations for a Western first strike, the KGB's primary task was to provide advance warning of any decision by the United States and its NATO allies to launch a nuclear attack. The Centre entrusted the planning of Operation RYAN to the FCD Institute for Intelligence Problems, established in 1978–9 to work on 'the development of new intelligence concepts'. The basis of the RYAN 'concept' developed by the Institute was the belief that deviations from peacetime routines in a wide variety of spheres – military, political, economic, health administration, civil defence – could provide preliminary warning of Western preparations for a first strike. In November 1981 the Centre despatched individual instructions to Residents in all Western countries, Japan and some states in the Third World. All were required to submit fortnightly reports on Western plans for nuclear war.

When he arrived to take up a post at the London Residency in June 1982, Gordievsky discovered that all his colleagues in the PR line viewed Operation RYAN with some scepticism. They were, and remained, less alarmist than the Centre about the risks of nuclear war. None, however, was willing to put his career at risk by challenging the FCD's assessment. RYAN created a vicious circle of intelligence collections and assessment. Residencies were, in effect, required to report alarming information even if they themselves were sceptical of it. The Centre was duly alarmed by what they reported and demanded more.

In February 1983 Residents were sent new and detailed instructions which reflected the Centre's belief in the steadily increasing nuclear threat and 'the growing urgency' of discovering the West's non-existent plans for a first strike. The importance of the directive was further indicated by the fact that it was addressed to each Resident by name, was marked 'strictly personal', and was ordered to be kept in the Resident's special file.

No. 373/PR/52   *Top Secret*
17.02.83   Copy No 1
                                          London
                  Comr[ade] Yermakov [A. V. Guk]
Permanent operational assignment   (strictly personal)
to uncover NATO preparations for
a nuclear missile attack on the USSR

In view of the growing urgency of the task of discovering promptly any preparations by the adversary for a nuclear missile attack (RYAN) on the USSR, we are sending you a permanently operative assignment (POA) and a briefing on this question.

The objective of the assignment is to see that the Residency works systematically to uncover any plans in preparation by the main adversary [USA] for RYAN and to organise a continual watch to be kept for indications of a decision being taken to use nuclear weapons against the USSR or immediate preparations being made for a nuclear missile attack. Carrying out this assignment is only one aspect, albeit an extremely important one, of the Residency's activity in connection with matters of military strategy. Work in this sector must be carried on side by side with the other tasks previously set for obtaining information on military strategy.

As information is obtained on the question of RYAN, the Centre proposes to supplement and clarify the permanent assignment accordingly.

Information obtained by the Residency relating to the assignments in sections I and II (immediate and future tasks), is to be sent to the Centre indexed 'I-VN', which will provide for distribution of telegraphic information as marked to: heads of service, subsections, information service; and see that information by bag is transmitted without fail to the information service. In order to specify the line of the official by whom the information was obtained, additional letters (PR, KR, X and so on) may be shown after the letters 'I-VN'.

The permanent operational assignment (POA) (Attachment No 1) must be studied by all operational staff of the residency. Specific suggestions and ideas evolved by the Residency with a view to carrying out this assignment as efficiently as possible, should reach Centre by 31 March 1983.

At the Residency, the POA must always be kept in the Resident's special file.

Attachments: 1) No 374/PR/52, 4 pages, Top Secret, PN 102
               2) No 6282/PR/52, 9 pages, Top Secret, PN 103

THE first part of the POA sent to Residents in NATO capitals laid down seven requirements (with time limits for fulfilment) for the collection of intelligence on likely indicators of preparations for nuclear attack, ranging from increases in the price paid to blood donors to heightened activity by Western intelligence and security services. (The Centre had failed to grasp that British blood donors are unpaid.) The second section of the POA instructed Residencies on how to carry out their assignments. Most of the instructions about the recruitment and use of KGB agents were fairly conventional. But the POA also reflects the Centre's sometimes bizarre conspiracy theories about the clerical and capitalist components of Western imperialism. It suspected that

Church leaders and heads of major banks might have been informed of plans for a nuclear first strike, and ordered Residencies to investigate.

Reference No 373/PR/52   Top Secret
                                                         Copy No. 1
                                                         Attachment 1

Permanent Operational Assignment
to discover NATO Preparations for
a Nuclear Attack on the USSR

Section 1 – Immediate tasks of Residencies for Collecting Information and Organising their Work

1. Collect data about places where Government officials and members of their families are evacuated. Identify possible routes and methods of evacuation. Make suggestions about ways of organising a watch to be kept on preparation and actual evacuation.   Time limit: 3rd quarter [by 30 September 1983]

2. Identify the location of specially equipped Civil Defence shelters or premises which could if necessary be used as shelters (underground garages and depots, basements, tunnels) and arrange for a periodical check on their state of preparedness to accommodate the population at a particular time.
                             Time limit: 3rd quarter [by 30 September 1983]
    Report to Centre immediately if shelters are being taken out of storage or a start is being made on preparing certain premises for accommodation of the population.

3. One important sign that preparations are beginning for RYAN could be increased purchases of blood from donors and the prices paid for it and extension of the network of reception centres, since the treatment of burns (the most widespread injury in a nuclear explosion) requires blood transfusions in very considerable quantity. In this context, discover the location of several blood-donor reception centres, and find out how they operate and the price of the blood donated, and record any changes.
                                Time limit: 2nd quarter [by 30 June 1983]
    If there is an unexpectedly sharp increase in the number of stationary and mobile blood donor centres and in the prices paid, report at once to the Centre.

4. Put forward proposals for organising a watch on individual civil defence installations.   Time limit: 2nd quarter [by 30 June 1983]

5. Identify several places which are most frequently visited outside working hours by employees of institutions and installations connected with taking and implementing decisions regarding RYAN, including military personnel. Put

forward your views about the possibility of regular observation of the places
selected.   Time limit: 2nd quarter [by 30 June 1983]

6. Keep under regular observation the most important government institutions,
headquarters and other installations involved in preparation for RYAN. Send
a list of immediate targets of observation to the Centre. Ascertain the 'normal
level of activity' of these targets in and out of working hours, i.e. the outward
signs of their daily activity in a normal situation (differences in the number of
cars collected there in the daytime and the evening, and in the number of
lighted windows in and out of working hours, and activity round these targets
on non-working days). Find out, on the basis of the 'normal level' ascertained,
any changes in the indicators during special conferences, when there is a crisis
situation (cars collected there out of hours, an increase in the number of lighted
windows at night in comparison with the 'normal level', or increased activity
on non-working days).

7. Set a regular watch for any significant changes in the police administration
system and the activity of the special [i.e. security and intelligence] services in
regard to Soviet citizens and institutions, which may be associated with preparation for RYAN.

On points 6 and 7 inform Centre of the existence or absence of any changes
of this kind regularly – once every two weeks.

Section II – Principal Prospective Directions for the Residency to Pursue its Work of Collecting the Information Needed to Discover the Adversary's Preparations for RYAN

1. Detailed description of the nature of measures being carried out in your
country of residence by NATO headquarters and agencies, American representations and military installations located there at a time of immediate preparation by the USA and NATO for RYAN.

2. Analysis of the possibility of co-opting existing agents to work on uncovering
preparation for RYAN and of using all available resources for this purpose.

3. Identifying and studying with a view to subsequent cooption for collaboration, a cadre of people associated with preparing and implementing the
decision about RYAN, and also a group of people, including service and technical personnel, who might be informed of the fact that this or that measure is
being taken in preparation for RYAN, even if they do not know its objective or
purport (the official chauffeurs of individuals involved in the decision about
RYAN, those working in the operating services of installations connected with
processing and implementing the decision about RYAN, and communications
staff involved in the operation and interaction of these installations).

4. Studying the possibilities of organising systematic observation of persons

associated with taking the decision about RYAN and those who might be informed of the preparation of such a decision.

5. Uncovering the lines of communication used for preparing for RYAN, their terminal points, switchboards and system of operating in normal conditions and in an emergency situation, technical characteristics and the possibility of interception.

6. Assessment of opportunities for keeping watch for changes in the pattern of operation of government institutions which are involved in taking political decisions regarding RYAN, and are responsible for the country's military preparedness and for contacts with NATO allies.

7. Collecting data about plans for preparing the special [intelligence and security] services for a particular time and for possible action at that time. Studying facilities for organising a systematic watch to be kept for changes in the operating routine of the central establishments of the special services.

8. Identifying the places where the country's leading military and political figures, and state institutions, including personnel from the central apparatus of the special services, are to be evacuated.

9. Identifying possible routes and methods of evacuating military and political leaders and state institutions. Studying the possibilities of discovering promptly when evacuation is in progress.

10. Gathering data about the location of control centres and headquarters of civil defence forces, shelters, depots and training posts of the civil defence system. Assessment of the possibilities of discovering immediate preparation of the civil defence system for war.

11. Defining the possibility of finding out with present resources what measures are being taken to bring military installations, which are accessible to our observation into a state of heightened operational preparedness. Collecting information about the main residential and recreational centres of the services, hospitals and other installations closely connected with military bases and headquarters.

12. Assessing the degree of likelihood that the heads of national churches and of international church organisations, and the leadership and institutions of the Vatican abroad would be aware of preparation for a nuclear attack and clarifying possibilities of obtaining information about RYAN from these circles.

13. Bearing in mind the very considerable knowledge possessed by the heads of international and the larger national banks, examine the possibility of obtaining information about RYAN from such circles.

The Residency must organise its work in a planned manner on the questions which have been enumerated. Please keep the Centre regularly informed as information is obtained.

No. 374/PR/52

THE second enclosure with the February 1983 directive to Residents in NATO capitals was a general, up-dated briefing on Operation RYAN. The deployment of American Pershing-2 missiles in West Germany would, it was claimed, greatly increase the nuclear threat. ICBMs launched from the continental United States allowed the Soviet Union about twenty minutes 'reaction time'. But, the Centre inaccurately claimed, Pershing-2s would need only four to six minutes to reach Moscow and other long-range Soviet targets. Had this been true, the Soviet leadership would have had insufficient time even to reach its bunkers before Moscow was obliterated.

Operation RYAN thus acquired 'an especial degree of urgency'. 'Uncovering the process of preparation by the adversary to take the decision for a nuclear attack and the subsequent measures to prepare the country for a nuclear war would', the Centre believed, 'enable us to increase the so-called period of anticipation essential for the Soviet Union to take retaliatory measures.'

The briefing went on to analyse the stages in NATO and United States alert systems which would signal the countdown to Armageddon. The Centre further alarmed itself by concluding that the first two stages of the NATO alert might be omitted. This, it told Residents, was 'a matter of particularly grave significance'. NATO's evident intention to achieve strategic surprise made it 'of the highest importance to keep a watch on the functioning of communications networks and systems since through them information is passed about the adversary's intentions and, above all, about his plans to use nuclear weapons . . .'

Reference No 373/PR/52   Top Secret
                                                             Copy No. 1
                                                             Attachment 2

The Problem of Discovering Preparation
for a Nuclear Missile Attack on the USSR

In view of the way in which the main adversary (the USA, NATO, the PRC) has stepped up the tempo and scale of military preparations, the need to deal with the central assignment of the KGB's foreign intelligence service at the present stage – not to overlook the immediate threat of a nuclear attack (RYAN) on the Soviet Union – has acquired an especial degree of urgency.

This task lies at the core of military strategy. It was emphasised in the instructions from the heads of the chief Directorate that in contemporary conditions 'the need to discover specific plans and actions by our adversary connected with his preparation for a surprise nuclear missile attack on the USSR and other socialist countries is now of particularly grave importance. In this context, the primary task is to obtain reliable documentary and other advance information about all aspects and details of military, political and strategic activity of the main adversary, revealing his secret preparations for war.'

The instruction defines in practice the main ways of dealing with our chief task, i.e. the need to uncover the adversary's plans and the measures he is taking in preparation for a nuclear missile attack, above all by exploiting and expanding agent access to the adversary's installations where secret information about military strategy is concentrated.

Information about strategic and operational plans to use nuclear weapons in war with the Soviet Union is of most serious and urgent significance for discovering the adversary's plans promptly for RYAN. This would include, for instance, such documents as the 'Single Integrated Operational Plan – SIOP' of the USA for waging a nuclear war, the 'General Defence Plans' of the NATO strategic and subordinate joint commands, NATO's 'Nuclear Support Plans – Supplan' and a number of NATO 'Contingency Operations Plans – COP', which anticipate deploying and utilising various types of armed forces and arms of service in operations zones in periods of tension or crises and at various stages of war, including nuclear components of these forces.

The intelligence value of the adversary's plans lies in the fact that it enables us to get clear, well in advance, the picture of his possible military operations against the USSR and other countries of the socialist community and his preparations for a nuclear missile strike.

An important element of the adversary's preparation for RYAN is specific action to bring the armed forces and the civilian sector from a peacetime on to a wartime footing, which is seen in implementation of *measures* which were planned in advance and subsequently ratified. At the stage when the measures are implemented, the most important section of which comes into effect after the adversary has taken the political decision in principle to go to war, he begins to step up his activity in both military and civilian sectors. Notwithstanding the fact that in order to make sure of a sudden attack the adversary counts on maintaining secrecy about his preparatory measures, the scale of activity involved in bringing military and civilian sectors from a peacetime on to a wartime footing entails the appearance of a whole series of revealing signs regarding the nature of the adversary's procedure.

Therefore one of the chief directions for the activity of the KGB's foreign service is to organise detection and assessment of signs of preparation for RYAN in all possible areas, i.e. political, economic and military sectors, civil defence and the activity of the special services.

Our military neighbours [the GRU] are actively engaged in similar work in relation to the activity of the adversary's armed forces. However, the fact that the adversary maintains a considerable part of his strategic forces in a state of operational readiness, capable of proceeding to execute military assignments in the shortest possible time (for instance, all American land-based intercontinental missiles, 70% of their naval nuclear facilities and 30% of the strategic air force are on duty, and in NATO, about 20% of nuclear missile facilities are detailed as duty forces) makes it essential to discover signs of preparation for RYAN at a very early stage, before the order is given to the troops to use nuclear weapons.

Uncovering the process of preparation by the adversary to take the decision for a nuclear attack and the subsequent measures to prepare the country for a nuclear war would enable us to increase the so-called period of anticipation essential for the Soviet Union to take retaliatory measures. Otherwise, reprisal time would be extremely limited. For instance, noting the launching of strategic missiles from the continental part of the USA and taking into account the time required for determining the direction of their flight in fact leaves roughly 20 minutes reaction time. This period will be considerably curtailed after deployment of the 'Pershing-2' missile in the FRG, for which the flying time to reach long-range targets in the Soviet Union is calculated at 4–6 minutes.

It is thus fully evident that the problem of uncovering the threat of RYAN must be dealt with without delay.

Immediate preparation for a nuclear attack begins at the moment when the other side's political leadership reaches the conclusion that it is expedient to use military force as the international situation becomes progressively more acute, and takes a *preliminary* decision to launch an attack on the Soviet Union.

Analysis of NATO's ideas on military strategy and the organisational procedures adopted in the North Atlantic Treaty Organisation, point to the fact that so-called nuclear consultations in NATO are probably one of the stages of immediate preparation by the adversary for RYAN.

To ascertain in good time the moment when nuclear consultations begin inside NATO is a most important problem for the information-gathering apparatus of Soviet intelligence, together with discovering the specific plans for RYAN of the individual powers constituting the main adversary and, in the first place, the USA.

Nuclear consultations begin after the NATO agencies (the Planning Council/Committee) have received notification from a nuclear power belonging to the grouping, of the intention to use nuclear weapons, or a request from a non-nuclear country in NATO or one of the main commands of the bloc (Supreme Command of NATO forces in Europe, Supreme Command of NATO Forces in the Atlantic or the NATO Command in the Channel) for the use of nuclear weapons. The aim of these consultations is to convey to the nuclear powers concerned, the views of the other members of the bloc on the questions of launching a nuclear attack, so that it should take them into account before taking its own *final* decision. NATO attaches great importance to beginning nuclear consultations at the earliest possible stage of a political crisis in East/West relations which is threatening to develop into armed conflict.

The forum for consultations, including nuclear ones, would be a meeting of the NATO Council/Defence Planning Committee, at the level of permanent representatives of the member-countries of the bloc at its headquarters in Evère (a suburb of Brussels), with the rank of ambassador. Joint meetings may also be called of the Council/Defence Planning Committee and the Military Committee of NATO, attended by military representatives of the member countries of the bloc.

The alert system serves to ensure military preparedness and provide for the transition of NATO armed forces and the civilian sector from a peacetime to a wartime footing, embracing a series of measures in military and civilian areas which must be implemented according to the degree of world tension and threat of the outbreak of war.

NATO's alert system consists of three mutually dependent and complementary components:

– a state of 'military alert' (preparatory measures of a military nature)

– a battle alarm system (an emergency 'system of military measures to forestall and break up a possible attack')

– an official alarm system (for putting on a war footing not only the armed forces, but also the NATO countries as a whole).

The state of '*military alert*' includes preparatory and preliminary measures of a military nature which may be implemented over a considerable period of time. It is designed to simplify the transition to a higher degree of preparedness and need not entail aggravation of international tension, since the corresponding measures must be carried out in maximum secrecy. A state of 'military alert' and the corresponding measures which form part of it are not in themselves indications of preparation for RYAN, but are largely a reaction to the beginning of complications in the international situation and are countermanded when there is an improvement in this situation. At the same time it is essential to discover what measures have been taken under the 'military alert', in order not to miss the moment of transition to a higher degree of readiness constituting a threat of RYAN.

The battle alarm system is a series of purely military measures implemented within an extremely short time in order to withdraw NATO armed forces from being under attack and maintain their fighting efficiency for action to carry out a surprise or retaliatory attack. This system comes into operation when owing to increasingly complicated circumstances, measures cannot be implemented as part of the official alert system, and the 'enemy attack has already begun or may begin in the immediate future'. It determines the order in which specific measures come into operation after receiving the warning signal of a 'possible attack'.

The battle alarm system envisages two states of readiness for action: an 'Orange' alert and a 'Scarlet' alert.

'State Orange' is declared when 'an attack may be expected' in the immediate future (within 36 hours), and 'State Scarlet' when military action has already begun or is expected to do so within minutes. When this alarm system has been introduced, the Supreme Command and the national authorities must undertake a series of operations under the official alert system, particularly if there is time to implement civil defence measures.

In view of the fact that the measures involved in 'State Orange' have to be carried out with the utmost secrecy (under the guise of manoeuvres, training etc) in the shortest possible time, without disclosing the content of operational plans, it is highly probable that the battle alarm system may be used to prepare a surprise RYAN in peacetime.

Following on from this it appears that the discovery that steps are being taken under a military alarm system, and there is a corresponding state of readiness for action in NATO armed forces, may in combination with a number of other factors point to the conclusion that RYAN is in preparation.

The official alert system embraces a series of civil and military measures aimed at switching the armed forces and the NATO member-countries as a whole from a peacetime to a war footing, and affects all potential fields of preparation for a nuclear attack – military, political, economic, civil defence, special service activity. The official system consists of three states:

Simple alert which is introduced in the initial stage of deterioration in the international situation but there is no 'immediate threat of attack' in the very near future. The steps taken under a simple alert are aimed at ensuring that the NATO armed forces are ready for action, in order that, if necessary, measures can be speeded up under a heightened alert and preparation completed to engage without delay in military operations. At this stage, immediate preparation begins to switch the civilian sector to a war footing. Discovery of this stage represents an extremely serious development from the point of view of early warning of immediate preparation for RYAN. The measures taken at this stage are kept secret but their scale and gravity enable signs of their implementation to be detected. Maximum attention must be devoted to ascertaining in good time that a state of simple alert has been introduced.

A heightened alert is declared in order to ensure that the NATO armed forces are in a state of maximum readiness and fully deployed in accordance with operational plans. At this stage, there is a large-scale operation to put the country on a war footing, and such measures can no longer be concealed. They will clearly indicate preparation for military operations. If the heightened alert is not called off, and is followed by proclamation of a *general alert*, then this will indicate the commencement of military action. It is a matter of particularly grave significance that a general alert may be declared without previously introducing the first and second stages of the official alert system in the period when states 'Orange' and 'Scarlet' are in operation.

The NATO alert system thus envisages measures to put not only the armed forces, but the country as a whole on a war footing. Opportune discovery of signs indicating implementation of a series of such measures, especially in conjunction with nuclear consultations, provides grounds for giving the Centre early warning of the possibility of RYAN.

The USA has its own system of military preparations for switching the American armed forces to a wartime footing. This system may be used by US armed forces deployed in NATO countries. It consists of five stages, any of which may be introduced according to the actual situation. It is also possible to switch the armed forces urgently to a heightened state of readiness, by-passing the intermediate ones.

Operational readiness No 5 is the normal state of the armed forces in peacetime conditions.

Operational readiness No 4 may be introduced if there is tension in certain parts of the world. Intelligence and counter-intelligence operations may be stepped up, with preparation for combating possible sabotage. All measures are carried out in secret, with no cancellation of leave for personnel.

Operational readiness No 3 is declared if tension in a particular part of the world may affect American interests and requires intervention by US armed forces. A specially detailed contingent of the armed forces is put into this state of readiness. Secret measures are carried out (in the guise of training and manoeuvres) to reinforce protection of installations and prepare military equipment and weapons for possible use, and intelligence and counter-intelligence is stepped up. Personnel are allowed leave or passes at the decision of the command.

This stage of readiness corresponds to that of 'military alert' in NATO's alert system.

Operational readiness No 2 is introduced when a threat of conflict develops which seriously affects the interests of the USA or its allies. The emerging situation is fraught with possibilities of military action. Operational deployment of selected contingents of armed forces begins. Arms and military equipment are put in a state of wartime readiness. Controls are instituted over the activity of the civilian authorities, shipping and airlines. Censorship is introduced, with safeguards for security of communications, and leave is cancelled.

This stage of readiness corresponds in general to that of simple alert in NATO's official system, including also a number of elements of a heightened alert.

Operational readiness No 1 is declared when there are obvious indications of preparation to begin military operations. It is considered that war is inevitable and may start at any moment. The armed forces are put into a state of complete preparedness for military action to execute operational plans. All activity of civilian agencies and undertakings is subordinated to military interests.

This stage of readiness corresponds in general to the 'Stage Orange' and a heightened alert in NATO's alarm system, with elements of the 'State Scarlet' and the general alert. It immediately precedes the proclamation of a state of military emergency (in the USA), or the 'State Scarlet' or a general alert (in NATO), signifying the start of military action.

Combat readiness is stepped up on instructions from the Committee of the Chiefs of Staff, and also on orders from the commanders-in-chief of the US armed forces in the zones (theatres of military operations) with the agreement of the Committee. The signals for introducing the corresponding degree of readiness are transmitted on the Committee's instructions through the main and reserve command centres and control points of the armed forces.

When a state of heightened readiness is introduced in the US armed forces or the alert system comes into operation in NATO, this must be accompanied also by a series of measures in the civilian sector of the United States to ensure that the country is put on to a war footing and the number of victims of a retaliatory attack is kept down.

One of the important means of safeguarding the process of preparing the decision to use nuclear weapons and controlling their use is provided by the various systems of communications: communications networks of the nuclear powers and NATO's combined systems of communication.

From a functional point of view the adversary's existing communications systems can be divided into general and military systems. However, irrespective of the distinctions laid down for the channels allocated, their subordination, the degree of secrecy and the specified subscribers, both types of communications are used for nuclear consultations.

Intelligence work carried out against the main communications agencies could make it possible to discover the adversary's overall plans for preparation for war. If information is obtained promptly about the activity of executive agencies at headquarters level in carrying out these plans, this may serve as an indication of enhanced readiness on the adversary's part for military action.

Any instructions which are discovered about rules for using the communication networks and their method of operating are also of practical significance.

In an emergency situation and when military exercises are taking place, operation of lines of communication may be switched to the 'minimise' system in which the volume of ordinary telephone calls and telegraphic messages is sharply curtailed and channels of communication cleared for transmitting urgent messages.

The 'minimise' system may be introduced selectively, in certain countries, for example, if there is deterioration in their internal situation, or it may apply to US and NATO communications systems. If this system is instituted in countries which have nuclear weapons, especially if it is on a global scale, this may provide a serious warning signal that the adversary is preparing for RYAN. The fact that 'minimise' had been introduced could only be discovered by means of intercept facilities.

It is of the highest importance to keep a watch on the functioning of communications networks and systems since through them information is passed about the adversary's intentions and, above all, about his plans to use nuclear weapons and practical implementation of these. In addition, changes in the method of operating communications systems and the level of manning may in themselves indicate the start of preparation for RYAN.

Information must be obtained about the organisation, location and functioning mechanism of all forms of communications which are allocated by the adversary for controlling the process of preparing and waging a nuclear war.

No. 6282/PR/52

THE enormously detailed intelligence requirements in the Centre's directive were too much for Arkadi Guk, the boastful but ineffective London Resident – though they may have served to enhance his already formidable alcohol consumption. Guk delegated responsibility for the regular census of official cars and lighted windows both in and out of normal working hours at government buildings and military installations suspected of involvement in preparations for a nuclear attack, as well as investigation of the evacuation procedures of government officials and their families, to a single junior KGB officer. The officer concerned did not even possess a car. (Had he done so, he would still have been unable to travel outside London without Foreign Office permission – an important detail which had curiously escaped the Centre's attention.)

The Centre's anxieties continued to mount as President Reagan regularly denounced the 'evil empire'. On 8 March 1983 he described the Soviet leadership as the 'focus of evil in the modern world'. A fortnight later the President announced the Strategic Defense Initiative (SDI), popularly known as Star Wars, a defensive shield in space which would use laser technology to destroy Soviet missiles in flight. Though the implementation of SDI lay far in the future, the rhetoric and television advertising with which the project was unveiled were interpreted by the Centre as further evidence of the US administration's attempts to prepare its citizens for nuclear war. Following Reagan's Star Wars speech, Soviet public pronouncements also changed dramatically in tone. 'For the first time since Stalin's death,' writes Michael MccGwire, 'the threat of war rather than the likelihood of avoiding war became Moscow's dominant theme.'[3]

On 16 June 1983 Andropov told the Central Committee that there had been an 'unprecedented sharpening of the struggle' between East and West: 'The threat of nuclear war overhanging mankind causes one to reappraise the principal goals of the activities of the entire Communist movement.'[4] Five days later the Centre sent a short and alarmist telegram to NATO Residencies, reporting that the United States was continuing preparations for a nuclear conflict, and stressing the priority of Operation RYAN. On 12 August it despatched a further directive 'relating to intelligence and counter-intelligence indications of enemy preparations for a nuclear attack'. The checklist of suspicious activities provided by the Centre was largely a mirror-image of Soviet contingency plans for war with the West. They included 'an increase in disinformation operations', infiltration of sabotage teams armed with nuclear, bacteriological and chemical weapons, and an increase in 'repressive measures by the punitive authorities'.

[ms notes: Please inform operational
               staff of residency   Incoming No 457/zh.180/

Leonov, [L. Y. Nikitenko] 24.8.83   Top Secret
                                                Copy No 1

No. 14953/KR
12.08.83   Bonn, Brussels, Copenhagen,
                                London, Osio, Paris, Rome, Lisbon

                                                To the Residents

Permanent operational assignment to detect
signs of NATO preparations for a nuclear
attack (RYAN) on the USSR as reflected in
the activity of special services of
member-countries of the block.

Ref. No. 373/PR/52 of 01.02.83

As a supplement to the permanent operational assignment, which the Residency already has for discovering NATO preparations for a nuclear attack on the USSR, we are sending you a more detailed version of Point 7 of Section 1, relating to intelligence and counter-intelligence indications of enemy preparations for a nuclear attack.

The task must be carefully studied by all members of the residency, especially the KR [Counter-Intelligence] Line, and borne in mind in practical work on the question of RYAN.

The results of work on the problem of RYAN from the KR-line standpoint should appear in the residencies' fortnightly reports.

Please keep this permanent assignment always in the resident's file.

Attachment: No 14954/KR of 11.08.83, 3 pages
              Top Secret, PN

ALYOSHIN [KRYUCHKOV]
15/9
ARTYOM

Attachment to No. 14953/PR   Top Secret
of 11.08.83   Copy No. 1

Permanent Operational Assignment to detect
signs of NATO preparations for a nuclear
attack on the USSR as reflected in the
activity of the special services of
member-countries of the block

When on the watch for changes in the pattern of counter-intelligence work
and police administration and for operations of the special services of NATO
member-countries and their activity in relation to Soviet citizens and institutions, attention should be concentrated particularly on signs of any secret measures, which in conjunction with other factors, may point to a decision being
taken by the military and political leadership of the member-countries of the
bloc to begin immediate preparations for a nuclear missile strike against the
USSR. The most important indications of preparation by the adversary for a
nuclear attack on the USSR which may find expression in the activity of its
special services are listed below:

1. Stepping up Information-Gathering and other Intelligence Activity

a) A sharp increase in the activity of all forms of intelligence, checking and
   elaboration of intelligence services' plans, stepping up efforts to obtain information about the fighting efficiency of the armed forces of Warsaw Pact
   countries;

b) an increase in secret dropping of agents and operational equipment into the
   USSR and other Warsaw Pact countries, starting to make use of agents 'put
   on ice' in socialist countries, intended to operate in wartime conditions;

c) increased activity on the part of the American CIA and NSA to establish
   close contacts with the special services of other NATO countries, in order
   to bring their resources closer to intelligence targets and also make use of
   the technical facilities of the allied intelligence services.

2. Various Subversive Operations

a) An increase in the number of disinformation operations against the USSR and other Warsaw Pact countries;

b) secret infiltration of sabotage teams with nuclear, bacteriological and chemical weapons into the countries of the Warsaw Pact;

c) expanding the network of sabotage-training intelligence schools and stepping up recruitment of émigrés from the socialist countries and persons who know the language of these countries; setting up émigré military formations and sabotage and intelligence teams.

3. Increased Counter-Intelligence Activity

a) A sharp exacerbation of the operational situation, including restrictions on the activity of embassy personnel and that of other institutions of socialist countries, introducing fresh prohibitions of travel round the country, especially in military areas;

b) reinforcement of repressive measures by the punitive authorities against progressive organisations and individuals, and also fitting out places for keeping politically unreliable persons subject to isolation;

c) instituting a strict counter-intelligence system in the more important installations in NATO countries and in individual areas and zones where first-stage mobilisation measures are planned;

d) replacement of local guards by special guard detachments at particularly important state and military installations;

e) restrictions on the use of the telephone and telegraph network by private persons;

f) reinforcement of military censorship and introduction of postal censorship, restrictions on the correspondence of forces personnel of all arms and the holding up of servicemen's letters;

g) mass discharge of servicemen and civilians from their duties and cancellation of their permission to work with nuclear weapons, in the interests of safeguarding security and reinforcing secrecy for the nuclear attack in preparation;

h) restrictions on rail, air, sea and road travel, especially in military zones and possible missile launching areas;

i) reinforcement of military security measures, also establishing a special counter-intelligence regime in military enterprises, at various headquarters and on the main forms of transport;

j) imposing much stricter frontier and customs controls on borders and at sea ports and airports of NATO countries.

Please organise your work systematically to detect indications of NATO preparations for a nuclear missile attack on the USSR.

No 14954/KR
MS signatures:
George 26/8
Gornov 26/8
Evans 26/8
Astakhov 29/8
Oliver 2/9

THE most serious moment of East–West tension since Reagan's election followed the shooting down in the sea of Japan in the early hours of 1 September 1983 of a Korean airliner, KAL 007, which had blundered badly off course over Soviet airspace. All 269 of the passengers and crew were killed. A telegram from the Centre to the London Residency on 4 September claimed that the tragedy was being used by the Reagan administration to whip up worldwide anti-Soviet hysteria. On 28 September the terminally-ill Soviet leader, Yuri Andropov, issued from his sickbed a denunciation of American policy couched in apocalyptic language unprecedented since the depths of the Cold War. The United States, he said, was 'a country where outrageous military psychosis is being imposed'.

By now the 'Strategic Section' established in FCD Service One (Political Reports) to assess RYAN intelligence was staffed by over fifty officers. Paranoia in the Centre reached its peak during the NATO command-post exercise Able Archer 83, held from 2 to 11 November, to practise nuclear release procedures. Soviet contingency plans for a surprise attack on the West envisaged using training exercises as a cover for a real offensive. The Centre was haunted by the fear that Western plans for a surprise attack on the Soviet Union might be the mirror-image of its own. On 5 November the Centre sent the London Residency a telegram revealing for the first time the timetable of the (non-existent) Western plan for a first strike: 'It can be assumed that the period of time from the moment when the preliminary decision for RYAN is taken up to the order to deliver the strike will be of very short duration, possibly 7 to 10 days.' The Centre added a checklist of likely indicators that the countdown had begun.

vn-1   Top Secret
No. 2132/PR   Copy No. 1
05.11.83

To London
Comrade YERMAKOV [A. V. Guk]
Ref no. 1673/PR of 24.10.83.

In response to your request we are sending you the information which the Centre has regarding possible operations by the USA and its allies on British territory in preparation for RYAN.

Attachment: Brief No. 2133/PR of 7 pages, Top Secret, PN.

SILIN
[G. F. TITOV]
[Head of FCD Third Department]

Attachment to No. 2132/PR   Top Secret
Copy No. 1

BRIEF
[Extract]

1. *The Nature of Possible Contacts and Consultations Between the United States Government and the British Leadership before RYAN*

If the US government were to hold consultations with its allies before RYAN, then the leaders of Great Britain, as one of the USA's close allies would take part. These consultations might take place both on a bilateral, and as is fully possible, on a multilateral basis (e.g. in NATO).

In our view, persons holding key positions in the country's leadership must necessarily be involved in preparing and establishing contacts with the US government on the eve of RYAN.

Consequently, a constant watch should be kept on the movements of their people, their residences, and their contacts in order to discover any possible contacts and consultations between the US government and the British leadership before RYAN.

2. *Possible Changes in the System of Operation of Central Departments and Institutions in Great Britain in the Period Starting from Preparation of the Preliminary Decision for RYAN to the Launching of a Nuclear Strike.*

Surprise is the key element in the main adversary's plans and preparations for war in today's conditions. As a result it can be assumed that the period of time from the moment when the preliminary decision for RYAN is taken, up to the order to deliver the strike will be of very short duration, possibly 7–10 days. It is however impossible that preparation for a nuclear attack should not be reflected in the pattern of work of the country's state institutions which are involved in safeguarding the defence capability and security. During this period attention must be paid especially to discovering indirect indications of preparation, which we think would be as follows:

- Unusual activity at the Prime Minister's residence at 10 Downing Street, where there will be energetic consultations without informing the press about who was at the meetings and what was discussed:
- Changes in the system of operation of the Ministry of Defence. Work may be carried on in the evenings and at night and also on non-working days. Obviously cars will be observed in large numbers at the administrative offices of the Ministry of Defence in London:

Main building, Whitehall, SW1;
Old War Office building, Whitehall, SW1;
Empress State Building, Lillie Road, SW6;
Old Admiralty Building, Spring Gardens, SW1;
Lansdowne House, Berkeley Square, W1;
Metropole Building, Northumberland Avenue, WC2;
Adastral House, Theobolds Road, WC1;
1–15 St Giles Street, WC2;
CAA House, 45/49 Kingsway, WC2;
Castlewood House, 77–91 New Oxford Street, WC1;
First Avenue House, High Holborn, WC1;
The Adelphi, John Adam Street, WC2;
Leysdown Road, SE9.

- Cancelling leave of MOD, intelligence, counter-intelligence, and police personnel and also service units;
- Appearance on the streets of military detachments and armed details of police in greater numbers than usual;
- Announcements of a military alert in units and at bases; military exercises;
- Activity on the air. Appearance of new channels of communications. Some existing channels may be cleared for use in future for military purposes;
- Restrictions imposed by the authorities on movement round the country of members of foreign embassies in Britain, in the first instance those of the USSR and socialist countries.

O N 8 or 9 November (Gordievsky is not sure which), flash (*molniya*) telegrams were sent both to KGB and GRU Residencies in Western Europe mistakenly reporting an alert at US bases. The telegrams clearly implied that one of several possible explanations for the (non-existent) alert was that the countdown to a nuclear first strike had actually begun. With the end of Able Archer on the 11th the alarm at the Centre eased slightly. It is reasonable to assume some connection between Gordievsky's warnings to British Intelligence of the Centre's reaction to the exercise and various attempts at indirect Western reassurance which followed. But there was no immediately visible easing of East–West tension.

Early in 1984 the Centre sent the London Residency further instructions on Operation RYAN which revealed, once again, the depth of its misunderstanding of British and Western society. Banks, post offices and slaughterhouses, it bizarrely believed, held clues to preparations for a nuclear first strike.

No. 6492/PR/52   Top Secret
18.01.84   Copy No. 1

                                                 To London
                              Comrade YERMAKOV [A. V. GUK]

Additional Guidance on the Problem of RYAN
[Extract]

. . .

In order to restore and regulate the country's ability to function in the period after a nuclear missile strike, the military and political leadership of capitalist states will pay particular attention to seeing that the system of financial credit operates uninterruptedly in the same form as at present. In this context more intensive activity may take place in the period of preparation for RYAN at branches of banks involved in insurance and credit operations. Banking personnel at any level may in these circumstances have at their disposal information of interest to us about the action being taken.

Apart from their activity on NATO's behalf post office institutions have an important role to play in helping to advance national mobilisation. These institutions are used to make a preliminary check on the addresses of mobilisation contingent and for measures to ensure that stable functioning of national communications channels is maintained, and other methods of a similar order . . .

The military and political leadership of the country regards the rehabilitation of food industry enterprises as a first priority objective. In this connection special steps will be taken to preserve them for emergency conditions, including increasing stocks of raw materials to the maximum laid down for current

production requirements and the capacity of storage space and area of the enter-
prise, establishing a stock of spare parts and equipment, mass slaughter of
cattle and putting meat into long cold storage, and number of other measures.
. . .

L ONDON cannot have been the only Residency in which some KGB
officers were now more concerned by the alarmism of the Centre
leadership than by the threat of surprise attack from the West. Over the
next few months they were encouraged to note the emergence in Moscow
of a less paranoid interpretation of American and NATO policy. The
change seemed to be assisted by Andropov's death on 9 February 1984.
Like Andropov, his successor and former rival, Konstantin Chernenko,
was already in failing health when he became General Secretary and had
only just over a year to live. But he was less morbidly suspicious of Western
conspiracies than Andropov had become at the end of his life. Gordievsky
learned from Kryuchkov's secretariat that he viewed Chernenko's election with consternation and feared that, as a former Andropov protégé,
he might be demoted. In March N. V. Shishlin, a senior foreign affairs
specialist in the Central Committee (and later an adviser to Gorbachev),
visited London and spoke at length on international relations to embassy
and KGB staff. He made no mention of a surprise nuclear attack.

By now, however, Operation RYAN had acquired a bureaucratic
momentum which took some time to wind down. When the London
Residency grew lax in early summer about sending in its fortnightly
reports, it received a reprimand from the Centre, and was told to adhere
'strictly' to the original directive. On 10 July Kryuchkov personally
informed Residencies of new 'combat readiness' procedures.

N 418

Top Secret
Copy No 1

No. 367/MP
10.7.84

To Residents
(as listed)

In order to shorten the delay in informing residencies about action to bring
our Service [the FCD] into combat readiness, the signal 'KOSTYOR 1' has

been instituted and will be transmitted when necessary to all organisations abroad. If this signal is received by a Residency (Embassy) it will mean that the central apparatus of our Service has been put on heightened combat alert, and the stations abroad must bring into operation the section of mobilisation plans for taking immediate operational measures to obtain and despatch to Centre without delay, information about specific signs of a surprise nuclear missile attack on the USSR and the countries of the socialist community; to safeguard the security of intelligence operations and the Soviet colony as a whole, clarify the details of communications with agents intended to be used at this particular time and prepare them to switch to the impersonal means already worked out; to step up coordination of activity with the heads of the Department and our military neighbours [the GRU], reserve channels of communication with Centre, prepare and operate communications arrangements between Soviet institutions abroad (where there are such), and also implement other measures designed to safeguard the vital activity of the apparatus abroad in an emergency situation.

This document is to be kept in the Resident's file.

ALYOSHIN
[KRYUCHKOV]

[MS. notes:]

Comrade Gornov [Gordievsky]
_____

Lavrov, 26.VII.84

MERCIFULLY, the signal 'KOSTYOR 1' was never transmitted. KGB officers returning from leave in Moscow during the summer of 1984 had the sense that the priority of Operation RYAN was steadily declining, and that the former obsession of the Centre leadership with the threat of nuclear surprise attack was no longer shared either by the International Department of the Central Committee or by the Foreign Ministry. Anxiety in the Centre, too, was visibly declining. RYAN was further undermined during the second half of 1984 by the disappearance of the two leading military alarmists. In September Marshal Ogarkov, Chief of Staff and Deputy Minister of Defence, was posted out of Moscow, allegedly for 'unparty-like behaviour'. Three months later the Minister of Defence himself, Marshal Ustinov, died. But though the Centre's fear of nuclear surprise attack had receded, its suspicions of the Main Adversary and its allies remained acute.

5

The 'Main Adversary'
The United States

T HE United States was the main target for KGB active measures as well as intelligence collection. The FCD conference to review operations during 1982–3 reaffirmed a priority which had remained unchanged since the end of the Second World War: 'Our chief task is to help to frustrate the aggressive intentions of American imperialism ... We must work unweariedly at exposing the adversary's weak and vulnerable points.'[1] The range of 'weak and vulnerable points' which the Centre believed required exposure was remarkable. It was concerned in 1976 that the bicentennial celebrations of the Declaration of Independence might raise the United States's international prestige. Residencies around the world were ordered to play their part in undermining the festivities.

In Copenhagen, where Gordievsky was stationed at the time, the Residency despatched, chiefly to the Third World, anti-American propaganda ostensibly emanating from a (non-existent) Danish-based organisation, 'The European Bicentennial Committee', in reality fabricated in Moscow by FCD Service A (Active Measures). The Centre supervised the circulation of its black propaganda with meticulous detail. The Residency was instructed not to put too much propaganda in any one letter-box lest it reveal 'our part in the operation'. It was also ordered to post copies to Soviet Bloc embassies in Copenhagen in order to check that their 'safe passage' was not being interfered with.

Service A was so pleased with the propaganda of the 'European Bicentennial Committee' that it continued sending it out after the bicentennial was over.

ob-1   TOP SECRET
No 450/A   Copy No 1
28 February 1977

Copenhagen
To: Comrade KORIN [M. P. LYUBIMOV]

Distribution of Booklet

We are continuing to put into effect measures to expose the reactionary internal and external policies of American ruling circles in connection with the US bicentenary. We have prepared a booklet entitled 'America's 200 Years' in which, using broadly based factual material, the acute social problems which are characteristic of contemporary American life have been revealed. A special place in the publication has been reserved for material relating to the discriminatory policies of the United States administration in its handling of national minorities, and to interference by Americans into the internal affairs of sovereign states in Africa, Asia and Latin America. The booklet is well illustrated and attractively reproduced. The publication has been issued in the name of the fictitious Danish organisation 'The European Bicentennial Committee' which has been used by us as a cover before for an analogous operation. We plan to distribute the booklet in several countries in Africa and Latin America. Bearing in mind the place of publication of the booklet it is appropriate to effect its distribution from Copenhagen.

In this connection we request you to distribute the attached envelopes containing copies of the booklet to the appropriate addressees, exercising the necessary precautions. Before that we ask you to affix stamps of the appropriate value to the envelopes which will ensure the unhindered passage of the letters to their destinations. We ask you to carry out the distribution of the booklet piecemeal which will help to cover up our part in the operation.

In order to keep a check on the safe passage through the postal channels we are also sending in the attachment some letters containing examples of the booklet addressed to the Soviet Embassy in Copenhagen and the embassies of socialist countries. We ask you to inform us whether these particular letters reach their addressees.

Please inform us by telegram when the operation is completed.

Attachment: As indicated in text, in separate packet, non-secret.

SEVEROV
[GRUSHKO]
[Head of Third Department, FCD]

THE 41-page booklet *America's 200 Years*, prepared by Service A, which accompanied this directive under separate cover, catalogued American crimes both at home and abroad since independence, and was lavishly illustrated with drawings and photographs of oppression and massacre. The United States was also portrayed in both text and illustrations as responsible for the crimes of the white regimes in South Africa. Photograph captions included the following:

- In Soweto a woman shot on [*sic*] the stomach rushing to hospital.
- Yet another mass grave of Nhazonia.
- Body of a brutally bayoneted Zimbabwean left in the bush by the Smith racist murderers.

The booklet concluded thus:

1976

The failure of the American intervention in Angola explains the hectic efforts by Dr Henry Kissinger* to 'mediate' between the leaders of the African Liberation Movements and the white racist dictatorship of Ian Smith in Rhodesia (Zimbabwe) and John Vorster in South Africa. The means and the methodes [*sic*] of the American intervention might change but not its objectives. These objectives are exactly the same as they ever have been since the 'richest nation on earth' was founded on slave-labour of the kidnapped people of Africa, considered an 'inferior' race by the Founding Fathers of the United States. And their successors, [*sic*] objectives were exactly the same, when they annihilated the aboriginal inhabitants of America, the Indians, when they robbed half of their neighbour, Mexico, while they razored villages in the Philippines, 'atomized' hundreds of thousands in Japan, destructed Korea, overthrow [*sic*] governments in Iran, Guatemala, Dominica, Chile, Iraq, Lebanon, Congo and in many other countries, and exactly the same in Vietnam where they tried 'to bomb back to the stone-age' a heroic nation. These objectives of the American foreign policy were very well defined by the eminent British historian, Arnold Toynbee, who said: '... America is today the leader of a world-wide anti-revolutionary movement in defence of vested interests. She now stands for what Rome stood for. Rome consistently supported the rich against the poor in all foreign communities that fell under her sway; and, since the poor, so far, have always and everywhere been far more numerous than the rich, Rome's policy made for inequality, for injustice, and for the least happiness of the greatest number. America's decision to adopt Rome's role has been deliberate ...' (Arnold Toynbee, America and the World Revolution, 1961)

* US Secretary of State, 1973–7.

The world-wide anti-revolutionary role of the United States is well recognized by those Afro-Americans who understand: they can win their freedom only by fighting together with their brothers abroad against the main oppressor of all poor peoples – the United States.

That thought was beautifully expressed by a courageous young Afro-American, General G. Baker of Detroit, when – replying to his draft board's instruction to report for a physical examination – he wrote:

'Gentlemen:

This letter is in regards to a notice sent to me, General Gordon Baker, Jr., requesting my appearance before an examining station to determine my fitness for military service.

How could you have the NERVE knowing that I am a black man living under the scope and influence of America's racist, decadent society??? You did not ask me if I had morals, principles, or basic human values by which to live. Yet, you ask if I am qualified. QUALIFIED FOR WHAT, might I ask? What does being 'Qualified' mean: qualified to serve in the US Army? . . . To be further brainwashed into the insidious notion of 'defending freedom'?

You stand before me with the dried blood of Patrice Lumumba on your hands, the defenseless Panamanian students, shot down by US marines: the blood of my black brothers in Angola and South Africa who are tortured by the Portuguese and South African whites (whom you resolutely support) respectively; the dead people of Japan, Korea and now Vietnam, in Asia; the blood of Medgar Evers, six Birmingham babies, the blood of one million Algerians slaughtered by the French (whom you supported); the fresh blood of ten thousand Congolese patriots dead from your ruthless rape and plunder of the Congo – the blood of defenseless women and children burned in villages from Napalm jelly bombs . . . With all this blood of my non-white brothers dripping from your fangs, you have the damned AUDACITY to ask me if I am 'qualified'. White man; listen to me for I am talking to you!

I AM A MAN OF PRINCIPLES AND VALUES: principles of justice and national liberation, self-determination, and respect for national sovereignty. Yet, you ask if I am 'physically fit' to go to Asia, Africa, and Latin-America to fight my oppressed brothers (who are completely and resolutely within their just rights to free their fatherland from foreign domination). You ask me if I am qualified to join an army of FOOLS, ASSASSINS and MORAL DELINQUENTS who are not worthy of being called men! You want me to defend the riches reaped from the super-exploitation of the darker races of mankind by a few white, rich, super-monopolists who control the most vast empire that has ever existed in man's one million years of History – all in the name of 'FREEDOM'!

Why, here in the heart of America, 22 million black people are suffering unsurmounted toil: exploited economically by every form of business – from monopolists to petty hustlers; completely suppressed politically; deprived of their social and cultural heritage.

But, all men of principle are fighting-men! My fight is for Freedom: UHURU, LIBERTAD, HALAGUA, and HARAMBEE! Therefore, when the call is made to free South Africa; when the call is made to liberate Latin America from the United Fruit Co., Kaiser and Alcoa Aluminium Co., and from Standard Oil; when the call is made to jail exploiting Brahmins in India in order to destroy the Caste System; when the call is made to free the black delta areas of Mississippi, Alabama, South Carolina; when the call is made to FREE 12TH STREET HERE IN DETROIT!: when these calls are made, send for me, for these shall be Historical Struggles in which it shall be an honor to serve!

Venceremos!
General G. Baker, Jr.'

(General G. Baker, Jr., Letter to Draft Board 100, Wayne County, Detroit, Michigan, 1964)

E VEN in May 1977 the KGB was still hard at work undermining the bicentennial of the previous year. So urgent did this work appear that the Copenhagen Residency was ordered to telegraph to the Centre the date on which it had despatched Service A's latest booklets.

fn.1   *TOP SECRET*
                                                                 Copy No 1
"   "   May 1977
No. 1026/A

COPENHAGEN

Comrade KORIN [LYUBIMOV]
Distribution of booklets

Please despatch by post the ready-wrapped booklets *'America's Years'* and *'Pocket Guide to the America's [sic] 200 Years'* after previously putting on the packets stamps of the requisite value obtained in the city.

Despatching must be carried out by operational staff from one place and in one day, observing the necessary precautionary measures. Please be meticulous

ф.н.1

"   " мая 1977 года
№ I026/A

Гор. КОПЕНГАГЕН

Тов. КОРИНУ

О рассылке брошюр

Просим отправить по почте законвертованные брошюры "*America's years*" и "*Pocket guide to the America's 200 years*", предварительно наклеив на пакеты марки соответствующего достоинства, приобретенные в городе.

Отправку следует
~~Бросок~~ произвести силами оперработников из одного места и в один день с соблюдением необходимых мер предосторожности. С конвертами просим работать аккуратно, не оставлять отпечатков пальцев.

О дате отправления просим телеграфировать.

ПРИЛОЖЕНИЕ: по тексту, в отдельном пакете, несекретно.
Только в адрес.

when handling the envelopes and do not leave fingerprints on them.

Please telegraph the date of despatch.

ENCLOSURE: as in text, under separate cover, non-secret

Only to address.

SEVEROV
[GRUSHKO]

B Y 1981 the main target of KGB active measures was President Ronald Reagan. At the beginning of 1983 Service A was already drawing up impracticable plans to sabotage Reagan's re-election in 1984 by branding him as a warmonger.[2] Residencies around the globe found it easy to claim the credit, frequently undeserved, for some of the anti-Reagan articles which flooded the world's press. But the limitations of KGB active measures were illustrated by the failure of a single Residency in a NATO country to popularise the principal slogan devised by Service A, 'Reagan means War!'

Service A's range of active measures against the Reagan administration included the dissemination of forgeries as well as hostile propaganda. The Centre maintained a large collection of official letterheads and signatures of prominent Americans and other Western leaders, which could be used with scissors and paste to construct forged letters in photocopy form. The forgeries were of two kinds. Some were 'silent forgeries' shown in confidence to Third World leaders to alert them to imaginary imperialist plots. Others were intended to promote media campaigns.

Among the chief victims of the forgers was President Reagan himself. While working at the Centre in 1981, Gordievsky learned of an active measure, involving Service A forgeries, to fuel opposition to Spanish membership of NATO. The main forgery, though he did not see it at the time, was a fabricated letter from Reagan to the King of Spain, putting pressure on him 'to act . . . with despatch to remove the forces obstructing Spain's entry into NATO'. In November 1981 copies of the letter were sent through the post to Spanish journalists and all delegations (excepting the American) attending the Madrid Conference on Security and Cooperation in Europe (CSCE).[3]

THE WHITE HOUSE

WASHINGTON

October 23, 1981

His Majesty
The King of Spain
Madrid

Your Majesty:

Permit me to bring to your attention a delicate and confidential matter which, I deeply believe, is highly important for both of our countries.

After our private talks, I learned that several persons close to you oppose Spain's entry into the North Atlantic Treaty Organization and have posed new conditions for the membership of Spain. The highly secret information I have received indicates that members of this group come from Spain's armed forces, political parties, the government, and even the Catholic Church. It is my good fortune to be able to enclose the draft text of a memorandum the group prepared for you, which I was given by a strictly confidential source.

I believe Your Majesty agrees that it is vitally important to the United States for Spain to enter NATO without delay, in fact, in 1981. Spain, after all, faces major tasks in this context: Suffice it to mention the role of the Canary Islands after the NATO Southern Command is set up. So, it is understandable that the United States is concerned about these doubts coming from influential and reliable individuals we regard as our friends. I believe in sharing conviction. We cannot permit another objectionable posture like the attitude of the French, which constantly creates problems for NATO in elaborating its new conceptions with reference to Latin America, Africa and the Mediterranean area. I have always believed Spain's absence from the Western system of defense to be a mistaken step, because your esteemed country would hardly feel at home among the self-styled "non-aligned" nations.

I respectfully ask Your Majesty to help disperse the uncertainty regarding Spain's NATO membership, created by the group influenced by the OPUS DEI pacifists. I believe it would help by granting those demands which do not directly conflict with NATO interests. For instance, my advisers inform me there are good grounds for destroying the left-wing opposition. In that event, the friendly relations between our two countries would improve. It would also neutralize the efforts aimed at creating difficulties for Spain's entry into NATO.

In such an instance, Your Majesty, I believe it imaginable that America might consider the final solution to Gibraltar in favor of Spain.

If necessary, the United States would undertake to dispel any anxiety in connection with Spain's new role which may arise, on the one hand, for the Mediterranean powers, and, on the other, on the part of the over-sensitive North African states with reference to Spanish territories in Africa and the Canary Islands.

I hope this message will strengthen Your Majesty's belief that Spain will benefit immensely by joining NATO. Such an act would enable Spain to once again assume the place she merits in history among the major World Powers. I urge Your Majesty to act, therefore, with dispatch to remove the forces obstructing Spain's entry into the NATO.

Yours truly,

Ronald Reagan

Ronald Reagan

THE WHITE HOUSE
WASHINGTON

October 23, 1981

His Majesty
The King of Spain
Madrid

Your Majesty:

Permit me to bring to your attention a delicate and confidential matter which, I deeply believe, is highly important for both of our countries.

After our private talks, I learned that several persons close to you oppose Spain's entry into the North Atlantic Treaty Organization and have posed new conditions for the membership of Spain. The highly secret information I have received indicates that members of this group come from Spain's armed forces, political parties, the government, and even the Catholic Church. It is my good fortune to be able to enclose the draft text of a memorandum the group prepared for you, which I was given by a strictly confidential source.

I believe Your Majesty agrees that it is vitally important to the United States for Spain to enter NATO without delay, in fact, in 1981. Spain, after all, faces major tasks in this context: Suffice it to mention the role of the Canary Islands after the NATO Southern Command is set up. So, it is understandable that the United States is concerned about these doubts coming from influential and reliable individuals we regard as our friends. I believe you share my conviction. We cannot permit another objectionable posture like the attitude of the French, which constantly creates problems for NATO in elaborating its new conceptions with reference to Latin America, Africa and the Mediterranean area. I have always believed Spain's absence from the Western system of defense to be a mistaken step, because your esteemed country would hardly feel at home among the self-styled 'non-aligned' nations.

I respectfully ask Your Majesty to help disperse the uncertainty regarding Spain's NATO membership, created by the group influenced by the OPUS DEI pacifists. I believe it would help by granting those demands which do not directly conflict with NATO interests. For instance, my advisers inform me there are good grounds for destroying the left-wing opposition. In that event, the friendly relations between our two countries would improve. It would also neutralize the efforts aimed at creating difficulties for Spain's entry into NATO.

In such an instance, Your Majesty, I believe it imaginable that America might consider the final solution to Gibraltar in favor of Spain.

If necessary, the United States would undertake to dispel any anxiety in connection with Spain's new role which may arise, on the one hand, for the Mediterranean powers, and, on the other, on the part of the over-sensitive North

African states with reference to Spanish territories in Africa and the Canary Islands.

I hope this message will strengthen Your Majesty's belief that Spain will benefit immensely by joining NATO. Such an act would enable Spain to once again assume the place she merits in history among the major World Powers. I urge your Majesty to act, therefore, with dispatch to remove the forces obstructing Spain's entry into the NATO.

Yours truly,
Ronald Reagan

C OPIES of the bogus memorandum referred to in the forgery, opposing Spanish entry into NATO and bearing forged signatures which included that of the Spanish Foreign Minister, were circulated with Reagan's letter.[4] The two documents were a classic example of Service A's attempts to fulfil the Centre's standing requirement to 'deepen the disagreements between the United States and its allies'.[5] As sometimes happened, however, the active measure was too crude to be effective. The forgeries had negligible impact. Several Spanish journalists publicly suggested that they were of Soviet origin. When the CSCE conference reconvened at Madrid a year later, Service A tried a different tack. The Centre instructed Residencies to arrange for articles and speeches accusing the Reagan administration of plans to turn Europe into a battlefield for nuclear, chemical and neutron weapons.[6]

The FCD conference reviewing Soviet operations during 1982 and 1983 was told that 'The range of questions dealt with by means of active measures has been continually widening.'[7] Among the anti-American operations in the early 1980s of which Gordievsky had personal knowledge were:

– Operation 'Chicory', begun in July 1981: based on Service A forgeries designed to expose a plot involving the CIA and West German Intelligence to supply nuclear weapons to South Africa.[8]

– Operation 'Sirena 2', begun in September 1982: based on a Service A forgery of a US National Security Council document, purporting to show American interference in Polish internal affairs.[9]

– Operation 'Dämpfer', begun in October 1982: designed to portray Western press reports that the Siberian gas pipeline was being built by forced labour as part of an American plot to disrupt East–West trade.[10]

A girl's best friend

Claudia Wright explores the often secret relationship between US Ambassador to the UN, Jeane Kirkpatrick, and South Africa

THE UNITED STATES Ambassador to the United Nations, Jeane Kirkpatrick, celebrates her birthday on 19 November. Last year the South African government sent a special courier to the Ambassador's New York office to deliver a birthday greeting. It was signed by Pieter Swanepoel, the Information Counsellor at the South African Embassy in Washington, who had just arrived from Pretoria. There were also 'best regards and gratitude' from Lieutenant-General P. W. van der Westhuizen, head of South Africa's military intelligence. With the letter (see illustration) came a birthday gift, a 'token of appreciation', honouring Kirkpatrick's 'activity for freedon and democracy'.

Now birthday presents are normal enough among friends and Kirkpatrick has been a friend, if not of freedom and democracy, at least of the parody version practised in South Africa. According to United States law, Mrs Kirkpatrick is obliged to report any gift to the Protocol Office of the Department of State. If it is of more than nominal value, she may not keep it for herself.

Kirkpatrick has not reported her gift from the South African government. In the annual list of gifts to US officials – published in the Federal Register on 26 March 1982 – Kirkpatrick remembered to record a small rust and green rug, worth $300, given to her on 30 August 1981, by General Mohammed Zia of Pakistan – but that was all. When I asked the Ambassador's office about a gift from South Africa in 1981, the response was there had been none. Swanepoel and the South African ambassador, Brand Fourie, also say that they 'know nothing about such a gift'.

Forgetfulness in reporting gifts has caused trouble for exalted officials in the Reagan Administration, among them the President's first Assistant for National Security Affairs, Richard Allen, who lost his job because of a Japanese watch and honorarium. More important, however, in the case of Mrs Kirkpatrick are the reasons General van der Westhuizen and the Pretoria government felt so grateful to the ambassador.

DURING 1981, General van der Westhuizen had several reasons for being personally grateful to Kirkpatrick. She was, for example, the most senior US official to meet him and four other South African military intelligence men on 15 March (see *NS* April 3, 1981). Until that meeting, the US had barred official visits by South African officers of brigadier rank or above. Early reports about Kirkpatrick's meeting were denied. She then admitted there had been a meeting, but lied about her knowledge of van der

Westhuizen's identity. The then Secretary of State, General Alexander Haig, intervened to tell the press that Kirkpatrick's meeting with van der Westhuizen had his personal authorisation.

The South African general returned to the US again, on 23-24 November, to attend a negotiating session on Namibia which was held near Washington. The State Department admits that Assistant Secretary of State for Africa, Chester Crocker, was at this meeting. Kirkpatrick's office denies meeting van der Westhuizen at that time. He returned for another visit (his third at least), this time to the State Department in Washington, on 22-23 February, this year. In Kirkpatrick's absence, the meetings were monitored by an official from her office.

Each of van der Westhuizen's visits have preceded major shifts in US policy, and large, usually secret, concessions to South African demands. Kirkpatrick's role on each occasion has been that of a 'go-between', according to officials at the UN, relaying South African requests to Washington, and helping to coordinate joint American-South African positions and negotiating tactics. According to a State Department official, she is one of several members of 'President Reagan's entourage (whose) furtive association . . . with some foreign governments, the South African regime in particular . . . will inflict serious damage to the long-term interests of my country'.

After the March 1981 meeting with van der Westhuizen, the administration sent Assistant Secretary Crocker to Pretoria. Summaries of his talks there were leaked and

published by the *Covert Action Information Bulletin*. The documents reveal that Crocker told the South Africans that 'top US priority is to stop Soviet encroachment in Africa. US wants to work with SAG (South African Government) but ability to deal with Soviet presence severely impeded by Namibia . . . USG (US Government) assumes Soviet/Cuban presence is one of (SAG's) concerns and we are exploring ways to remove in the context of Namibia settlement.' This was the beginning of a US-South African shift on the terms of the settlement for Namibia, undermining the current UN resolution on Namibia and ending the effective negotiating role carried out so far by the Namibia 'contact group' – the US, UK, Canada, France and Germany. It was also the beginning of the 'linkage' in US and South African policy between the withdrawal of South African forces and the independence of Namibia on the one side, with a simultaneous withdrawal of Cuban forces from Angola to the north. According to South African officials, the idea of this 'linkage' was 'something the Americans initiated, wanted, and pursued'.

The Kirkpatrick and Crocker meetings in early 1981 were also the green light for General van der Westhuizen and his fellow generals to widen their military operations in Namibia and Angola and to escalate covert operations against Mozambique and Zimbabwe. As South African troops advanced into southern Angola in August 1981, Kirkpatrick played the role of public defender at the UN. The draft resolution requested by Angola condemning the South African invasion had overwhelming support in the Security Council on 31 August. But Britain abstained and Kirkpatrick cast the American veto. The justification she gave was that South Africa's attack was a legitimate reprisal for SWAPO raids from Angolan bases into Namibia – the same view Crocker had privately offered in Pretoria on 15 April.

Kirkpatrick was to play the same role protecting South Africa from UN votes on sanctions through the autumn of 1981, and

– Operations, begun in October 1982, to discredit the 'Popular Tribunal on Afghanistan', due to be held in Paris the following December. Residencies were ordered to spread reports that the CIA and 'Zionist circles' were behind the organisation of the Tribunal.

– Operation 'Golf', begun in October 1982: based on a forged letter to the US Ambassador to the United Nations, Jeane Kirkpatrick, from a Counsellor at the South African Embassy in Washington conveying 'best regards and gratitude' from the head of South African military intelligence and allegedly enclosing a birthday present 'as a token of appreciation from my government'. The use of the word 'priviously' [sic] indicates that, as sometimes happened with its forgeries, Service A had forgotten to check its English spelling. However, the letter was successfully planted on, among others, the unsuspecting Washington correspondent of the *New Statesman* (see p. 101).

In January 1985 L. F. Sotskov, First Deputy Head of Service A, told the London Residency that there were three main active measure priorities: first and foremost, attacking all aspects of American policy; second, promoting tensions between the United States and its NATO allies; third, finding ways to encourage Western peace movements to concentrate their fire on the United States.

Though Service A scored occasional successes such as Operation 'Golf' in the West, its main triumphs occurred in the Third World where it was able to tap a rich vein of anti-Americanism and anti-imperialism, combined with a receptiveness to conspiracy theories about the West. Perhaps its most successful active measure was the attempt to blame Aids on American biological warfare. In 1983 Service A began to disseminate the claim that the Aids virus had been 'manufactured' during genetic engineering experiments at Fort Detrick, Maryland. The story was slow to take off. But from late 1985 onwards it swept the Third World as well as taking in some of the Western media. In the first six months of 1987 alone, the Aids fabrication received major news coverage in over forty Third World countries.[11]

As well as organising deception operations about the 'Main Adversary', the Centre also fell victim to self-deception. Its tendency to alarm itself by imagining Western plots to subvert the Soviet Bloc survived the end of Operation RYAN – albeit, mercifully, in a less apocalyptic form. During the early 1980s the Centre became progressively more concerned by the Soviet Union's growing dependence on Western grain imports and by speculation, especially in the United States, about using these imports to exert political pressure on the Soviet Union. Whereas the West believed that it was supplying grain at bargain prices, the KGB convinced itself that the prices were deliberately inflated. Reports of deterioration of some grain imports from the USA, due no doubt chiefly to the notorious inadequacies of food transport and storage in the Soviet Union, led the Centre to devise a conspiracy theory somewhat reminiscent of the tendency during the 1930s to blame the problems of the Five Year Plans on economic 'sabotage'. Early in 1985 the FCD warned Residencies of the danger that the CIA and other Western intelligence services were 'deliberately infecting grain imported by the Soviet Union'.

No 91

Secret

Copy No 1

No. 934/KR-8   To Representatives and Residents

21.01.1985   as listed

Stepping up work on uncovering and
stopping subversive action by the adversary
against the USSR through the grain trade
(ref No 49786/EK of 23.11.1984)

According to information in the Centre, the USA administration regards export of agricultural produce to the USSR and other socialist countries as an effective instrument for inflicting serious damage on their economies. By exploiting certain difficulties which we are having in the field of agricultural production, the USA is attempting to pursue a line which would make the USSR dependent on grain imports, the aim being to make use of the food weapon in future to exert pressure on the Soviet Union. Thus, as acknowledged by the US Secretary for Agriculture, D Block, 'an embargo or the threat of using one, may become a real means of bringing political pressure to bear on the USSR if Soviet grain purchases in the US amount to about 35 million tonnes a year'.

An important role is also assigned to the USA, Canada, Australia, and the EEC countries, establishing some kind of 'grain cartel'. According to American intentions, this plan, if implemented, would make it possible for them not only to control the main sources of grain supplies for the USSR, but also to raise prices sharply.

Evidence of the scale of the adversary's intelligence effort in regard to the USSR's grain trade with Western countries, is provided by the 'list of priority tasks for gathering economic intelligence about the USSR', prepared by the Economic Intelligence Council of the director of the CIA, in which the following points, in particular, are especially singled out: the Soviet Union's requirements in imports of grain and other kinds of agricultural produce; the quantitative indices of imports of these commodites (by countries); real interest on the part of the USSR in supplies of farming products and plans to expand

imports; the USSR's foreign exchange resources to provide for import requirements; credits made available to the USSR for financing of food imports:
capacity of Soviet ports, facilities for receiving, processing and transporting
imported foodstuffs, losses sustained in the process etc.

The adversary is trying to obtain information on these points through overt
Soviet publication, by the use of technical devices and also by organising agent
activity through the USSR's economic connections abroad with Western countries. For instance, the interest shown by the West's special services in officials
of the USSR Ministry of Agriculture and scientific research institutes working
in the agricultural field has markedly increased in recent times. The adversary
is actively studying Soviet scientists, agrarian specialists, and representatives of
Soviet foreign trade organisations, especially 'Export-khleb' who are en poste
abroad, in order to acquire sources of intelligence information among them.
The methods used by the special services in regard to Soviet representatives,
include handing them expensive presents and paying all expenses involved in
their stay abroad; also included is agent study from vantage points in grain
trading firms etc.

Analysis of operational material has shown that when organising subversive
operations against the USSR through the grain trade, the adversary devotes a
great deal of attention to utilising, for its own ends, any slips or omissions on the
part of Soviet foreign trade organisations in commercial talks with foreign firms
about purchases of grain and other kinds of produce, which lead to considerable
losses in foreign exchange for the Soviet side. For instance, the United States
Department of Agriculture considers it essential to 'consolidate and expand the
practice adopted for Soviet grain purchases', in which the 'Export-khleb' foreign
trade organisation and the USSR Ministry of Foreign Trade as a whole are con-
fined to a limited group of large-scale grain-trading firms. This enables the
Americans to obtain considerable surplus payments from the Soviet Union for
grain imports. In the words of the president of the firm 'Louis Dreyfus', 'the
Russians are easy to work with, they don't haggle, they overpay by 8 dollars a
tonne'. (Altogether this amounted in individual years to a sum of the order of 80
million US dollars a year in the transactions with this firm alone.)

The quality of grain imported by the Soviet Union still remains an unsolved
problem. The Centre is continually receiving information about shipments to
the USSR by foreign firms, especially American ones, of dirty, infected and
even stale grain from stocks carried over from previous harvests. The Soviet
side has sustained considerable financial loss as a result of this, from having to
carry out additional processing of agricultural produce and organise storage and
reprocessing in specially detailed enterprises, with shipping kept idle beyond the
standard time limits. There is also the danger of quarantine pests, weeds and
diseases of agricultural crops and livestock not previously encountered on the
territory of the Soviet Union being brought in. Nor must it be excluded that
the adversary's special services may use grain delivery firms for deliberately
infecting grain imported by the USSR, even in the trans-shipment ports.

In view of what has been said, and also having regard to the instructions from the authorities to the USSR Ministry of Foreign Trade to purchase a considerable quantity of grain from the USA, Canada, Argentina, Australia and a number of other countries in 1984–1985, please step up operational action designed to uncover and put a stop to subversive operations by the adversary and to ensure that the Soviet Union's economic activity in the grain trade can be safely carried on. The principal effort must be concentrated on dealing with the following operational tasks:

– expose departments of the adversary's special services which prepares and implements operations connected with the Soviet Union's trade in grain with Western countries;

– uncover the means and methods used by the adversary to inflict economic damage on the USSR and step up action to acquire agents and confidential contacts among foreigners representing farming businesses, banking circles, scientists and specialists from Western countries, with real facilities for cooperation in ensuring the safety of commercial activity of Soviet organisations in this sector;

– expose instances of the despatch of poor quality grain to the USSR, drawing attention especially to the possibility of it being deliberately infected in storage, trans-shipment, loading and while in transit;

– reinforce counter-intelligence safeguards for Soviet colonies and for delegations travelling on USSR Ministry of Foreign Trade business, in order to prevent attempts by the adversary's special services to make recruitment approaches to Soviet citizens, and to stop leaks of secret information about the USSR's agriculture and grain trade;

– inform the Centre promptly of instances of incompetence in the conduct of negotiations held by representatives of Soviet foreign trade organisations with foreign firms about purchasing foodstuffs, attempts to hand over expensive presents or bribes to Soviet specialists, and any economically unsound contracts signed by them: more active use should be made of agents and reliable persons among our Soviet nationals for this work.

– Analysis of information on the subject of grain which has reached the Centre indicates that, unfortunately, in a number of cases, this information is overt in character and relates mainly to the market situation in grain and other types of produce.

In this context please concentrate your attention chiefly on obtaining intelligence information on the following points:

– intentions of governments of capitalist countries exporting grain to make use of the grain trade to exert political and economic pressure on the USSR and other socialist countries;

– attitudes (possible disagreements) of the principal grain-exporting countries regarding establishing a so-called 'grain cartel';

– the adversary's knowledge of confidential aspects of the activity of Soviet foreign trade organisations and trade delegations going abroad for negotiations on the purchase of grain and other foodstuffs;

– competitive proposals from Western firms, which may be helpful in concluding contracts for deliveries of grain and other foodstuffs to the USSR on terms which are more advantageous to the Soviet side, etc.

Please see that all operational staff are informed about this briefing.

ALEKSEEV
[GRUSHKO]
[First Deputy Head, FCD]

[MS notes:]

Gornov/Comr Gornov	James	?10.3
〃 Patrick	Oliver	
〃 Vadim	11.3	[other illeg.
& all oper. staff of the Residency		names etc]

Lavrov 26.11.85

T HE FCD was more conscious than perhaps any other section of the vast Soviet bureaucracy of the vast economic gulf between East and West. It was well aware that even scientific and technological espionage on an unprecedented scale was failing to prevent the Soviet Union from falling still further behind. The Centre's loss of faith in Soviet ability to match Western technology led it to fear that advances in American weapons systems would give the United States 'military superiority over the Soviet Union'.

During the second half of 1984, however, the Centre's plans for countering that threat were in some confusion. Though the acute alarmism of Operation RYAN was subsiding, no coherent alternative approach to the nuclear arms race with the West had yet emerged. As it became increasingly plain that the Soviet leader Konstantin Chernenko was terminally ill, the Politburo showed itself reluctant to make major policy decisions. The London Residency, among others, expected from the summer of 1984 onwards a major directive from the Centre on SDI (American 'Star Wars'). None arrived until February 1985.

The Centre then announced that 'military strategy', in particular American attempts 'to gain military superiority over the Soviet Union', were to be henceforth 'the top priority in Residencies' work'. An accompanying brief listed three main specific areas of concern: the military implications of the Space Shuttle programme, the ASAT anti-satellite system and SDI. The brief showed that the Centre remained uncertain whether the primary aim of current US policy on SDI was to use it to extract bargaining concessions from the Soviet Union. Its instructions to Residencies to report back by 20 March indicated that it intended to use their replies to help brief Soviet negotiators before the next round of Arms Control negotiations with the United States opened in Geneva.

The chief reason why SDI and alleged American plans for the 'militarisation of space' preoccupied the Centre was that its faith in the ability of American technology to achieve apparent miracles (paradoxically, greater than among many Western politicians and scientists) persuaded it that they might well succeed. The GRU agreed. In April 1985 Colonel A. I. Sazhin, head of the military attaché section at the Soviet Embassy in London, told a meeting of diplomats and intelligence officers that Moscow believed SDI systems might eventually be able to intercept 90 per cent of Soviet strategic missiles. He saw little chance of Soviet SDI research keeping pace with that of the United States.

[Ms notes:]
Comrade Gornov   No 75
Comrade Feliks
& operational staff of line.
Pl. allocate the subject according
to existing facilities and carry
out tasks within the time limit.

Comr James How do we advise [illegible]
                        Lavrov [Nikitenko] 22.2.85
vn-1   Top Secret
                                                          Copy
No 337/PR
13.02.85   To Residents

In view of the increasingly tense international situation and the American administration's persistence in striving to gain military superiority over the Soviet Union, the Centre is making military strategy the top priority in residencies' work.

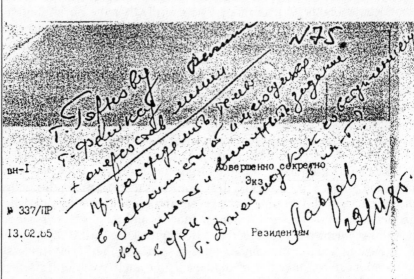

вн-I

№ 337/ПР

13.02.85

Совершенно секретно

Экз. №

Резидентам

В условиях обострившейся международной обстановки, настойчивого стремления американской администрации добиться военного превосходства над Советским Союзом, Центр придает первостепенное значение работе резидентур по военно-стратегической тематике.

В соответствии с указанием руководства нашей Службы просим Вас принять соответствующие меры и до 20 марта с.г. направить в Центр информационные материалы по вопросам, изложенным в прилагаемой ориентировке-задании.

Приложение: ориентировка-задание № 453/ПР/52, экз. № 3, на 10 л., сов.секретно, ПН.

In accordance with instructions from the heads of our Service, we are asking you to take appropriate action and despatch material to the Centre by 20 March this year on the points set out in the attached briefing.

Attachment: Briefing No 453/PR/52, Copy No 3, 10 pages,
      Top Secret, PN.

SVETLOV

[GRIBIN]

[Two illeg signatures] 28.2

Attachment to No 337/PR   Top Secret
of 13 February 1985   Copy No 3

American policy on the militarisation of space

Analysis of information at the Centre shows that the USA is carrying out militarisation of space on the following basic lines:

– deployment in space of systems for supporting military operations in nuclear and conventional wars (early warning of missile attack, reconnaissance, communications, meteorological and navigational support, control of delivery of nuclear strikes)

– equipping the reusable space transport system 'Shuttle' with the capability of attacking ground targets and space installations;

– establishing the 'Asat' anti-satellite system;

– developing a large-scale anti-missile defence system with elements based in space.

Even if the first of the lines mentioned does not run counter to the international agreements on the use of space, the action of the USA in the other directions is aimed at undermining these agreements and eroding the foundations of the Soviet–American Anti-Ballistic Missile Treaty (1972) and represents a threat to the state security of the USSR.

Equipping the 'Shuttle' system with strike capabilities is to be achieved by placing on the board reusable space transport craft a weapon for putting the transmitters of Soviet satellite orientation systems out of action, and using this craft as a bomber. (The United States Air Force concluded a contract with the firm 'Science Application' for research on the strike capabilities of the 'Shuttle' in August 1984.) Furthermore, the manoeuvrability characteristics of the 'Shuttle' craft already enable it to be used for inflicting damage on Soviet satellites in low orbits (especially optical reconnaissance satellites and piloted orbital stations of the 'Salyut' type).

One should note particularly that in connection with the Treaty governing for action by states to explore and exploit space, including the moon and other heavenly bodies (1967), the USA and the other participating states assumed an obligation not to launch into space any installations with nuclear weapons or any weapons of mass destruction. Therefore plans to use the 'Shuttle' as a space bomber can be regarded as a precondition for violation of the afore-mentioned agreement.

According to existing information, during a 'Shuttle' flight on 25–28 January this year the United States Air Force began to try out certain elements which would provide the strike capabilities of this system.

The Centre is anxious to obtain from residencies information on the following points connected with the 'Shuttle' system:

1) Specific contents of plans to use the 'Shuttle' craft in a strike variant to destroy targets in space and on the ground (in the air, on water and on land).

2) The attitude of Congress, political parties, public and academic organisations to these plans.

3) The degree of involvement of the USA's West European allies in NATO in implementing these plans and their attitude towards them.

4) Possibility of the Americans including the question of the 'Shuttle' as a subject in the forthcoming talks with the Soviet Union on space and nuclear weapons.

5) Content of the experiments carried out during the 'Shuttle' flight on 25–28 January this year.

A start was made in the USA to set up the *'Asat' anti-satellite system* designed for combating space installations in low orbits (up to 1,000 km) in 1977 by the firms 'Vought', 'Boeing' and 'McDonnell Douglas'.

The 'Asat' system is an air-launched missile interception system consisting of an F-15 carrier aircraft, a two-stage 'Asat' missile and the Spadats space checking apparatus (at the NORAD command post in the Cheyenne Mountains, Colorado).

The F-15 series fighter is used as a carrier aircraft with a specially modified ventral attachment point from which the 'Asat' missile is suspended. About six hours are required to re-equip a standard fighter aircraft to carry the 'Asat' missile.

The two-stage 'Asat' missile is 5.5 m long and 0.5 m in diameter, all-up weight 1.22 t. The missile is fitted with an inertial guidance system and onboard computer. The pay load is the most important element of the whole 'Asat' system, a compact interceptor equipped with infra-red homing head and micromotors for orientation and manoeuvring. Satellites are destroyed by the strike principle with the kinetic energy of the interceptor.

The 'Asat' missile is launched as the aircraft reaches a previously calculated altitude of 18–20 km. Successful test launchings of the 'Asat' missile were carried out on 21 January and 13 November 1984. Altogether twelve launchings are planned, the next one for spring this year.

(above) General Vladimir Aleksandrovich
Kryuchkov, head of the FCD from 1974
to 1988, the first foreign intelligence
chief to become Chairman of the KGB;
one of the leaders of the abortive coup of
August 1991.

(right) General Gennadi Fyodorovich
Titov, head of the FCD Third
Department from 1979 to 1984, shown
here on the right with his celebrated
agent, the Norwegian Arne Treholt.
Early in 1991 Titov was made head of
Second Chief Directorate (Counter-
Intelligence) of the KGB.

KGB DEAD LETTER BOXES AND SIGNAL SITES IN LONDON

Brompton Oratory, the site of a KGB 'DLB', located behind the right-hand of the two columns situated just to the left of the altar (page 59).

DLB at the base of a tree to the left of a statue of St Francis of Assisi (page 59).

Signal site on a lamp post in Audley Square. A light blue chalk mark was placed below the figure 8 to indicate that a DLB had been filled (page 60).

Signal site on park bench. A chalk mark was placed on one of the benches to indicate that the signal on the lamp post had been read and understood (page 61).

Signal site code-named 'Koran' on a post at the intersection of Guilford Street and Gray's Inn Road (page 63).

Signal site near the Ballot Box Public House in Sudbury Hill, north-west London. The signal consisted of a piece of chewing gum placed on the top of the concrete post (page 62).

DLB on a verge between a path and a fence on the northern edge of Coram's Fields in Bloomsbury. In May 1985 Gordievsky left on this site an artificial brick containing £8,000 for an Illegal code-named 'Dario' (page 62).

If the tests are successfully completed, the 'Asat' system may become operational towards the end of 1986. The first combat squadron of 'Asat' missile carrier-aircraft (14 aircraft, 28 missiles) is to be deployed at Langley Air Force Base, Virginia, in 1987. A second squadron of the same strength will be deployed at the McCord base in Washington by 1989. The plan is for the number of 'Asat' system aircraft to reach 56, with 112 missile units in the 1990s.

If this carrier aircraft system is based solely on the continental part of the USA it can only ensure that 25% of Soviet satellites in low orbit are intercepted. The Reagan Administration is trying to create a global anti-missile system and to this end talks are taking place about the right to use foreign territory for deploying the 'Asat' system (especially in the Falklands and New Zealand).

In practical terms work is being done on questions of refuelling the 'Asat' missile-carrier aircraft in the air and re-equipping as carrier the deck-launched F-14 fighters, which may expand considerably the extent of the zones for carrying out anti-satellite operations.

The cost of setting up the 'Asat' anti-satellite system is estimated at 4,200 billion dollars, including 1,400 billion dollars for development, 2,500 billion for purchases and the rest for building infrastructure installations.

The Reagan Administration declined a Soviet proposal put forward in 1983 for introducing a moratorium on testing anti-satellite weapons, giving as the reason for the refusal the 'endeavour to reduce the extent of the lag-behind the USSR in the field of anti-satellite weapon system'.

During A. A. Gromyko's* talks with G. Shultz† in Geneva on 7–8 January this year the American side, having agreed in principle to discuss questions of space weapons at the Soviet–American talks to begin on 12 March this year, tried to reduce them to so-called 'nuclear defensive weapons', meaning primarily the existing anti-satellite systems in the USSR. Obviously this approach will also be reflected in the attitude adopted by the USA at the talks in Geneva where the Americans can try to deflect the Soviet proposals on banning anti-satellite systems.

The Centre is anxious to obtain information on the following points connected with the 'Asat' system:

1) The United States administration's plans for deploying the 'Asat' system, especially information about measures taken to deploy it on the territory of foreign states.

2) The administration's intentions in regard to using elements of the 'Asat' system (especially the compact interceptor) for anti-missile defence tasks and for inflicting strikes from space against ground targets. Assessments by foreign experts of the possibilities of making this kind of use of elements of the system.

* Long-serving Soviet foreign minister and Politburo member.
† US Secretary of State.

3) Prospects of expanding the combat facilities of the 'Asat' system to use it against satellites in high and geostationary orbits (up to a height of 3636,000 km) by making a more powerful rocket or carrying elements of the 'Asat' complex into space.

4) Attitude of the Reagan administration to including the 'Asat' system as a subject of discussion at the talks on space and nuclear weapons. On what conditions might the USA agree to ban deployment of the 'Asat' system.

5) The attitude of Congress towards construction and deployment of the 'Asat' system.

Development of a large-scale anti-missile defence system with elements based in space the idea of which was announced by Reagan in a speech on 23 March 1983, began in January 1984 after the Presidential Directive No 119 was signed.

With the aid of this system the Americans expect to be able to ensure that United States territory is completely invulnerable to Soviet intercontinental ballistic missiles, which would enable the United States to count on mounting a nuclear attack on the Soviet Union with impunity.

Research is being carried out in this field in conformity with the 'Strategic Defence Initiative' (SDI) programme, under the guidance of Lieutenant-General G. Abrahamson. This includes numerous previously uncoordinated pieces of fundamental research and experimental developments of prospective means of destroying ICBM and ICBM warheads (beam-power weapons; lasers and beam weapons; kinetic weapons; antimissile missiles and electromagnetic guns), early warning, target indications, guidance and tactical control, of use in setting up an anti-missile defence system. At present the work is at the stage of examining the feasibility of the actual concept of setting up such an anti-missile defence system (this draft plan has not yet been drawn up in its final form). The present stage should continue up to the 1990s.

The planned appropriations for the programme in the financial years 1985–1989 amount to $21 billion, including $14 billion allocated to the military budget for the 1985 financial year and about $4 billion requested for the budget for the 1986 financial year. The overall cost of setting up a large-scale anti-missile defence system with space-based elements is estimated by American experts at $500–1,000 billion. The approximate date for deployment (at all events in the form in which it is now outlined) will not be before the beginning of the twenty-first century.

The principal effort under the 'Strategic Defence Initiative' programme is concentrated in the following areas (appropriations fixed for the period up to the 1989 financial year):

– tracking systems for following targets ($75 billion);

– beam-power weapons ($57 billion);

– kinetic weapons ($6 billion);

– support systems ($18 billion).

The anti-missile defence system being developed is designed above all for destroying an ICBM, in the powered phase of its flight path (during the first five minutes after launching and flight up to a height of 300–400 km) by putting this stage of the ICBM out of action with beam-power or kinetic weapons. The prospects are also being considered for destroying the warhead platforms and the warheads themselves in the free-flight phase of the flight path and on entering the atmosphere.

The 'Strategic Defence Initiative' has been widely publicised as an effective method of defence of the whole population of America in a nuclear war. Particular stress is laid on extravagant praise of the advantages of beam-power weapons. However, the information available enables one to judge that the Americans attribute considerable prospects in the field of anti-missile defence above all to the use of kinetic weapons, which were first successfully tested for use in anti-missile defence on 10 June 1984 when the warhead of a 'Minuteman' ICBM was destroyed by a direct hit from an anti-missile missile.

Opposition to Reagan's 'star wars' plan is now forming in the US Congress and in scientific circles. A number of American political and public figures (including Senators Kennedy, Proxmire and Chaffy, and scientists of world repute Sagan, Bet and others) are expressing grave doubts about the possibility of setting up an effective anti-missile defence system. They hold the view that some Soviet ICBMs will be able to penetrate the outer limits of this anti-missile defence and inflict unacceptable damage on the USA. It is not fully believed in political and scientific circles that the administration is in fact setting itself the target of setting up a large-scale anti-missile defence system with space-based elements. They are advancing the opinion that the real aims are different: firstly, to secure enormous profits for the military-industrial complex; secondly to draw the USSR into a costly arms race in areas where according to American estimates it is lagging behind the USA; thirdly, to try to use the question of the anti-missile defence system for 'trading' with the Soviet Union at the Geneva talks. One also must not exclude the possibility that the USA is planning to carry out research for other purposes under the guise of working for anti-missile defence (for instance, producing means of attacking ICBM launchers from space, and increasing the effectiveness of their general purpose forces in conventional war).

The opposition's activities in Congress are in fact leading to actual slowing down of the planned tempo of research. For instance, the administration originally asked for $31 billion for the SDI programme for the 1985 financial year and Congress endorsed only $14 billion. Estimates testify that even if twice the appropriations for 1985 are allocated for work on this programme in 1986, this too will be inadequate for completing the first stage within the projected time limit.

The countries of Western Europe are also coming out against creating and deploying an anti-missile system with space-based elements. Under pressure from the USA, however, they are on the whole supporting research in this field.

These considerations provide a basis for believing that the 'strategic defence initiative' (especially the part involving producing beam-power space weapons under its auspices) may be the chief subject for political 'bargaining' at the Geneva talks – for obtaining from the USSR concessions in the area of actual nuclear weapons in exchange for abandoning developments of a large-scale anti-missile defence system, at present only existing in the form of an untested concept. In addition, one must not exclude the possibility that while working on this programme the Americans may get results which they can use for altering strategic parity in favour of the USA.

The Centre is therefore very anxious to obtain the following information in connection with the 'Strategic Defence Initiative':

1) The Reagan administration's plans for producing an anti-missile defence system. Possible evolution of these from the point of view of targets, dates and expected financial outlay. Assessments by those developing the system of the successes and difficulties encountered in this field.

2) The principal arguments of the opposition (especially in Congress and scientific circles), testifying to the political and technical inexpediency of continuing work in the USA on producing a large-scale missile defence system with space-based elements.

3) Specific results obtained by American specialists in achieving technical characteristics of operational and supporting components to enable them to be used in the missile defence system.

4) Estimates confirming or disproving the proposition regarding the United States' prospects of creating an anti-missile defence system, especially one based on kinetic weapons.

5) The Reagan administration's attitude towards including the subject of research on missile defence systems in the Geneva talks. In what context will it place the question of the SDI programme in the talks. Conditions on which the administration might agree to stop research on this programme.

6) How accurate are views which hold that the SDI programme is a large-scale disinformation operation of the Reagan administration calculated to obtain, in exchange for abandoning concessions from the USSR in the field of nuclear weapons.

7) The attitude of government circles and political parties of West European countries towards 'star wars' plans. Their views in regard to the realism of the Reagan administration's efforts to create a large-scale anti-missile defence system with elements based in space.

8) Suggestions of possible active measures on the Soviet side designed to

promote opposition to American 'star wars' plans and support for the attitude of the USSR at the Geneva talks.

9) Assessment by Western government and political circles of possible initiatives from the Soviet Union in connection with the Geneva talks on space and nuclear weapons.

Please send replies to all the questions posed in the brief/assignment to the Centre by 20 March this year.

No 453/PR/52

T HE last meeting at the Centre which Gordievsky attended before his interrogation began was on 21 May 1985. The speaker was Y. A. Kvitsinsky, chief Soviet negotiator on SDI, who addressed an audience of 800 senior KGB officers on the subject of the Geneva arms control negotiations. His tentative conclusion was that the United States had no serious desire at present to reach an agreement with the Soviet Union.

All the Centre's many and varied directives for operations against the 'Main Adversary' during the decade before Gorbachev's rise to power ran up against the same obstacle: the problem of recruiting American agents. Discussions of this problem within the FCD invariably resulted in recriminations against Residencies concerning the 'low standard of this work' and in instructions for 'a radical improvement'. On 21 February 1985 Kryuchkov himself complained to an FCD Party meeting about 'the lack of appreciable results of recruitment against the Americans in most Residencies'. There followed what the official report of the meeting described, perhaps euphemistically, as 'a lively discussion'.

[Ms notes:] Comr. Gornov
           Comr. Oliver   No 63
           & PR Line operational staff
                Lavrov [Nikitenko], 21.III.85
vn-1
No 495/PR   Secret
07.03.85   Copy No 1
                                    To Residents

Party Bureau letter: 'Tasks of
Party organisations in carrying out
the instructions of the heads of the
Department and Service in working against
the US'

A Party meeting took place in our section on 21 February with the following agenda: 'Tasks of Party organisations in mobilising communists in stations abroad to carry out the instructions of the Heads of the Department and Service in working against the USA'.

As was mentioned in the report, the various successes obtained in working against the Americans are not commensurate with the tasks facing our Service. The speaker dwelt particularly on the results of the operational conference of top personnel of the Service held recently on the question of working against the USA. During the conference Comrade ALYOSHIN [KRYUCHKOV] expressed serious uneasiness over the lack of appreciable results of recruitment against the Americans in most residencies. There was criticism of the low standard of this work, which does not match up to the demands being made at this stage. The speaker drew communists' attention to the point brought out in Comrade ALYOSHIN's address that 'active intelligence work against the USA is a matter of professional honour and an official and Party obligation for every member of the Service'.

This remark of Comrade ALYOSHIN's became the leitmotiv of a lively discussion among communists in our section on the position in the sector working against the USA.

Some speakers remarked that the greater tension in the operational situation in most of the countries we are dealing with cannot justify the lack of initiative and often lack of activity of certain officers and stations abroad in working against the Americans. It has been established that there is considerable reserve capacity for improving this work, and above all in producing a change in communists' approach to this matter. Recruitment work against the USA and NATO must become the central point, not only in words, but in practice, in the activity of every communist in the department and must be the chief criterion for his work en poste abroad – all those present reached the same conclusion.

One important sector of the activity of stations abroad and of the Centre itself must be improving the organisation of their work on the basis of well-thought out and realistic planning, strict accounting and the requirement of communists for the matter entrusted to them. A special role in improving cooperation and ensuring continuity in working on the Americans is assigned to the residents' assistants dealing with the 'main adversary'. In this context the plans for working against the USA submitted by the Copenhagen and Canberra residencies were subjected to criticism in that they were too formal and excessively general and did not provide facilities for continuous checking on fulfilment. There was a certain amount of criticism of the Helsinki residency for not making full use of existing facilities for working on the Americans.

An official from the department specialising in working against the USA [the FCD First Department], who took part in the meeting, emphasised in his address the need to make determined efforts to combat all manifestations of formalism, as shown in mere passive study of American targets, compiling repetitive background papers about them, and establishing superficial contacts with official representatives of the USA and putting them down as operationally significant.

All communists endorsed the idea expressed in Comrade SVETLOV's [GRI-BIN's] speech that the principal way of dealing with the tasks facing our stations abroad and Centre itself in this important sector is to recruit auxiliary agents, to acquire agent-recruiters and to make more purposeful use of existing agent access in working against the USA.

The resolution adopted to sum up the discussion of the report notes that the measures taken by the heads of our department, the Party Bureau and the organisations it looks after abroad, are required to ensure a real improvement in the position in the sector for working against the USA, intensifying the factor of personal responsibility of each member of operational staff for achieving results in recruitment work. The main drive in the activity of both residencies and the Centre must be to acquire agents in principal and intermediate American targets, using agent-recruiters and auxiliary agents.

The plan for the Party Bureau's work includes listening to residents' assistants working against the 'main adversary' from the Helsinki, London, Stockholm and Copenhagen residencies* while they are at the Centre on leave.

The Party Bureau expresses its confidence that communist-officials of the 'PR' Line of the Residencies under its charge have a proper understanding of the tasks in front of them, which require a radical improvement in work on the 'main adversary' and that they share the aspiration expressed by communists during the meeting to achieve results in recruitment work against the Americans.

Please inform 'PR'-line communists about this letter.

[for] Party Bureau
SVETLOV
[GRIBIN]

---

* Groups within each Residency coordinating operations against the USA. In the London Residency the group was headed by Mikhail Yurievich Bogdanov.

6

The Main Ally of the 'Main Adversary'
The United Kingdom

THE major turning point in post-war Soviet intelligence operations in the United Kingdom was the unprecedented mass expulsion from London in 1971 of ninety KGB and GRU officers. Another fifteen on leave in the Soviet Union were told that they would not be permitted to return, making a grand total of 105. Moscow Centre was stunned. The London Residency never recovered. Contrary to the myths generated by media revelations about past Soviet moles, both real (like Blunt) and imaginary (like Hollis), during the next fourteen years up to Gordievsky's escape from Moscow in 1985 the KGB found it more difficult to collect high-grade intelligence in London than in almost any other Western capital. The greatly reduced number of KGB and GRU officers found themselves under much tighter surveillance. Largely as a result of the surveillance and several rounds of expulsions, during Gordievsky's three years in London from 1982 to 1985 the Residency ran only a handful of agents and 'confidential contacts', none of major importance. The only secret documents acquired during that period were a small quantity of Chinese ones.

The London Residency's reputation in Moscow in the early 1980s derived chiefly from its political reporting. It pleased the Centre by producing political forecasts which were substantially more accurate than those of the Embassy. In the months preceding the general election campaign of June 1983, the Ambassador, Viktor Ivanovich Popov, hedged his bets, searching for evidence that Labour could do well. The Residency, by contrast, consistently forecast a large Conservative majority. Once the campaign had begun, the Embassy accepted that the Conservatives would win, but Popov and his minister counsellors, V. I. Dolgov and V. L. Bykov, exaggerated the likely strength of the Alliance parties. Gordievsky's final pre-election assessment predicted twenty to thirty seats for the Liberals and five or six for the SDP. (In the event the Liberals won 17 and the SDP 6.) The London Residency also enhanced its reputation in Moscow by consistently forecasting Reagan's re-election well ahead of the 1984 presidential campaign and by predicting from the outset that the 1984 miners' strike in Britain would fail.

The Annual Review of the PR line for 1983 illustrates the style of reports from the London Residency. Reasonably objective analysis was combined with the crude rhetoric expected by the Centre, denouncing Mrs Thatcher's 'chauvinist, anti-Communist activity and efforts to solve Britain's economic problems at the expense of the workers' as well as 'her complete dependence on Reagan'.

1936/PR   Top Secret
5 December 1983   Copy No. 1
from London   to Comrade SILIN [TITOV]

1983 ANNUAL REVIEW OF PR LINE, LONDON RESIDENCY

[Extract]

POLITICAL SITUATION

The period under review has been largely characterised by the intensification in British political life of tendencies designated as 'Thatcherism' and expressed in Government reliance on the most reactionary forces among the British public, combating progressive forces inside the country and beyond its border, whipping up chauvinist, anti-Communist and anti-Soviet attitudes, encouraging the activities of large-scale capital and striving to solve Britain's economic problem at the expense of the workers' interests.

In the area of foreign policy the Thatcher Cabinet, adopting its usual, openly anti-Soviet attitude, has been constantly seeking opportunities to undermine Soviet positions on the international scene, unreservedly supporting the US Administration's actions to intensify world tension to a still greater extent and taking an active part in preparing and implementing NATO and US plans for achieving military superiority over the Soviet Union, including the plan for deployment of new American medium-range missiles in Western Europe. The Conservative Government proceeded to put into effect plans for modernising British nuclear forces in 1983, aiming at markedly increasing their powers of destruction and at the same time refusing to agree to include these forces in the INF talks. This largely contributed to the failure of these talks.

Continuation of the British policy of all out support for the United States in international affairs, especially in East–West relations, has been combined with various manifestations of friction between the Thatcher Cabinet and Reagan Administration, finding expression in dissatisfaction among Conservatives with the fact that Washington has in some cases taken action in the international arena without taking British interests into account and sometimes directly ignored their advice, as was the case in the course of the American invasion of Grenada or their action in the Lebanon. These factors, together with increasing criticism of Thatcher in regard to her complete dependence on Reagan, the continuation of the anti-war movement's activity, especially in connection with deployment of American Cruise missiles in this country, have induced the British Prime Minister to take a number of tactical measures, expressed particularly in statements about making efforts to develop a dialogue with the USSR. According to evidence from reports received by the Residency, this dialogue is seen by the Conservative Cabinet chiefly as a means of demonstrating that Britain has an 'independent' foreign policy and is trying to 'make her contribution towards lessening international tension', but not as a way of actually improving Anglo–Soviet relations.

Britain has continued her efforts in the period under review to achieve a leading position in the EEC, but opposition from France and the FRG and also disagreements with her partners in the Community on the question of the amount of the British payment into the 'Ten's' budget, have prevented these plans from being realised. Nor have British attempts to introduce discord into relations between the FRG and France and convert the Paris–Bonn 'axis' into a London–Bonn 'axis' or a London–Bonn–Paris 'triangle' been successfully developed.

In domestic politics the Thatcher Cabinet has achieved a certain amount of success in the recent period and this was seen in a reduction in the level of inflation, some increase in business activity, a rise in the popularity of the ruling party and some weakening of the position of the opposition parties and progressive social organisations, including the anti-war movement. Utilising these findings, the Conservatives held parliamentary elections ahead of time in June 1983 and won a convincing victory. Supported by an overwhelming majority in Parliament, Thatcher carried out a reorganisation of her Cabinet, in which the key positions were given to her people.

The Labour Party has found itself in a difficult position during the current year, having lost a considerable number of its seats in the House of Commons as a result of the parliamentary elections. Drawing the inferences from this defeat Labour members have elected a new leader and deputy leader of the Party and made certain changes in its policy, which has led to a notable increase in Labour's authority among the population and to some abatement of the internal struggle between its right and left wings. Centrist forces relying on the support of leaders of the larger British trade unions have begun to play a leading role in the leadership of the Labour Party.

The 'Alliance' of Liberal and Social-Democratic Parties has not been strengthened in the period under review and they have not been able to achieve their plans to turn themselves into the leading opposition force in the country. Some increase in the Liberal faction in the House of Commons as a result of the elections has not compensated for a considerable reduction in the number of SDP members. Following their defeat the Social Democrats were not only obliged to change their leader, but also to agree to take the role of junior partner in the union with the Liberals.

Analysis of the political situation developing in Britain shows that Thatcher continues to maintain full control over the government and the ruling party. In this context one must expect that in 1984 the main tendencies in the country's domestic and foreign policy will remain unchanged. Some tactical manoeuvres on the part of the Conservatives, and, in particular, critical pronouncements addressed to the USA, or statements in favour of developing relations with the USSR will not lead to any change in the substance of this policy or deterioration of Anglo–American relations or actual improvement of Britain's relations with the USSR . . .

GORNOV
[O. A. GORDIEVSKY]

Like all Residencies, London was expected to draw up each December its 'Plan of Work' for the following year. The priority accorded by the Centre to Operation RYAN meant that the Plan for 1983 inevitably gave pride of place to American and NATO military planning.

– –/PR   Top Secret
– – December 1982   To Comrade SILIN (Titov)

PLAN OF WORK OF THE PR LINE OF THE LONDON
RESIDENCY OF THE KGB FOR 1983*

[Extract]

1. Information Work
In 1983 the Residency's forces and resources are to be concentrated on procuring secret intelligence on military strategy, world economic problems, the plans of the main adversary, and NATO, the EEC and China with regard to the

* Draft submitted by Gordievsky.

USSR and developments in parts of the world which are of serious significance for the Soviet Union's interests. In this context it is planned to carry out specific work on the following lines:

Problems of Military Strategy: To obtain a regular supply of intelligence information on indications of United States and NATO preparations to launch a nuclear attack on the Soviet Union; plans and action on the part of the United States to step up its military potential; designs of the Reagan Administration and the NATO Command to make use of their military power, including rapid deployment forces, to obtain unilateral military and political advantages in various parts of the world; NATO plans to conduct military action in Europe using conventional forces; progress in modernising NATO's medium-range missiles and tactical nuclear forces; the possible formation of new military blocs allied to the West and the degree of the adversary's knowledge regarding the USSR's war industrial potential and the Soviet armed forces. To continue to gather information about the approach of the United States Administration and the governments of the main NATO countries to the negotiations on MBFR, INF and CSCE. To collect information about the results of the meetings of the NATO Council and the bloc's Defence Planning Committee and nuclear planning group, and also about the activity of its central headquarters . . .

World Economic Problems: The main effort will be directed to obtaining intelligence regularly about the plans and intentions of the United States, NATO, the EEC, and China to make use of economic methods to disrupt the economy of the USSR: the West's credit policy with regard to the Soviet Union and the other socialist countries; United States and EEC plans to make use of commercial and economic contacts with socialist states in order to achieve their political aims; the possibilities for using situations arising in world markets to the advantage of the Soviet economy; the prospects for using some forms of Western technology to increase the efficiency of Soviet industry and agriculture and afford the utmost assistance in carrying out the Food Program. To continue to gather information about the development of West European integration within the EEC, the attitude of the countries of the Community towards prospects for developing relations with the USSR and the CMEA, the disagreements between the Ten and the USA and also within the EEC. To inform the Centre regularly about the outcome of meetings of ministers of Community countries and the meetings of the European Council . . .

The Main Adversary: In the task of gathering information about the main adversary attention must be concentrated on the following problems: the position and trends in the development of relations between the United States and Western Europe, the USA and Japan, and the USA and China; the economic and political rivalry between them and the possibility of making use of existing contradictions to the advantage of the USSR; tendencies shown in the disposition of forces in the United States Administration and their influence on the shaping of Washington's foreign policy; the economic situation in the USA and its effect on the world economy . . .

Line 'K' [China]: Systematic attempts will be made to clarify the Peking leadership's plan with regard to the USSR and other socialist countries; their intentions to establish a political and military alliance with the West; plans to step up the PRC's war industry potential; the internal political situation in China and the struggle for power within the Chinese leadership . . .

Britain: Systematic work is to continue on gathering intelligence about the British Government's plans and intentions with regard to the USSR and other socialist states; Conservative policy regarding the USA, China, NATO and the EEC; British activity in the 'Third World'; the internal situation in the country; the position in the leadership of the main political parties and their preparations for possible parliamentary elections . . .

Oceans, etc: The Residency is planning to work on obtaining intelligence on important questions such as the prospective exploitation and utilisation by the adversary of the natural resources of the seabed, the status of the Arctic and Antarctic and plans of the West to change it . . .

The Residency is planning to step up work on procuring intelligence on the questions of the world's oceans, the Arctic and Antarctic (your No. 1967/PR). In this field attention will be directed mainly to obtaining data about United States and NATO Military strategy in the world's oceans; the designs and actual operations of the USA, the other advanced capitalist countries and 'Group of 77' with regard to the implementation of the international Convention on the Law of the Sea; attempts by the USA to undermine this convention and damage the interests of the USSR; the national programs of the USA, Britain, France, the FRG, Japan, Norway, Italy, Brazil and other countries for the exploitation of the resources of the world's oceans and seabed; the contradictions and competitive struggle between individual capitalist countries on questions of economic activity in international waters; the military plans of the USA, Canada, Denmark and Norway with regard to the Arctic and their attempts to 'internationalise' the Arctic; possible Western plans to undermine the 1959 agreement on the Antarctic and intentions to divide up the territory and exploit the natural resources of the Antarctic . . .

Analytical Papers: On the basis of information accumulated in the Residency, the following consolidated papers to be prepared in 1983:

1. The position and prospects for the development of Anglo-Soviet relations . . .
2. British policy with regard to the Arctic and Antarctic . . .
3. The internal situation in Britain and the prospects for early parliamentary elections . . .
4. Britain's attitude towards East–West economic relations . . .

Sources: An analysis carried out by the Residency of the 'PR' Line's information facilities has shown that as yet we have no sources capable of regularly procuring secret information about United States and NATO military policy, mutual relations between the West and the PRC, or the secret decisions of the Western countries designed to disrupt the unity of the socialist community.

LARIN

T HOUGH forced to admit that it had no regular access to secret information about US and NATO military policy, the Residency gained the Centre's approval for a series of competent reports on this subject. It failed to tell the Centre that its chief sources for these reports were publications of Chatham House, IISS and RUSI, combined with overt discussions with Western military commentators. The Residency also won approval for reports on movements in the grain and gold markets, again derived from open sources.

No. 1936/PR	Top Secret
5 December 1983	Copy No. 1
from London	To Comrade SILIN [TITOV]

1983 ANNUAL REVIEW OF PR LINE, LONDON RESIDENCY

[Extract]

INFORMATION AND ANALYTICAL WORK

The Residency continued during the period under review to direct its main efforts towards obtaining intelligence information about the military strategy plans of the USA and NATO, the most important world economic problems of possible interest to the USSR, designs of the USA, NATO, the EEC and China to undermine the international position of the Soviet Union and other socialist countries, the situation in the PRC, and Britain's foreign and domestic policy. The proportion of information on priority problems in the overall volume of the Residency's information work increased from 56% in 1982, to 59% in the year under review.

Operational personnel in all lines of the Residency's work were enlisted to gather 'PR' information. The practice was continued of systematically analysing the information-gathering work of all operational personnel and the access of agents, persons undergoing study and official contacts. This has enabled us to improve the quality of information despatched to the Centre and to concentrate our attention on the most important matters and especially on gathering information on military strategy. World economic problems and the actions of the United States Administration have been systematically clarified. Most of the reports dealing with these questions despatched to the Centre received a favourable evaluation. During the period under review the Residency informed the Centre in good time about the possibility of parliamentary elections taking place in Britain before the term was out and subsequently supplied details of preparations for them, the way they were held and the effect on the internal situation in the country and its foreign policy.

The basic indices of the Residency's information work in the eleven months of this year (compared with the corresponding period in 1980, 1981 and 1982) are as follows:

	1983	1982	1981	1980
Overall number of reports	385	469	328	326
Including:				
Information on questions of military strategy	76	68	58	48
Information on world economics	55	69	34	29
Information on the main adversary	64	76	74	55
Information on China	24	25	31	32

Some decrease in the quantity of information despatched to the Centre is connected with the fact that the Residency has tried to send more reports of a consolidated nature and also with the after effects of the British Government's provocations, resulting in considerable curtailment of 'PR' Line personnel and other lines in the Residency. At the same time it should be noted that in the period under review there has been a considerable increase in the average number of reports per member of the 'PR' Line operational personnel. In 1983 the number was 73, by comparison with 56 in 1982 and 42 in 1981. 82% of the material despatched to the Centre was used, which fully matches up to the figure for 1982.

The Residency has also supplied the Centre with reports on British foreign and domestic policy, especially about the Thatcher Cabinet's policy in regard to the USSR and British action in Cyprus and the Lebanon, Western policy regarding Yugoslavia, Poland and other CMEA countries, and the situation in the EEC.

Information-gathering through recording British television broadcasts has continued. In all, up to 1 December this year 48 video-cassettes were despatched to the Centre.

At the same time there are still shortcomings in the Residency's work of information-gathering. This applies especially to the lack of regular information on China and also on specific United States and NATO plans for preparations of a surprise nuclear strike against the USSR.

GORNOV
[O. A. GORDIEVSKY]

vn-1
No. 168/PR
01.02.84

Top Secret
Copy No. 1
to London
Comrade YERMAKOV [A. Y. GUK]

[THE CENTRE'S] ASSESSMENT OF THE LONDON RESIDENCY'S PR LINE REPORT FOR 1983

[Extract]

Information-gathering and analytical work

The work of supplying and analysing information attained a fairly high standard in the year under review. 386 reports were despatched to the Centre and the percentage of these used reached 82%. There was some reduction in the number of information telegrams (this was 469 in 1982) owing to the fact that the post compiled more comprehensive reports, and also to the considerable cut-back in the number of PR Line personnel as a result of the provocation operations of the British special services. There was some increase in the quantity of reports compiled by individual PR Line officers during the year (73, in comparison with 56 in 1982).

The increased activity shown in gathering information on military-strategic and economic problems, particularly with regard to implementation of the Food Program in the USSR, deserves our approval. Useful work was also done to keep the Centre informed in good time about the preparation of proceedings for holding parliamentary elections in Britain before they were actually due.

At the same time the plan for work on information and analysis was not carried out to the full extent in 1983. In particular, arrangements were simply not made to obtain regular information on the Chinese question, or on specific United States and NATO plans for preparing a sudden nuclear strike against the USSR. Virtually no documentary material was despatched to the Centre. An insufficient quantity of information was received on the questions of the Arctic, the Antarctic, and the World's Oceans which, following an instruction from the head of our Service dated 04.11.82, was designated as a priority matter for the London Residency. The supply of information on the activities of the EEC and the Socialist International was poor . . .

... The proportion of information on priority matters, including military strategy, world economic problems, and important topical events (Soviet foreign policy initiatives, parliamentary elections in Britain, etc) increased in relation to the total volume of the Residency's information output from 56% in 1982 to 59% in the year under review ...

SILIN

[G. F. TITOV]

As well as receiving annual assessments on their performance, Residencies also received comments from time to time on individual reports. A standard form of praise, as in the following example, was to say that a report had been passed to, or incorporated in a briefing for, 'higher authority' (a phrase which always included the International Department of the Central Committee and sometimes referred to the Politburo).

vn-1   No 329
                                                         Secret
No 1001/PR   Copy No 1
07.05.85

                                                        London
                                      Comrade Gornov [Gordievsky]
Evaluation of information

1. *Use in generalised information*
   No 594 – 'Western Experts' assessment of the situation on the oil market'. The telegram contained interesting assessments of the position on the oil markets in the first quarter of 1985. It was used in analytical documentation for the political leadership. It would be useful to obtain information about the effect on the EEC's oil-refining industry of increasing exports of petroleum products to Western Europe from the Persian Gulf countries and the changes in the import structure of West European countries in this context, in favour of petroleum products, and also the consequences of this process for prospects of Soviet oil exports to the countries of Western Europe. Please also gather material on the so-called simulation of an oil shortage (in the form of an exercise involving NATO's information system and the larger oil corporations), planned for October under the auspices of the International Energy Agency.

No 603 – 'The British reaction to the death of the Albanian leader' [Enver Hoxha].

The evaluations in the telegram were used to prepare a generalised document on this subject for the political leadership.

No 608 – 'The position in Albania'. The report contains interesting forecasts and was taken into account in compiling a generalised report for the political leadership.

No 611 – 'Pakistan's work on producing an atomic bomb'. The material corroborates and to some extent, supplements existing information on the position work has reached in Pakistan on producing nuclear weapons. The data on work to produce a nuclear microbomb for use in F-16 aircraft is of interest as a new aspect of Pakistan's nuclear programme. This information must be substantiated and clarified.

No 622 – 'The British assessment of Howe's* visit to the GDR, Czechoslovakia and Poland'.

The information about British efforts to link questions of economic cooperation with the demand for some political concessions from the socialist countries deserves attention. The material was used as a whole in an analytical memorandum for the higher authorities.

No 629 – 'The British assessment of the results of Thatcher's visit to the countries of South-East Asia'.

The points concerning Thatcher's efforts to play the role of an emissary of the EEC during her trip were taken into account in an analytical report. The item about the conclusion reached by the British on the ineffectiveness of Commonwealth machinery in guaranteeing influence on former colonies requires further substantiation. The Centre is interested in obtaining information of an analytical nature about British policy in various areas of the 'Third World' and – on a wider scale – about the British approach to expanding relations with the developing countries in general.

No 631 – 'The British evaluation of the results of Thatcher's visit to Sri Lanka and India'. The telegram is quite well factually substantiated and contains assessments by the British of the results of Thatcher's talks in Delhi and Colombo which deserve attention. Please keep an eye on the implementation of the agreements reached and London's attitude to developing relations with India and Sri Lanka.

No 654 – 'The British assessment of future prospects in Soviet–Chinese relations'. The British opinions quoted on this issue were of interest. Source's views about alleged reports existing in the British Foreign Office regarding a softening of the Chinese attitude in the consultations on the issues hampering the development of Soviet–Chinese relations have not been confirmed.

No 663 – 'Prospects of a revision of NATO's military strategy'. The information about a possible radical change in NATO strategy deserves attention

---

* Sir Geoffrey Howe, British foreign secretary.

but is regarded as doubtful, since it is not confirmed by the information from other sources. Please will you, where possible, check and clarify the information on this subject.

2. *Retained pending further information*

No 585 – 'Modernisation of the Chinese People's Army [the PLA] and Anglo–Chinese military contacts'. Information already known from commentaries in the overt press.

No 634 – 'Thatcher's visit to Saudi Arabia'. The material does not contain any essential new elements and is already known from overt sources.

No 659 – 'The problem of implementing Britain's defence programme'. The information has already been received from other sources. It would in future be advisable to obtain information of a documentary nature about postponement of dates for carrying out individual military programmes mentioned in the report from the Chief of General Staff (priority projects in first place).

3. *Evaluation of information by bag*

No 68/PR – Selection of material about the situation in Latin America. This was of interest and has been used in current analytical work and in generalised form for reporting to higher authority.

SVETLOV
[GRIBIN]

THE Centre was certainly unaware, however, how frequently the London Residency sought to pass off information from open sources as coming from confidential contacts or agents in order to disguise its failure to obtain secret intelligence. A KGB co-optee in the Soviet Embassy gave the Residency regular advance copies of the Embassy's lengthy 'political letters' which analysed various aspects of British foreign policy. The Residency's PR line officers prepared a digest of each Embassy letter, made a few changes, added some details of their own, and telegraphed the result to the Centre. The plagiarised KGB versions of the Embassy reports were circulated in Moscow a fortnight ahead of the originals which went by diplomatic bag. The Residency's sourcing telegrams gave the impression that it had relied chiefly on its own contacts rather than on its co-optee in the Embassy.

The PR line in London, as in other Residencies, was expected to spend 25 per cent of its time on active measures. Both Yakov Konstantinovich Lukasevics, Resident from 1972 to 1980, and Arkadi Vasilyevich Guk, his successor from 1980 to 1984, had an exaggerated belief in what active measures could achieve. Gordievsky was told that in 1977 or 1978 Lukasevics had been asked by Andropov, then KGB Chairman, whether his Residency possessed the means to influence British policy. 'Why yes, we can exercise influence,' Lukasevics replied, 'We have such channels.' 'I do not think you can,' Andropov told him. 'I think you are too hasty in answering that question.'

The active measures targeted on Britain as on other Western countries were also sometimes marred by the crudity of the material prepared by FCD Service A. Some of the first active measures against Margaret Thatcher were based in Denmark. Gordievsky had personal knowledge of a case involving Arne Herløv Petersen, a Danish agent of influence recruited in 1973. Petersen agreed not merely to write articles along lines suggested to him by his case officers, but also to publish under his own name occasional articles and pamphlets written for him in the English language by Service A. The first of the KGB/Petersen co-productions attacking Mrs Thatcher, published in 1979, gave her pride of place as Europe's leading anti-Soviet crusader. Though the Centre was unaccountably proud of its composition, the pamphlet was crudely constructed and had negligible influence.

Magaret [*sic*] Thatcher

Great Britain today has her first female prime minister – the Conservative leader Margaret Thatcher.

If one prefers to do so, one might conceivably regard this as a victor of sorts for women's lib. But the three previous female prime ministers that we have seen – Golda Meir, Indira Gandhi, and Sirimavo Bandaranaike – clearly show that also female politicians are able to follow an iron-handed power policy. Examples of female politicians pursuing a reactionary and inhuman policy on lesser levels are numerous.

So there is no reason to see any importance in Margaret Thatcher's sex. It is much more important to look at the policy she is advocating.

When the British Conservative Party went through a crisis of leadership in February [*sic*] 1975, and Edward Heath was replaced by Margaret Thatcher it was in effect a victory for the extreme right wing of the party.

Margaret Thatcher has never hidden the facts that she feels herself to be a crusader against the Communist menace – at home and abroad. In a speech she held in Hannover, Germany in 1976 at a conference for the Christian Democrats she advocated a rightist attitude which should among other places be expressed in the European parliament after the first direct elections in June 1979.

'I am convinced that the Christian Democratic conservative, and centre parties in Europe should now join together in an effective working alliance', she said on this occasion.[1]

She proposed as the name for this alliance the European Democratic Union (EDU).

'This co-operation needs to be improved and strengthened if our different parties are to be able to fight a co-ordinated campaign across the whole of Western Europe and then form a cohesive alliance within the new directly elected European parliament', she went on to say.

She asserted that there are only two possibilities: the Marxist Socialist one and the policy of the West German Christians Democrats, the British Tories and their allies.

At the same occasion she warned strongly against the belief that the Socialist countries mean it seriously when they say that they want détente and peace in Europe.

'Of course we hope that their oft-proclaimed change of heart is genuine. But every child in Europe knows the story of Little Red Riding Hood and what happened to her in her grandmother's cottage in the forest.

Despite the new look of these Communist parties, despite the softness of the voices, we should be on the watch for the teeth and the appetite of the wolf'.[2]

In this connection it might be mentioned that Thatcher is the first Conservative leader of Great Britain since Chamberlain to have had no experiences with foreign policy whatsoever. In the former Conservative cabinet she served as Minister of Education.

The crusader mentality is strongly emphasized whenever Margaret Thatcher speaks about the 'Russian danger':

'The Russians are bent on world dominance, and they are rapidly acquiring the means to become the most powerful, imperial nation the world has seen', she says.[3]

During her visit to Singapore in September 1976 she stressed the need of Great Britain to 'always stand fully ready to meet Soviet expansion everywhere in the world'.[4]

Even Margaret Thatcher is aware that the military strength of Great Britain is no longer what it was in the great days of the empire, and therefore she advocates close collaboration with USA.

'An isolationist Britain would encourage an isolationist America', she says. 'The Conservative Party rejects any such course . . . It is just as much our duty to help keep America in Europe as it is to help Europe maintain its close links with America'[5].

Margaret Thatcher is of the opinion that reactionary forces anywhere can look to a bright future:

'I see some encouraging signs of a clearer vision and firmer resolve on the part of the western alliance. The Americans are stepping up their defence expenditure. France is reported to be increasing her defence budget. West Germany, too, is putting up her defence spending. But what of Britain? . . . The national executive of the Labour Party are calling for an additional cut of

£1,000 million ... The Conservatives will fight these last cuts in every way ... I believe it is only when they see that the West is militarily prepared that the Soviet leadership will begin to realise their own massive investment in armaments is leading nowhere.'[6]

Time and again Margaret Thatcher has asserted that the Soviet Union is on the threshold of gaining the upper hand militarily over the Western powers, and that the only solution for the West is heavier spending for armaments. The Conservative newspaper 'The Times' comments that 'Approximate parity at present exists between East and West and has done so for several years'[7].

The former Defence Secretary Roy Mason calls Margaret Thatcher a 'cold war warrior' and goes on to say

'Great endeavours are under way to lessen the tension between the world's most powerful military alliances. We and our allies have the power, the might, the solidarity and the will to deter. We do not have to provoke.

The Thatcher thesis is ill-timed and provocative. It is a repetition of old-fashioned reactionary Tory dogma and if heeded could jeopardise the peace we have so successfully established for all our people and bring back that awful spectre of nuclear war'.[8]

Also the former Liberal leader Jeremy Thorpe, who can in no way be accused of Socialist attitudes, warns strongly against the cold war-attitude of Margaret Thatcher. He calls her remarks:

'An unashamedly hawkish collection of cliché-ridden statements which would have done credit to Senator McCarthy or Senator Goldwater in their prime'.[9]

The rightist Labour politician* Reginald Maudling adds that the Western World 'will get nowhere by shouting at Russia'.[10]

The Liberal newspaper 'The Guardian' wrote in a political comment that she seems bent on destroying the state of balance existing between the West and the Soviet Union, and noted that this could create real difficulties if she were to become Prime Minister.[11]

In a commentary by Peter Jenkins the same newspaper sums up its attitude to the contributions made by Margaret Thatcher to the present foreign policy-situation thus:

'We are in poor straits as a nation when a speech as glib and frivolous as Mrs Thatcher's is vaunted into a major contribution to the debate about détente which in other countries is conducted with meaningful and informed seriousness'.[12]

One has to admit that the political convictions of Margaret Thatcher form a cohesive unity. Abroad she wants to call for a crusade against 'Red wolves'. At home she will wage war against the 'Socialists'.

'Under the Socialists rapid strides has been taken toward an Iron Curtain state,'[13] she told the House of Commons. Followed by Labour laughter.

---

* In reality, of course, a former Conservative cabinet minister.

What is to be done she showed in her time as Education Secretary when she abolished free milk and lunch for school children and introduced entrance fees for the art museums.[14]

Now she has wider aims. She deeply understands racist sentiments and the people who want to throw out all immigrants from Great Britain:

'It is a problem of endless numbers in a country which is more densely populated than Pakistan or India', she says.[15]

And first and foremost she demands that private capitalists take over again pall industries that have been nationalised. She takes a special interest in the British state-owned oil company which she wants to be put back under capitalist influence.

In this connection one may note that Margaret Thatcher's husband was director of the large Burmah-Castrol oil company until 1975.[16]

Thatcher's predecessors as chairmen – Eden, Macmillan, Douglas-Home and Heath – often advocated an aggressive and reactionary policy. But Thatcher is the first British Conservative leader since Churchill who openly and vigorously calls for a crusade against the Socialist countries and war against the British working class.

Sources

1. 'The Morning Star', May 26, 1976
2. Ibid.
3. 'The Times', January 20, 1976
4. Ibid., September 8, 1976
5. Ibid., July 28, 1975
6. 'The Sunday Times', August 1, 1976
7. 'The Times', January 20, 1976
8. 'The Guardian', January 26, 1976
9. 'The Times', January 23, 1976
10. 'The Sunday Telegraph', April 17, 1977
11. 'The Guardian', April 11, 1977
12. Ibid., January 29, 1976
13. 'The Times', June 9, 1976
14. 'The Financial Times', February 8, 1975
15. 'The Times', September 7, 1976
16. 'The Sunday Times', September 12, 1976

ARNE HERLØV PETERSEN

TRUE BLUES

The Thatcher that couldn't mend her own roof

JOE HILL PRESS
1980

T HE next Petersen pamphlet ghosted by Service A, *True Blues*, published in 1980, was solely devoted to attacking Mrs Thatcher. It made the mistake of attempting satire – usually a weak area of the KGB's heavy-handed active measures – and carried the feeble subtitle 'The Thatcher that couldn't mend her own roof'. The Service A author had an even feebler grasp of English geography, and believed Mrs Thatcher's birthplace at Grantham in Lincolnshire to be 'in the suburbs of London'.

MS. THATCHER AND HER POLICIES

'Whatever you won't hear (about Thatcher) in casual conversations: A terrible ogress . . . I'm fond of her obstinacy . . . She has a nice hair-do. An energetic wench . . . A nasty woman . . . I'll never vote for a woman at the menopause age . . . I'll vote for her to annoy men . . . A charming, well-educated woman, but a Prime Minister? She is an impudent woman . . . We already have a woman at the head of the kingdom, that's enough.'* That is how a correspondent of the impartial French daily *Le Monde* reported conflicting, ironic and even insulting remarks, which, he says, the Britons made about Margaret Thatcher when she was running for the job of the Prime Minister of Great Britain at the Parliamentary elections in May 1979.

This diversity of views, however, did not prevent Thatcher from coming to power. The Conservatives won an impressive victory, getting an absolute majority of 339 seats. The Labor won only 268 seats, that is, even with the support of all other parties that are not represented in the Government the Conservatives would still have a 43-seat majority.

Thus, the Parliamentary elections of May 1979 gave the Conservatives a sufficiently stable majority for the next five years, when Parliamentary elections are to be held in May 1984.

Although all political observers share this view, they are far from being unanimous in that the present Conservative leader – Margaret Thatcher – will be able to stay in power through this term. And not without reason.

First, many Britons associated Margaret Thatcher with the attractive image of an ideal England and small private ownership. Thatcher was presented as a woman born into the family of a modest businessman who had a small grocery

---

* 'Que n'entend-on pas au hasard des conversations: Terrible ogresse . . . Je l'aime pour son obstination . . . Elle est si bien coiffée . . . Une pouliche rapide . . . Une sale bonne femme . . . Je ne voterai jamais pour une femme qui a l'âge de la ménopause. Je voterai pour elle, rien que pour embêter les hommes . . . Une femme charmante, bien eduquée, mais premier ministre? Elle a du toupet . . . Nous avons déjà une femme à la tête du royaume, cela suffit' (*Le Monde*, 24.4.79, page 5).

shop in the suburbs of London. So, many people expected her to protect the interests of rather numerous middle classes of Britain, of people who are modestly but more or less solidly well off. And yet their well-being has not shown any signs of improvement over the last few years and the prospects are growing more and more gloomy. This section of the British society is not entirely satisfied with the Labour whose policies it regards with caution and concern for the future, on the one hand, and is subjected to pressure from big business, on the other. Now this section is receiving numerous evidence to show that Thatcher's background is only a suitable façade used by big business to further its interests. Therefore, the exposure of Thatcher as a representative of big business interests may ultimately compromise her in the view of the general public and lead to her removal from the post of the Prime Minister (by the Conservatives themselves).

Secondly, Thatcher came to power not so much because the British had associated her name with expectations of a better economic position of the country but rather as a result of the discontent with the Labour economic policy. Now wider circles in Britain have come to believe that the current policy of the ruling right wing of the Conservative Party has not only failed to improve, but, on the contrary, has had a more adverse effect on the living standards of the working people. Inflation and unemployment have grown, the rights of the trade unions have been curbed, social security funds have been cut, the prospects of de-industrialisation have become more visible. The British economy has reached the state of a chronic crisis. In this context, the Conservatives may quite naturally be tempted to duly change the façade and make the Iron Lady the scapegoat.

Thirdly, Thatcher's adamant belligerency is actually nothing more than a calculated risk and a pose. Britain is more visibly toeing Washington's line and thus living up to her image of the US Troyan horse in Europe. Thatcher expresses more rabidly and more vociferously than anybody else her support for whatever foreign policy initiatives Carter finds fit to make. But since these initiatives are more often than not changed and just as often prove self-defeating, Thatcher's toeing of Washington's line has only made Europe to grow suspicious of her. Neither Schmidt, nor Giscard d'Estaing, Thatcher's major EEC partners who are just as concerned for the future of Europe, have demonstrated such a 'line toeing'. A tilt to Washington has complicated Britain's standing in Europe and especially the settlement of a series of economic problems within the European Economic Community. Thatcher's attemps, now to behave like a 'good European', now to show herself 'iron' and make an ultimatum to the EEC demanding a solution to the specifically British problems, have brought no results. These problems can hardly be solved in the first place, since Britain's claims hit the interests of France and other EEC partners. What is possible are only half-baked compromises, which can hardly console the British.

So, both in the home and foreign policy the present Conservative Government has made very serious miscalculations which may ultimately lead to the removal of Thatcher before the economic bonanza she promised may come. The time of its coming is being postponed to a more and more distant future by Thatcher herself.

O N this high point, the KGB/Petersen co-productions ended. Petersen was arrested in November 1981 and charged with collaborating with the KGB. In 1982, however, the Danish Minister of Justice, noting that the main guilty parties, the KGB officers concerned, had left the country, granted Petersen *tiltalefrafald* (a waiver of charges).

During Gordievsky's term at the KGB London Residency from 1982 to 1985, the anti-Thatcher material prepared by Service A never quite matched the crudity of the Petersen pamphlets. Nor did he encounter any fabricated documents bearing Mrs Thatcher's signature comparable with the Reagan forgeries. In the course of these three years, however, Gordievsky noted over forty subjects on which the London Residency was asked to promote active measures. Some were long-term operations such as that to discredit President Reagan. Other operations were short-term and tactical; in November 1982, for example, the Residency was ordered to try to depress Western grain prices by spreading rumours, especially to the International Wheat Council, that Soviet grain purchases were to be only 35 million tonnes instead of the anticipated 44 million.

Among the Residency's most important active measures campaigns was that to oppose the deployment of Cruise Missiles. At the end of September 1982 the Centre sent a telegram to London (noted but not copied by Gordievsky), listing four main active measures 'theses':

1. Cruise missiles were offensive, not defensive, weapons.

2. The Americans insisted on their deployment and refused serious negotiations about them.

3. The Soviet Union would detect their dispersal from British bases during an East–West crisis, interpret this as a signal of impending nuclear attack, and be likely to respond with a nuclear strike of its own.

4. US deployment of Cruise missiles in Britain thus risked involving Britain in a nuclear war begun, against its wishes, by the United States.

The Residency was instructed to use these theses in meetings with all its contacts, both 'confidential' and otherwise.[1]

In mid-November 1982 the London Residency sent the Centre its operational plan for active measures against Cruise missiles. It proposed to organise both mass demonstrations and parliamentary protests against the deployment in Britain of Cruise and Pershing missiles. The Residency's proposals were as unrealistic as they were grandiose. There were no plans to station Pershing as well as Cruise missiles in Britain. Nor is there any evidence that the KGB had more than a marginal influence on the campaign against Cruise conducted by the peace movement. The London Resident, Arkadi Guk, however, was not the only KGB officer to claim credit for anti-nuclear protests which owed little or nothing to active measures.

Among the anti-American active measures in Britain which the Centre counted as successes was Operation 'Azalea'. In the summer of 1983 Service A informed the Residency that it was preparing a forged document (which, it later transpired, was a bogus memorandum by President Mobutu's Special Adviser in the Zaïre National Security Council) and asked for the addresses of African groups and journalists in London to whom to send it. The Residency replied with a list of nine addresses, including those of the London offices of the ANC and SWAPO. A telegram from the Centre in December confirmed that copies of the forgery had been despatched to all of the addresses. At least some of the recipients were taken in and gave the forgery the publicity for which Service A had hoped. The Observer duly reported American claims that the document was fabricated but gave greater weight to evidence for its authenticity (see opposite page).

The Centre saw part of the function of active measures as defensive: to counter anti-Soviet campaigns in the West. Service A's usual response in such cases was to begin by asking the appropriate KGB Residency in the West for information (preferably compromising) on those behind the campaign. A typical example was Operation 'Kodex' launched late in 1982 to counter well-founded Western charges concerning the abuse of psychiatry in the Soviet Union. A telegram from the Centre (noted but not copied by Gordievsky) put four main questions to the London Residency:

1 Who were the initiators and main supporters of the campaign against the alleged abuse of psychiatry in the Soviet Union?

2 What statements had the Royal College of Psychiatrists made on this subject?

3 What links did the Royal College have with the CIA?

4 What cases had occurred in Britain of the abuse of psychiatry? Was there reason to suspect political motives in any of these cases?[2]

Further telegrams from the Centre made clear its wish, never fulfilled, to expose the campaign against Soviet psychiatry as a CIA or SIS plot.

(opposite) reproduced from The Observer, 22 January 1984.

'US and S Africa in Angola plot'

by GODWIN MATATU

A CONFIDENTIAL memorandum, smuggled out of Zaire, claims that envoys of the United States and South Africa had a secret meeting to discuss destabilisation of the Cuban-backed Government of Angola.

Plans were drawn up to supply more arms and equipment to the rebel UNITA forces of Dr Jonas Savimbi.

The document, if proved genuine, will cause a storm in the United States, where aid for rebel Angola movements is prohibited by the Clark Amendment passed by Congress in 1977.

A spokesman at the US Embassy in London refused to believe that the document was genuine. 'I am positive that no such meeting took place,' he said.

'The document is a forgery. The people who are peddling it want to discourage the MPLA (the ruling party in Angola) from continuing negotiations with the United States.'

Sources close to Nguza Karl i Bond, a former Zaire Prime Minister who now lives in Brussels, have told *The Observer* that the meeting did indeed take place. It was, they claim, part of a series of discussions. As far as they could tell, the document was genuine.

The document is headed with the insignia of the Zairean National Security Council and is addressed to President Mobutu of Zaire. The memorandum is filed from the office of the President's special adviser, Seti Yale.

The document reports that the meeting in late November was attended by a US 'special envoy,' three representatives of UNITA movement, and military and intelligence officers from South Africa. An adviser from the Israeli military mission in Kinshasa was also present as an observer.

Among the topics discussed were:
● The supply by America and South Africa of arms and money for rebel groups in Angola.
● Ways of stirring up popular

US officials say the secret memo is a forgery.

feeling against the Angolan regime of Eduardo dos Santos and 'destabilising the situation in the capital (Luanda).'
● Sabotage against factories and transport systems within Angola.
● The best means of bringing pressure to bear on Cuba to withdraw its troops.

The main aims of the meeting, according to the document, were to review the military and political situation in Angola and discuss aid for the rebels. Another was to forge a common front between the anti-government movements in the former Portuguese colony. The special US envoy, the document says, called on UNITA and other opposition groups to 'consolidate their authority and influence in the liberated areas.' They should also 'speed up social and political measures to deepen the population's discontent against the regime of dos Santos, the Cuban and Soviet presence and other Communist countries in Angola; destabilise the situation in the capital; organise acts of sabotage against principal economic installations and seize strategic points as well as important roads.'

The American official also stressed the need to disrupt joint Angolan and Soviet projects and undermine the relations between the dos Santos Governmeunt and the Cubans and Russians.

The rebel movements were also encouraged to sow divisions in the ranks of the MPLA

leadership in Luanda and infiltrate agents into the Angolan Army. The aim is to force part of the Angolan leadership to negotiate with UNITA.

He also called for more military pressure against the Luanda regime by the South Africans, who did indeed launch a military operation, deep into Angola last December. The document says the US emissary suggested creation of a 'democratic government in the liberated areas which would include representatives of all the struggling movements.' The United States, for its part, would increase 'military and financial assistance' to the rebels and apply pressure to stem the flow of foreign investment in Angola.

Marcos Samondo, UNITA's representative in Washington, would neither confirm nor deny that the meeting took place. However, he said UNITA had 'contacts with US officials at all levels on a regular basis.' Savimbi visited Washington in 1981 and held discussions with top officials in the Reagan administration, including Mr Alexander Haig, then Secretary of State. UNITA's secretary for foreign affairs, Jeremiah Chitunda, is a regular lobbyist in Washington, Samondo said.

Chitunda left the jungle headquarters of UNITA early in November and later travelled to the United States. Zairean sources in Brussels say he travelled as usual through Kinshasa and may have been available to attend the meeting.

7

*The European Community**

U NTIL 1976 the Centre had little interest in the EC, unlike its leading member states. Residencies in Western Europe were told to limit intelligence collection in Community institutions to matters of major political significance. The report to the Community in December 1975 by the Belgian Prime Minister, Leo Tindemans, caused a major reassessment within the FCD. Tindemans condemned as 'schizophrenic' the contradiction between the EEC's economic integration and its political fragmentation. He called for the Community's transformation by 1980 into a European Union with common foreign and defence as well as economic policies. Though his report was politely received, it was clear from the moment it was presented that the political will to create a European Union did not exist. During the mid-1970s European leaders were preoccupied instead by an economic crisis which confronted them with the simultaneous problems of inflation and mass unemployment. The Tindemans report was left to gather dust on Community shelves. The so-called Three Wise Men's report on European institutions in 1979 did not even mention it.

The Centre, however, took the Tindemans report much more seriously than the Community itself. It interpreted the proposal for European Union not as a visionary project for a distant future but as the result of 'objective processes' which were already leading to political and military, as well as economic, integration. KGB anxieties were heightened by the emergence of what it saw as a Brussels–Beijing axis.

---

* The European Community (EC) or, more properly, the European Communities were established in 1967 when the 'Merger Treaty' of 1965 came into force, bringing together the European Economic Community (EEC), the European Coal and Steel Community, and the European Atomic Energy Community. At least until the mid-1980s, however, KGB documents (like some in the West) referred to the EEC, rarely to the EC.

№ 3825/ПР-52
от 27 августа 1976 г.

Р Е З И Д Е Н Т А М

О некоторых новых моментах политического и военного сотрудничества стран ЭЭС

По полученным сведениям, на проходившей 12-13 июля с.г.
в Брюсселе встрече глав государств и правительств стран ЭЭС
обсуждался, в частности, вопрос о состоянии и перспективах развития политического и военного сотрудничества в рамках сообщества. Участники встречи высказались за дальнейшую активизацию
такого сотрудничества. При этом руководители стран "девятки"
исходят из того, что в современных условиях лишь совместные
действия стран "Общего рынка" дают западноевропейцам шанс обеспечить свое участие в принятии решений всемирного значения.
Кроме того, как считают в руководящих кругах ЭЭС, политическое
единство позволит "девятке" преодолеть известные экономические
трудности и послужит толчком к дальнейшему развитию интеграции.
Руководствуясь указанными соображениями, премьер-министр Бель-
гии ТИНДЕМАНС в докладе о перспективах развития ЭЭС рекомендо-
вал как можно быстрее перейти от координации политики к прове-
дению единой внешней политики с тем, чтобы сообщество выступало
"одним фронтом перед лицом внешнего мира".

Важнейшей задачей, которую ставят страны ЭЭС, является
подрыв внешнеполитических позиций стран социалистического со-
дружества. При этом предусматривается, в частности, обязатель-
ная координация политики стран сообщества в отношении социали-
стических государств; активное использование некоторых выгодных
Западу аспектов Заключительного акта Совещания по безопасности
и сотрудничеству в Европе; критика политики мирного сосущество-
вания; оказание давления на страны-участницы Варшавского Дого-
вора в вопросе о военных аспектах разрядки с целью дальнейшего

In September 1975 the first Chinese Ambassador was accredited to the Community and promptly began trade negotiations. On 8 July 1976 the Centre issued, under Kryuchkov's signature, its first major directive on the EEC and demanded the fullest possible intelligence on Community policy.[1]

Reports on the meeting of Community Heads of State and Government in Brussels a few days later strengthened the Centre's conviction that 'The most important aim of the countries of the EEC is the undermining of the foreign policies of the socialist states.' State Department documents obtained by the KGB confirmed its fear of US–Community plots against the Soviet Bloc. The FCD continued to attach a deeply sinister significance to the Tindemans report, and in particular to his conclusion that 'the European Union will be unstable until it has a common defence policy'.

To: Residents

No 3825/PR-52   Top Secret
27 August 1976   Copy No. 1

New Aspects of Political and Military Cooperation
Between EEC Countries

According to reports we have received, the present situation regarding political and military cooperation within the framework of the European Community, and the possibilities for its future development, were discussed at the meeting of Heads of States and Governments of the EEC countries held in Brussels on 12–13 July 1976. The representatives taking part gave support for further development of this cooperation.

In so doing, the leaders of the 'Nine' countries are working from the premise that under present conditions only a united stand of the countries of the Common Market will give the West Europeans a chance to participate in the process of decision-making on problems of world-wide significance. The leading circles of the EEC also consider that political unity will allow the 'Nine' to overcome their well-known economic difficulties and will provide the impetus for the further development of integration. Guided by these considerations, Belgium's Prime Minister Tindemans suggested, in his report on prospects for developing the EEC, that the EEC should switch as soon as possible from the coordination of political view-points to the introduction of a common foreign policy, in order that the Community could present 'a united front to the outside world'.

The most important aim of the countries of the EEC is the undermining of the foreign policies of the socialist states. In particular, in order to achieve this a strict coordination of the policy of the countries of the EEC is envisaged

towards the socialist states; also the active exploitation of certain points in the
Final Act of the CSCE [Conference on Security and Cooperation in Europe]
which are useful to the West; criticism of the policy of peaceful co-
existence; the exertion of pressure on the member-countries of the Warsaw
Pact concerning the military aspects of détente, in order further to strengthen
the military potential of the West; and the consolidation of its position at the
talks on the reduction of armed forces and arms in Central Europe. The leading
circles of the EEC consider that the whole complex of these measures will
allow them to influence the internal system and foreign policy of the countries
of Eastern Europe. As a result, the EEC views the suggestion made by the
CMEA [Council for Mutual Economic Assistance]* in February this year for
an agreement on the basis of mutual relations between these two organisations
as 'inadmissible', because such an agreement could only strengthen the international position of the CMEA. At the same time the leaders of the EEC
consider that in the present state of détente they cannot reject outright the
CMEA suggestion, as this would give the Socialist countries a powerful weapon
in their propaganda war against the West. In view of this the 'Nine' are delaying
at all costs their final decision on this question, insisting on the necessity for
'intermediate negotiations'.

According to an assessment by the US State Department, the Community
is at present carrying out an effective coordinated policy directed to 'the defence
of the common interests of the West' in the developing countries. Special
attention is being paid by the 'Nine' to the strengthening of the Community's
position in the area of the Middle East and Northern Africa, which according
to the EEC Commission represent a 'natural zone of influence for Europe'.
Besides this, according to available reports, the Community is planning 'to take
on itself a more active role' in the area of South-East Asia also. At a meeting
of the Ambassadors of the countries of the 'Nine' in Bangkok in December
1975 it was noted that the unusual 'political vacuum' produced in this region
favoured the strengthening of the Community's economic and political influence there.

In the above-mentioned report by Tindemans it is stated that 'the European
Union will be unstable until it has a common defence policy'. In this connection
it is worth stressing that the countries of the Community have recently been
trying to bring about military cooperation as well within the framework of the
EEC, with the ultimate aim of forming a European armed force. According to
experts in the West, the first step in attaining this aim must be 'the harmonis-
ation and integration' of the European armaments industry coupled with the
adoption of a common position in the negotiations with the East on all questions
of security. In order that the actions of the 'Nine' in this 'extremely delicate
sphere of European development' should not create tensions with the socialist

---

* Also known as COMECON, the CMEA was founded in 1949 to strengthen Moscow's hold
over the economies of the Soviet Bloc.

states, the countries of the Community consider it essential to substantiate carefully in the press, and through diplomatic channels, the idea that military integration in the EEC is compatible with the policy of detente. According to reports available to us, the FRG government is the most active country in the EEC in supporting the development of defence cooperation in the EEC, and is insisting on a speedy realisation of plans for the military integration of the Community countries.

With the object of giving further depth to political and military cooperation in the EEC, the countries of the 'Nine' intend to strengthen 'the institutional system' of the Community. An important step in this direction is considered by the leaders of the 'Common Market' countries to be the agreement reached at the above-mentioned meeting in Brussels in July this year, for the holding of direct general elections to the European Parliament in 1978. It is assumed that in its first stage this parliament will only concern itself with supervising the general budget of the EEC but that later its functions will be enlarged so that it will become, as stated in Brussels, 'the engine of evolution' of the Community.

In the opinion of the US State Department, one can expect in the future some further extension of the political and military cooperation of the countries of the EEC, embracing an ever wider range of subjects. This prospect is in general well received by the United States. It is reckoned by the US State Department that with the 'Nine' carrying out a common policy they will be able to share with the Americans 'the responsibility for maintaining the position of the West in all parts of the world' and will be able to act even more effectively against the policies of the countries of the socialist community. The USA is also not opposed to the creation of a military organisation within the framework of the EEC, since they believe that this will lead to an increase in 'the contribution' of the Community countries to the defence of the West and further the reintegration of France into a single 'Atlantic' system of defence.

SEVEROV
[V. F. GRUSHKO]
[Head of the Third Department]

A CIRCULAR to Residents in EEC capitals in February 1977 emphasised 'the great importance that the leadership of our service attaches to the organisation of work against the European Economic Community'. It repeated the conspiracy theory that 'the most important task which the governments of the EEC countries have set themselves is the undermining of the foreign policy positions of the Socialist countries'. To guide Residencies in agent recruitment and intelligence collection, the Centre enclosed a briefing on 'the main organs of the EEC, which are targets for deep study by Soviet external intelligence'. The brief demonstrated a surprising degree of confusion about Community institutions. The Centre had failed to grasp that the EEC conducts only external *economic* relations; foreign policy is the responsibility of European Political Cooperation (EPC), first launched in 1970, which is formally distinct from the EEC and operates through regular conferences of Foreign Ministers and their officials as well as through summit meetings of heads of government ('European Councils') two or three times a year. The FCD confused the two. According to its brief, 'The meetings of the Council of Ministers are held in turn in the countries of the EEC member-states'. In reality, the Council of Ministers met in Brussels; it was the EPC Conference of Foreign Ministers which moved between European capitals as the Presidency changed from one country to another. During the 1970s the British, French and Danes all sought, with varying degrees of determination, to maintain the distinction between EPC and EEC business. On one occasion during the Danish Presidency in 1978, the Foreign Ministers met at Copenhagen in the morning, then took a midday flight to Brussels where they reconvened as the EEC Council of Ministers.[2] The Centre failed to grasp the distinction. The FCD's belief that General Directorate E of the Council of Ministers' General Secretariat held secret intelligence on 'the EEC's foreign policy' was similarly based on a confusion between EEC and EPC. It is fair to add, however, that over the next decade the demarcation between the two institutions became increasingly blurred.

The KGB also misunderstood the powers of the European Parliament which, it claimed, could 'take decisions' on issues placed before it by either the Council of Ministers or the Commission. In reality, Parliament could only delay legislation though it could show its displeasure either by sacking the Commission (which it has never tried to do), or by throwing out the budget. The Centre was further confused about the 'special establishments of higher education preparing personnel for EEC organs', whose students it regarded as potential targets for recruitment. The European Institute in Amsterdam is a Dutch institution, not, as it believed, 'a specialised higher education establishment of the EEC countries'. The FCD brief claimed that graduating students at the European College at Bruges were 'posted to "Common Market" establishments and to NATO'. In reality, students who wish for such jobs have to apply for them in competition with others.

The Centre's most basic misunderstanding, however, was its conviction that there was a serious prospect of the EEC becoming 'a constituent part of NATO' and 'a military-political union in which aggressive revanchist circles may play the leading role'. Much of the secret intelligence which the Centre sought on plans to achieve these ends did not exist. 'The sessions of the Economic and Social Committee', it reported, 'are held behind closed doors'. In fact the Committee members, who felt generally ignored, usually welcomed enthusiastically any sign of interest in their activities. The Committee did not, as the Centre believed, possess a 'specialised section' which had material on foreign policy 'of intelligence interest'.

vch.1
No 411/PR   Secret
28 February 1977   Copy No. 1

To: Residents

Taking into account the great importance that the leadership of our Service attaches to the organisation of work against the European Economic Community (EEC) (our letter no 1666 of 8 July 1976), we are sending you for your operational use and to help expand your Residency's intelligence activities against the 'Common Market', a guidance paper entitled *The European Economic Community as a target for study by Soviet external intelligence*, together with a list of diplomatic missions accredited to the EEC.

We request you to take measures to gather material that will throw light on the activities of the European Community and which will contribute towards a more clear-cut organisation of work against the 'Common Market' targets.

Attachment: No. 481/PR/5, copy no. 1, 12 pages, secret
              No. 482/PR/5, copy no. 1, 4 pages, secret

SEVEROV
[V. F. GRUSHKO]
[Head of FCD Third Department]

et-2   Secret
Attachment to No. 411/PR   Copy No. 1

THE EUROPEAN ECONOMIC COMMUNITY (EEC) AS A
TARGET FOR STUDY BY SOVIET EXTERNAL INTELLIGENCE

Introduction
The idea of West European integration was embodied in the Schumann Plan for the creation of the Coal and Steel Community, which was signed in Paris in April 1951 by France, the FRG, Italy, Belgium, Holland and Luxembourg.

In March 1957 in Rome these countries concluded a treaty for the creation of the 'Common Market' and the establishment of EURATOM. In 1965 it was agreed to amalgamate the executive organs and to create single organs; the Council of Ministers, the Commission of the European Community, the European Parliament, the Economic and Social Committee and the European Court.

As of 1 January 1973 the United Kingdom, Denmark and Ireland joined the 'Common Market'. At the present time nine countries of Western Europe compose the EEC with a population of about 260 million, occupying a territory of more than 1.5 million square kilometres. These nine EEC countries represent more than 30% of the industrial capacity of the capitalist world, more than 40% of exports and imports, and 35% of gold and hard currency reserves.

The EEC has attained marked successes in the economic sphere; a common market for labour, services and capital and a single agricultural market has been created. At the present time the countries of the EEC are working towards the creation of an economic and currency union.

The EEC in itself represents a real economic force which by the conclusion of agreements is drawing into its orbit many of the countries of Western Europe, Africa, Asia and Latin America. The EEC has treaty agreements with 69 countries; and the member countries conduct trade with 106 countries, in all influencing one way or another the foreign political direction of its trading partners.

In the last few years the governments of the member countries of the EEC have been working on plans for the formation of a European Union (the Tindemans Report) on the basis of a broad economic, political and military integration. According to the intentions of its authors, the eventual aim is to use the 'Common Market' as the basis for creating a political, military and monetary-economic union, appearing on the world stage as a unified whole and forming a constituent part of NATO. Special anxiety is aroused by the prospect of the creation of a common European military organisation which may transform the EEC into a military-political union in which aggressive revanchist circles may play the leading role.

According to available information, the most important task which the governments of the EEC countries have set themselves is the undermining of the foreign policy positions of the Socialist countries. In this respect the coordination of policy among the EEC countries towards the socialist community, and communist movement and countries of the 'Third World' will continue to develop.

What is taking place among the countries of the 'Nine' directly affects the state interests of the Soviet Union and other socialist states. In the circumstances of détente and the development of cooperation between states with different social systems, the problems connected with industry, finance, trade and economic activity become subjects for negotiation between capitalist and socialist countries and assume more and more a political significance.

That is why Soviet external intelligence considers the EEC a target for active study and is placing on the services' component parts the requirement to achieve agent penetration of the principal organs of the Community in order to obtain intelligence revealing the true plans and intentions of the governing circles of the member countries towards the socialist countries in the economic, political and military spheres. In the period of establishing and developing contacts between the Council for Mutual Economic Assistance (CMEA) and the EEC, secret reliable information on the position of the 'Nine' during the negotiations with representatives of CMEA is of special value.

The main organs of the EEC, which are targets for deep study by Soviet external intelligence:

According to details available at the beginning of 1976, the EEC employed 12,200 staff; however not all these are of interest to Soviet foreign intelligence. First of all the holders of secret intelligence or those civil servants who due to the nature of their work have direct access to it are of operational interest. In connection with this, when organising operational agent measures, the correct choice of targets for deep study is of paramount importance.

At the present time, of the greatest operational interest for the Soviet external intelligence is a deep study of the following EEC organs; the Council of Ministers, the Commission of the European Community, the Committee of permanent representatives, the European Parliament, the Economic and Social Committee and the permanent missions of member-countries to the EEC.

Council of Ministers (located in Brussels, at Rue de la Loi 170, 1048 Bruxelles, Telephone: (02) 736-1900 and 736-8940, Telex: Consil B 21711). All governments of the member-states are represented in it. It meets every month. The main members of the Council of Ministers are the Ministers of Foreign Affairs, but other Ministers can take part in the work of the Council depending on the subject under discussion.

The function of President of the Council is carried out for a period of six months by each of the Ministers of Foreign Affairs in turn according to the Latin alphabetical order. From 1 January to 31 June 1977 [*sic*] the job of President of the Council of Ministers is held by the British Minister of Foreign Affairs, Mr Crosland* [crossed out in the original text] and as from 1 July the Belgian Representative will take over.

The competence of the Council of Ministers includes decisions on all the important problems of the activities of the EEC. It adopts the final decisions in the spheres of external and internal policies and these are binding on all member-countries. Discussions affecting national interests of the member-countries have to be adopted unanimously, less important ones by majority vote.

The meetings of the Council of Ministers are held in turn in the countries of the EEC member-states.

* Tony Crosland died suddenly on 19 Feburary 1977, and was succeeded as Foreign Secretary by David Owen.

The working organ of the Council of Ministers is the General Secretariat. According to dates available in 1974 it employed 1,152 people, that is: Germans – 166, French – 182, Italians – 251, Dutch – 88, Belgians – 237, Luxemburgers – 17, British – 111, Danes – 74, Irish – 16, representatives of other nationalities – 10.

The General Secretariat consists of five general directorates and a number of services. The most likely units to hold secret information are:

a. *General Directorate A.* (Administrative and budgetary matters.) Deals with administrative and budgetary problems. Compiles the appropriate working documents; prepares draft decisions and has them translated into the languages of the member-countries. This directorate has an important function in the activities of the EEC because it prepares schemes for decisions by the Council of Ministers.

b. *General Directorate E.* (Foreign relations and contacts with associate countries.) Deals with foreign relations and contacts with associated nations. Secret intelligence is stored here on the EEC's foreign policy.

c. *General Directorate F.* (Economic and financial relations, relations with the European Parliament, problems of information, documentation and publications.) Deals with the problems of economic and financial relations. Carries out working contacts with the European Parliament. Secret information is concentrated in this directorate pertaining to the economic and financial policy of the EEC, as well as on questions of the relations between the Council of Ministers and the European Parliament.

The Press and Information Service is responsible for the accreditation of foreign journalists. Prepares and organizes press-conferences, maintains contacts with the representatives of the mass information media, publishes reports and speeches as well as press-releases.

The Legal Office checks that the contents of documents conform with national legislation and the Treaty of Rome. In practical terms, all important documents pass through this office.

The Official Library of the EEC is located in the Main Building; a special unit has been created there in which EEC secret material is stored.

In order to concert and coordinate the activities of the member-countries, a Committee of Permanent Representatives (COREPER) has been established attached to the Council of Ministers. This consists of the Ambassadors of the member-countries who are accredited to the EEC; they meet once a week. In fact preliminary agreement and the drawing up of decisions for the Council of Ministers is carried out with the direct participation of the permanent representatives. In recent times the growing importance of the COREPER in the activities of the EEC has been noteworthy, due to the increase in political consultation within the Community.

The Council of Ministers has formed a number of committees; amongst these the one which is of main interest to Soviet external intelligence is the *Political Committee* (PC). Each state appoints as a member of this committee a responsible official of its Ministry of Foreign Affairs and his job is to maintain contact with other countries' representatives who have a similar function. The PC works out the main foreign policy documents of the EEC: in the course of this work it can apply to the Ambassadors accredited to the EEC with requests for whatever documents and information are necessary, and in this way it contributes towards the cooperation on the diplomatic representative level of the member-countries. The Committee compiles periodic reports on its activities for the Ministers of Foreign Affairs.

The PC has the right to form working groups. At the present time a special working group is busy working out the position of the member-countries for negotiations within the East–West framework. The PC and the special working group maintain working contacts with the corresponding committees in NATO in order to reach concerted decisions. It is known from the activity practised by this group that representatives of the member-countries of the Council of NATO can take part in meetings of this group.

The PC has the right to pass to the member countries information which may be of interest to them.

In December 1974 in order to concert and coordinate the main direction of EEC policies, the European Council was set up consisting of the Heads of States and governments of the member-countries of the Community. The European Council meets three times per year (in the spring, summer and autumn) and takes decisions on questions submitted by the Council of Ministers and the Commission.

The Commission of the European Community (CEC) located at Rue de la Loi 200, 1049 Bruxelles, is the executive organ of the EEC. It consists of thirteen members, appointed by agreement of the governments of the member states (two members each from France, Italy, the FRG, Britain and one each from Belgium, Holland, Luxembourg, Ireland and Denmark). From these the governments elect a President of the Commission and five vice-presidents for a period of two years. From 1 January 1977 the President of the Commission is an Englishman, Roy Jenkins. His appointment to the leading post in the Commission has resulted in staff changes. According to incoming reports, the new staff of the Commission consists mostly of anti-communist inclined individuals. The imminent hardening of the Commission's policy towards the CMEA is linked to the appointment of R. Jenkins as well as to the increase in the activities of the counter-intelligence components inside the EEC.

In accordance with the Treaty of Rome, the Commission keeps a watch on the clear-cut fulfilment of the terms of the treaty by the member countries, as well as on the execution of decisions made by the Council of Ministers. The Commission takes decisions, makes recommendations or draws conclusions on problems pertaining to the main directions of the activities of the EEC organs. It is empowered to act as the initiator of the common policy of EEC and to see that this policy is implemented. The Commission works out draft schemes for decision on various subjects and presents these to the Council of Ministers for ratification. The Commission represents the Community during negotiations and on the signing of trade agreements with third countries.

The Commission has a vast staff, numbering 7,605 employees (as at February 1976). It consists of twenty general directorates, a secretariat, a number of services and more than 100 working groups. In these various units experts are engaged in preparing documents and proposals, and when necessary other national specialists are invited to take part giving their views on the draft documents under consideration. The employees of the Commission are international civil servants. Their pay is very much higher than that of NATO officials.

Among the main units of the Commission, in which secret political and economic information is concentrated and which are consequently of intelligence interest, it is worth mentioning the following:

– *Directorate General of External Relations*. It deals with questions of relations with third countries and with international organisations. It also handles the problems of foreign trade policy with capitalist and socialist countries. It supervises the EEC mission to the OECD in Paris, the EEC mission to the UN office in Geneva, the EEC mission to the US government in Washington, to the UN Headquarters in New York, to the Canadian government in Ottawa, and the EEC missions in Latin America in Santiago (Chile), and in Tokyo (Japan).

– *Directorate General for personnel and administrative questions*. (Some units of this Directorate are located in Luxembourg.) Personal files of EEC employees are kept here.

– *Directorate General of Information*. Conducts all the propaganda activities of the EEC and supervises the work of the Press and Information Bureau in Community member countries, as well as in Santiago (Chile), Washington, New York, Geneva, Ottawa, Tokyo, Athens and Ankara.

– *Directorate General of Energy*. Works out the energy policy of the member countries of the Community.

– *Legal Service*. Its functions are similar to the duties of the corresponding service at the Council of Ministers.

– *Security Service*. According to available information, there are two security services within the EEC; one attached to the Council of Ministers, the other attached to the Commission.

According to available details, the Bureau of Security has recently been organisationally strengthened and placed under the control of the President of the Commission of the European Community. It has worked out a directive to strengthen security measures and the protection of the most important secret documents concerning the conduct of political consultations within the EEC framework, the development by the Community of trade and economic policies towards other countries, as well as documents concerning negotiations with Socialist states. It is envisaged that there will be a more thorough check on persons coming to work at the Secretariat of the Council of Ministers and in the Directorates of the Commission where documents are compiled on external relations, and on trade and financial policy. The check on new staff will be carried out by the national security services and additionally with the help of the facilities of the NATO security services in Belgium. EEC civil servants with access to secret documents are obliged to report to their Chiefs about their contacts with representatives of the Socialist states.

This branch has available a list of Commission Security Bureau personnel.

Public Information Group is the official voice of the EEC. Its employees can act on behalf of the Commission as well as on behalf of the President and Vice-Presidents.

General Secretariat of the Commission. Deals with all business correspondence in the Commission, the organisation of all work in the Commission and checking the location of documents in the units of the Commission.

Offices of Commission members. Every member of the Commission has a personal secretariat, through which all documents are passed, directly concerning him. In the secretariat secret information is held, not only relating to the activities of Commission members but on practically all other subjects.

European Parliament. (Located at Centre Européen, Luxembourg. Plateau du Kirchberg.) It is composed of 198 deputies, elected from Members of Parliaments of the member states. At the present time it consists of 198 deputies, 36 each from Britain, France, the FRG and Italy; 14 each from Belgium and the Netherlands; 10 each from Ireland and Denmark and 6 from Luxembourg. Within the Parliament political groupings independent of their national affiliation have been formed. In February 1976 these groupings numbered 66 Socialists, 51 Christian-Democrats, 25 Liberals, 17 Conservatives, 17 Democrats supporting European progress, 15 Communists and their supporters and 7 Independents.

The Parliament possesses limited powers; it discusses the activities of EEC on the basis of the yearly Commission Report; when necessary it makes oral requests to the leadership of the EEC; it has the right to pass a vote of no-confidence on any executive organ of the Commission. Besides this the Parliament can submit recommendations on questions of Community policy, and at the request of the Council of Ministers or the Commission it can take decisions on problems placed before it by these two bodies. Within the framework of the activities of Parliament, debates are held with Ministers of Foreign Affairs of the EEC member countries taking part as well as the members of the Parliament, in order to discuss those points which are the subject of consultation in the framework of the Community in the sphere of foreign policy. Besides this unofficial meetings are held to discuss urgent problems. The Parliament meets six to eight times per year; these sessions usually last not more than one week. In the period between sessions, all the work is carried on in the parliamentary commissions. The parliamentary sessions are held in Strasbourg (in France) and Luxembourg. The commissions are held in turn in the various member countries of the EEC.

Every year the European Parliament elects a Presidium consisting of a President and ten Deputies. The Parliament has created a Committee of Chairmen, its members being the President of Parliament, his Deputies, the Chairmen of the twelve Commissions and the Chairmen of the six political groups. The European Parliament has its own *general secretariat* which is located at the Centre Européen, Plateau du Kirchberg, Luxembourg, Telephone: (01) 352-47711, Telex: 494 Parleurolux 1.

Economic and Social Committee (located at Rue Ravenstein 2, 1000 Bruxelles), is an advisory organ. The senior institutions of the EEC must consult this committee on agricultural policy, the free movement of labour, labour regulations, social policy, education etc. The Committee is composed of 144 representatives: 24 each from Britain, the FRG, France and Italy; 12 each from Belgium and Holland; 9 each from Denmark and Ireland and 6 from Luxembourg. Members of this Committee are appointed for four years by the Council of Ministers at the suggestion of the national governments. The leading organ of the Committee is the Bureau. The Committee has its own secretariat and nine specialised sections, amongst which the section for foreign relations is of intelligence interest. It has 53 employees. This section prepares recommendations for the Council and the Commission on foreign policy problems of the Community; besides this it establishes links for the Economic and Social Committee with countries abroad.

The sessions of the Economic and Social Committee are held behind closed doors.

Permanent Missions of the member countries to the EEC. (Located in Brussels.) All nine countries forming the EEC have their own permanent representations to the EEC headed by Ambassadors. Their main function is to coordinate the activities of their own country with the other member states within the framework of the EEC. The employees of these permanent offices are used in compiling working documents for the EEC organs and have access to the Community's secret material. The bigger of these missions are Britain – 43 employees, the FRG – 37, Italy – 31, France – 26, Belgium – 24, Ireland – 24 and Holland – 22.

An examination of the composition of the permanent missions shows that these are basically filled by personnel from the national Ministries of Foreign Affairs, the Ministries of Economics and Finance, of Foreign Trade and Agriculture. In this connection it is worthwhile to study and cultivate the employees of those components of national government establishments who handle the problems of their country's relationship with the EEC.

Special establishments of higher education preparing personnel for EEC organs:

1. *The European College in Brugge* (located at Dijver 11, B-8000 Brugge, Belgium). The instruction period is for one year (from 27 September to July), with a yearly intake of 58 persons with higher education in three faculties: political, economic and diplomatic. On completion of their studies the students are posted to 'Common Market' establishments and to NATO.

   Citizens from the Socialist countries are also admitted to this college. It is known that representatives from Bulgaria, Czechoslovakia, Romania and Yugoslavia have been admitted to the European College.

   In the College building seminars are periodically held for NATO employees, financed by the appropriate NATO institutions.

2. *The European Institute in Amsterdam* (Holland). A specialised higher education establishment of the EEC countries. Located at Herengracht 508, Amsterdam, Telephone: 020-5252951. The instruction period is two years with a yearly intake of about 100 persons.

   The graduates of the institute are accepted for work in diplomatic services, parliamentary offices and other important restricted political and economic organisations in Western Europe.

   This Institute organises special courses for EEC countries' institutions.

3. *The European University Institute in Florence* (Italy). Located at Via di Roccettine 5, 50016 San Domenico di Fiesole. Established in September 1976. Seventy students a year, citizens of the member countries of the EEC, are admitted for study.

No. 481/PR/5
28 February 1977

THE Centre's next major circular, dated 15 April 1977, on 'Intelligence Work against the EEC', still failed to grasp the distinction between the EEC and the EPC, which excluded the Commission and was organised at an intergovernmental level. It also greatly exaggerated, once again, the pace of political integration. 'The foreign policy of the "Nine",' it claimed, 'is now already nothing less than the upshot of agreed decisions taken at the highest level.' (One British diplomat in 1977 privately put a rather different view about the Nine's efforts to arrive at a common foreign policy. 'It doesn't,' he claimed, 'add up to a row of beans.') The Centre saw even plans for direct elections to the European Parliament in 1978 as a threat to Soviet security, and ordered 'active measures' to prevent them. (In the event it was British foot-dragging rather than KGB operations which delayed them until 1979.)

What most concerned the KGB, however, was the allegedly 'real possibility' of the military integration of the EEC. 'The prospect of the appearance on the Western border of the Socialist community of an exclusively military organisation which will considerably increase the already vast military-economic potential of NATO can only give rise to alarm.'

Residencies in all EEC countries were ordered to appoint a senior officer to coordinate operations against the Community. Though his main priority was agent recruitment, he was also burdened with a number of more humdrum tasks: among them providing the Centre with EEC telephone directories, lists of diplomats and journalists accredited to the Community, and details of EEC officials travelling to the Soviet Union.

zt-1
No 1058/PR/61   Top Secret
15 April 1977   Copy No. 2

To the Residents (according to list)

THE ORGANISATION OF INTELLIGENCE WORK
AGAINST THE EUROPEAN ECONOMIC COMMUNITY (EEC)
FROM THE STANDPOINT OF 'LEGAL' RESIDENCIES

At the present time the EEC must be considered as a real political force and an important factor in present-day international relations. By means of various agreements some 70 countries of Western Europe, Africa, Latin America and Asia have been incorporated into the sphere of economic, political and ideological influence of the European Community. Ambassadors from 106 of the world's states are accredited to the EEC.

The ruling circles of the EEC member-countries are at present taking steps to strengthen further the political aspects of the organisation and gradually transform it into a 'European Union' with a 'single centre for decision making' on all the Community's problems including foreign policy and defence.

Within the framework of the 'Nine', the 'European Council' has been created – this is the highest political organ, consisting of Heads of States and governments, dealing with the internal political problems of the EEC as well as with important international matters. On the internal plane preparations are being made to hold direct general elections to the European Parliament in 1978, in order to give this organ real power and to use it as a means of stimulating the development of integration in various spheres.

The foreign policy of the 'Nine' is now already nothing less than the upshot of agreed decisions taken at the highest level. In working out a single foreign policy for the countries of the EEC a tendency is reflected among the ruling circles of the EEC to move gradually away from a coordinated foreign policy to a common foreign policy. This policy is particularly marked in the relationships of the member countries towards the socialist states. The dominant thrust of the foreign policy activities of the EEC member states is to weaken the economic integration and political unity of the countries of the socialist community on the international plane, as well as to make use of the negotiations with CMEA to exert pressure on the socialist countries in order to obtain from them unilateral concessions. The Community has become a centre for coordinating collective economic, political and ideological actions, aimed at undermining the international prestige of the Soviet Union and other countries of the socialist community.

The events of the last years have shown that the EEC, even before the official creation of the European Union, was beginning to operate on the international scene as a sort of political unit, continually widening its spheres of interest. The 'Nine' are showing in this guise when taking decisions relating to the problems of cooperation and security in Europe, in the events in the Middle East, in the North–South dialogue, in the UN and so on.

At the present time one can speak of a real possibility of the creation of a military-political union of the 'Nine', with a possible increase in the number of member-countries from among those Western European states who at this moment are striving for full membership of the Community. According to the intentions of the initiators of the creation of this military-political union, it will play an independent role on the world stage, while remaining at the same time part of the North Atlantic Bloc. The present policy of the Community in this connection is determined by the gradual accumulation of elements with military integration through consultations on a constantly expanding scale about the problems of security and the development of cooperation in the arms industry and the sphere of military technology.

The integration processes taking place within the EEC in the political and economic fields affect the vital interests of the Soviet Union in a most direct way. The prospect of the appearance on the western border of the socialist community of an exclusive military organisation which will considerably increase the already vast military-economic potential of NATO can only give rise to alarm. As a definite embodiment of the ideas connected with the military integration of the EEC member-countries, one must examine the activities of the Eurogroup and the Independent Planning Group. According to reliable information, the leadership of NATO is stimulating the development of contacts between the EEC and the [NATO] bloc on the military side and overall. The NATO Secretary-General, J. Luns, stated that he contemplated with satisfaction the process of 'mutual penetration of the "Nine" and the fifteen countries of NATO'.

The main tasks of Soviet foreign intelligence in organising work against the

EEC were laid down in the instructions in letter no 1666 of 8 July 1976 from Comrade Alyoshin [Kryuchkov]. This gives the agent-operational and organisational measures, which are designed to stimulate all work against the EEC. In particular, these foresee the need to keep a close watch on the main tendencies in the development of West European integration and the elaboration of definite measures to increase the exploration and purposefulness of agent possibilities in order to penetrate the targets in which intelligence is concentrated, as well as in order to carry out active measures.

Soviet foreign intelligence is faced with various responsible tasks, the main one of which is to obtain secret EEC documents, which will reveal the plans and concrete actions of the 'Nine' vis-à-vis the Soviet Union; also intelligence about the contents of decisions by the leading organs of the Community, which are aimed to counterbalance the foreign policy and economic initiatives of the Soviet Government, and to undermine the economic and defence potential of the countries of the socialist community, is required.

In the sphere of active measures, the main efforts of Soviet intelligence must be directed towards holding back the integration process by making use of reliable and secret intelligence about contradictions and differences between the EEC member-states on the one hand and between the EEC and USA on the other: active measures must also help to establish legal treaty relations between the CMEA and the EEC on the basis of CMEA's proposals. The task also includes obstructing direct elections to the European Parliament, opposition to the election into it of delegates from West Berlin, and the prevention of a Conservative majority in Parliament in the event of direct elections being held. One of the most important objectives of the Residency's activities must be measures directed towards the possible frustration of, or the complication of, joint actions which the governments of the EEC member-countries, the USA and Japan are striving to put into effect in their dealings with the Soviet Union, its allies, and the countries of the 'Third World' . . .

IRTYSHOV

[Y. I. SHISHKIN, Deputy Head FCD]

THE high priority given by the Centre to operations against the Community was underlined by a circular of 1 August 1977 which made clear that European integration, in all its forms, was regarded by the KGB as a threat to Soviet security.

vk-1   Secret
No. 1582/PR   Copy No. 1
1 August 1977

To Copenhagen
Comrade KORIN [M. P. LYUBIMOV]

Reference No. 464

We are sending you a list of questions which are of top priority interest to the Centre in relation to intelligence coverage on the EEC and which have been compiled in conjunction with the appropriate sub-sections of the Service:

Political Intelligence
    1. The situation and prospects for West European integration in the monetary-economic, political and military spheres.
    2. Strains within the Community with relation to the basic problems of West European integration.
    3. The balance of forces between the proponents and adversaries of European unity in governmental, political and social circles of the 'Nine'.
    4. The influence of the processes towards West European integration on the attitudes of the EEC countries in their dealings with the rest of the world. The problems which exist in the relationships of the 'Nine' with the USA, Japan and China.
    5. The probable consequences of the creation of a European union as far as the USA's economic, political and military position in Western Europe is concerned.
    6. The position of the EEC and of those countries who are joining it with relation to CMEA and individual socialist states.
    7. An assessment of the possible consequences of West European integration on the political, economic and military positions of the USSR and of the countries of the socialist community.

SEVEROV
[V. F. GRUSHKO]
[Head of the Third Department, FCD]

T HE Centre returned to the threat of EEC 'military-political integration' in a circular of 20 April 1978 which continued to confuse EEC and EPC. Its particular fear on this occasion was the creation of a European Security Council. It failed to grasp that the two main NATO powers in Europe, Britain and Germany, feared that any such scheme would provide unwelcome ammunition for those in the US Congress anxious to reduce the American military commitment in Europe.

nm.5
No 2041/PR/52
20 April 1978

Top Secret
Copy No. 1

To: Residents (according to list)

PLANS TO STEP UP MILITARY-POLITICAL COOPERATION WITHIN THE EEC

According to reliable information, plans to strengthen military-political cooperation among the countries of the Nine are presently being mooted among some leading countries of the European Economic Community (EEC). In particular, aspirations towards concerted action by the member-countries of the community in the fields of military-political planning and armaments production have been expressed. Trustworthy sources have indicated that in some EEC countries concrete means are being worked out to develop military cooperation within the framework of the community. A document prepared by experts of one of the West European countries at the behest of that country's Ministry of Defence shows that the process of détente, or more precisely, the absence of open confrontation between the USSR and the USA, and the unlikelihood of arriving at an agreement on arms control more far-reaching than those projected at the present time, creates the most favourable conditions possible for posing the question of the development of military-political cooperation in Western Europe.

In this connection it is proposed to set up a special body, a European Security Council, which is to meet at the same time as the ordinary sessions of the European Council (regular conferences of heads of state and governments of the EEC member-countries) i.e. three times a year. To service this, it is planned to establish a group of high-ranking officials, mainly from the Ministries of Foreign Affairs and Defence, who would be charged with making the preparations for these sessions. Security problems are also to be discussed in the EEC political committee (at the level of director of the political departments from the Foreign Ministries of the 'Nine').

The purpose of creating the above-mentioned organs is to strive to reconcile points of view through regular consultations and, eventually, to evolve a joint attitude on the problems of defence policies, in particular in the field of arms control. It is envisaged extending this joint approach to questions concerning, directly, defence organisation, and also the structure and competency of NATO institutions. If an agreed position can be established in advance within the European Security Council, then consultations on measures for arms control which are carried on within the NATO framework and in which representatives of France participate, will take on an entirely different character.

The creation and functioning of a European Security Council will, in the opinion of experts, compel Washington to take more notice of the opinions and interests of the European allies of the USA. This will also allow an end to be put to the situation whereby the governments of each of the allied countries present themselves independently before the American administration to plead their cases.

An intensification of the 'European tendency' is also recommended in the course of increasing cooperation in the fields of scientific research, the development and production of weapons and military technology. With this in view it is proposed that the countries of the 'Nine' should establish a European Armaments Committee which would rely on the experience of the Independent European Programme Group (EPG) set up in Rome in February 1976. This Armaments Committee would take the form of a council made up of government representatives at State Secretary level from the Defence Ministries (Armaments Departments) or persons performing analagous duties, a general secretariat responsible for coordination and administration, and groups of experts, set up in accordance with the existing plan of work of the EPG and handling the various branches of the armed forces.

The above-mentioned body must enjoy full powers in working out programmes for future weaponry for the member-states of the EEC, deciding the length of time for existing arms and military technology to stay in service before replacement and perfecting the forms of inter-governmental cooperation in these fields.

In communicating this information to you we wish to draw your attention to the fact that, on the basis of what is known to the Centre, the plans for intensifying military-political integration are being discussed in the organs of the EEC and the ruling circles of the member-countries. The Centre is interested in obtaining intelligence on the following questions:

– the positions of the governments of the countries of the Community with regard to the future intensification of military-political cooperation within the EEC framework;

– the attitude of the USA to the drawing up of plans for military-political cooperation within the EEC and the future prospects for their coming into effect;

– the course of the discussions in the EEC organs and in the government departments of member-countries on the above mentioned plans; possible disagreements among community members; and concrete proposals or decisions taken with relation to these questions.

SEVEROV

[V. F. GRUSHKO]

[Head of the Third Department, FCD]

EUROPEAN political and military integration seemed all the more alarming in the Centre as a result of 'active collaboration' between the EEC and the Chinese People's Republic (PRC). The five-year trade agreement signed in April 1978 giving the PRC most favoured nation status appeared an ominous precedent for further Chinese attempts 'to exploit Western European integration against the Soviet Union'.

One compensation, however, for the increasing PRC presence in Brussels and the countries of the EEC was a growing number of Chinese targets for KGB recruitment, who were all the more important in the Centre's view because of the immense difficulty of conducting intelligence operations within China itself.[3]

zk-1
1087/PR   Top Secret
11 April 1978   Copy No. 1

To: Residents (according to list)

We are sending you some background guidance for your Line 'K' work.* Please keep the Centre informed in good time about the problems mentioned in the guidance and formulate proposals for stepping up work against Chinese nationals, both from the point of view of the development of relations between the Chinese People's Republic and the EEC itself, and also with individual member-countries of this closed grouping.

Attachment: as indicated in text, 3 pages, No. 1091/PR/5

IRTYSHOV

zk-1   Top Secret
             Copy No. 1

LINE 'K' WORK TACKLED FROM
THE STANDPOINT OF THE EEC

The first signs of a reappraisal by Peking of its attitude towards the European Economic Community (EEC) occurred in 1973. As a first step, a number of visits to China by top officials of the 'Common Market' took place, among them those of the Dutch Foreign Minister, van der Stoel (in January 1975), and the Chairman of the EEC Council of Ministers, Tindemans (in April 1975). As a result of these visits official relations were established between the EEC and the

---

* Operations against China.

Chinese People's Republic. In September 1975 the Ambassador of the Chinese People's Republic presented his letters of accreditation in the EEC.

Immediately after the establishment of relations there began technical discussions to work out a formula for a trade agreement between the Community and the Chinese People's Republic. In February 1978 a five-year trade agreement was initialled which granted most favoured nation status to China, and in April of the current year the signing of the agreement took place.

The Chinese representatives do not hide the fact that, in concluding the agreement, the People's Republic is pursuing political objectives first and foremost, striving to exploit Western European integration against the Soviet Union. Side by side with this the Chinese count on gaining access to advanced Western techniques and technology with the help of the EEC, also to arms and military hardware markets. In order to build up their armaments industry potential; likewise they hope to make use of the EEC to establish relations with NATO on the basis of anti-Sovietism. Almost at the same time as the trade agreement was initialled, the Chinese signed contracts with a number of West European countries to buy goods with a military application. Visits of various Chinese delegations took place to EEC countries to study the possibility of cooperation in military matters.

As far as the EEC is concerned, it is attracted by the future potential of the Chinese market and the possibilities of gaining access to sources of raw materials. An important consideration for the EEC is the future utilisation of China's good relations with some developing countries for the benefit of the 'Common Market'. Besides this, the political interests of the EEC coincide with Chinese anti-Sovietism.

The signing of the trade agreement between the EEC and the Chinese People's Republic is seen in leading circles of the Community as a kind of precedent for future negotiations with European socialist countries (notably Romania) inasmuch as the EEC Commission acted as a juridical entity in the negotiations with the Chinese People's Republic and not the Council of Ministers. In agreeing to grant China most favoured nation status, the countries of the EEC wish to demonstrate to the USSR and the countries of the Socialist community that it is in their interests to recognise the EEC as quickly as possible and to seek ways of conducting direct negotiations with its organs, as did the Chinese.

The active collaboration between the EEC and the Chinese People's Republic has created additional scope for work against the Chinese target in Europe. The impending opening of new Chinese institutions abroad and the expansion of already existing ones, the increased exchange of delegations, exhibitions, students and graduates etc, between the Chinese People's Republic and the EEC will significantly broaden the field of recruitment in our work on Chinese nationals.

On account of the foregoing, it is already essential that Residencies, in their Line 'K' work, should keep in mind the following points:

- the opening of new Chinese missions and the expansion of existing ones in your country of residence;

- the purchase of strategic materials by China from the EEC countries and the signing of contracts for the delivery of goods to the PRC which have a military significance or military application;

- Chinese contacts with representatives of NATO and other Western military-political organisations;

- visits to your country of residence of Chinese delegations, the organising of exhibitions by the Chinese and their participation in public debates etc; the aim of which is to influence the development of commercial, economic and political relations between the Chinese People's Republic and your country of residence;

- the identification and study of officials of Chinese institutions who are dealing with questions related to EEC activities and their contacts with the representatives of local business, party and government circles;

- the possibilities of activating as Line 'K' agents citizens of those 'Third World' countries which have good relations with the Chinese People's Republic and corresponding trade agreements with the EEC.

7 April 1978
No. 1091/PR/5

L ITTLE had changed in the KGB's attitudes to the Community (which it still referred to as the EEC) by the mid-1980s. A circular in the spring of 1984 rehearsed the conspiracy theories first elaborated in 1976 with, if anything, added emphasis. Growing cooperation between China and the Community was causing 'alarm' in the Centre; the EEC was pursuing far-reaching plans to undermine the international prestige and political unity of the Soviet bloc; plans by 'reactionary groups' for European military integration presented 'a special danger'. In all its aspects, the Centre concluded, 'The integration of Western Europe runs counter to the interests of the Soviet Union.' The Politburo had named the EEC as one of the 'main targets for intelligence penetration'.

It was an ironic tribute to the progress achieved in European integration since the signature of the Treaty of Rome in 1957 that the Community found itself elevated by 1984 to virtually the same target status as NATO and China.

lp-1   Secret
                                                       Copy No 1

[ms notes:]
Incoming No 227
Comrade Gornov
Comrade Yelin, and
PR Line operational personnel

                    Yermakov [A. V. Guk], 18.4.84

1025/PR/61
                        To Residents
5.03.84   (according to list)

Guidance – Requirements for carrying out our work with regard to the Euro-
        pean Economic Community.

At the present time the European Economic Community must be regarded as
a real political and economic force comprising the ten states of Western Europe,
and as an important factor in international relations. Progress in the integration
of EEC member countries, their concerted action in the fields of foreign policy
and economics and the impending expansion of the 'Common Market' as a
result of the admission of Spain and Portugal, attracting new countries in
Western Europe, Asia, Africa and Latin America within its sphere of influence,
have greatly enhanced the role of the Community in the international arena
and its influence on resolving important world problems.

The 'Ten' have already adopted a united attitude on many major international questions, such as East–West, North–South, Mediterranean, EEC–
Japanese, and EEC–American relations. This stands out particularly clearly in
matters involving the 'Common Market's' relations with the socialist states.
One of the principal lines pursued by the EEC in its foreign policy is that of
undermining the international prestige of the Soviet Union and other countries
belonging to the socialist community and their political unity, and drawing them
into the sphere of its own economic policy.

EEC attempts to achieve closer co-operation with the People's Republic of
China (PRC) in political and economic fields are rightly arousing alarm. The
leaders of the 'Ten' have considerable hopes of making use of Soviet–Chinese
rivalry in their own interest; seeing in China not only a powerful military and
strategic counterweight to the Soviet Union, but also a future reserve for execut-
ing commercial and economic manoeuvring and bringing pressure to bear on
CMEA.

The plans of the most reactionary groups within the 'Ten' to promote
European military integration harbour a special danger. In recent times they
have been pursuing the matter more and more actively with the aim of transforming the 'Common Market' into a 'European Union', investing its agencies
with supra-national powers in all the more important questions, including

foreign policy and some aspects of military industrial co-operation among West European countries.

Obviously, progress in the integration of Western Europe, especially in the military-political field, runs counter to the interests of the Soviet Union.

The policy of the EEC leadership is fraught with even greater adverse consequences in a situation where the Reagan administration has adopted a policy of confrontation with the countries of the socialist camp and has begun the actual deployment of medium-range missiles on the territory of a number of West European states. In this situation it has become a matter of great urgency to step up and improve still further our intelligence effort with regard to the EEC.

Following the instructions of the authorities,* the leadership of our Service has earmarked the European Economic Community as one of the main targets for intelligence penetration, first of all in view of the fact that important political, economic, scientific and military information is concentrated in its agencies.

The 'Common Market' is also of particular interest to us because it is an organisation affording footholds from which it is possible to carry on intelligence work successfully against the USA, NATO and the PRC. The existence of sharply conflicting rivalry among the three main centres of imperialism (the USA, Western Europe and Japan) enables the EEC to be used to reinforce contradictions among the imperialists advances in all directions. The EEC can at the same time serve as a unique 'foreign flag' in recruitment work in regard to nationals of the USA and the PRC and NATO employees.

In addition, work on the EEC target is at present acquiring particular immediacy in view of the fact that it is regarded as an integral part of economic intelligence as a whole.

In view of the importance which the leadership of our Service attaches to the question of working on this target for intelligence penetration, the central apparatus and stations abroad have been specifically tasked to penetrate the directing elements of the EEC, to obtain intelligence information revealing the actual plans and intentions of the ruling groups of the EEC with regard to the USSR and the other countries of the socialist community, and also to prepare and carry out active measures to counter these plans. For a number of years, our agencies abroad have carried on intelligence work purposefully against the EEC in dealing with these tasks. At the same time, in view of the particular features of the present international situation, the fresh impetus in developing the integration process in Western Europe and other substantive factors, a more thorough and profound approach is required to the question of organising and carrying out work against the 'Common Market'.

In accordance with Comrade Alyoshin's [Kryuchkov's] instructions, work

* The 'Instantsiya', in KGB documents, denotes the political leadership, in particular the Politburo.

on the problem of the European Economic Community must be regarded as one of the priority lines and carried on in immediate association with work on the Main Adversary.

Following this instruction, action must be taken to step up intelligence activity with regard to the EEC in all sectors in order to carry out the set tasks.

In the area of information gathering, attention must be concentrated chiefly on clarifying the following problems:

1. The integration process in the EEC:
- the situation with regard to the integration of West European countries at this stage and new factors in the integration process in the political, economic and military fields;
- the attitudes of individual governments of the EEC countries and differences of opinion with regard to the forms and directions for integration;
- problems facing the EEC in connection with the admission of new members to the community;
- co-operation and rivalry in the Bonn–Paris–London triangle in the struggle for the leading role in the EEC and the attitude of the other countries of the community towards this rivalry.

2. Foreign policy of the EEC:
- assessment of 'Common Market' co-operation with regional international, political and economic organisations, in particular with ASEAN; problems of co-operation and ways of solving them;
- the ideas of individual EEC countries on the problem of developing relations with the USA;
- the EEC's Mediterranean and Middle East policy;
- relations between the EEC and Japan and the EEC and the USA;
- plans for developing relations between the EEC and the PRC and their political and military consequences;
- the attitude of individual members of the community and of the directing elements of the EEC towards dialogue with the CMEA;
- EEC plans and specific measures designed to unify the community's policy with regard to the main international problems, and above all in relation to the socialist countries;
- the most promising sectors, in the West's opinion, for co-operation with European socialist countries.

3. The United States' attitude to integration in Western Europe:
- the USA's position with regard to the development of European integration and the policy of individual member countries of the EEC;
- United States' policy regarding the EEC at the current stage, and use of pressure levers, especially NATO.

4. Evaluation of the EEC's economic potential.

5. The present position and prospects for COCOM's* activity:

– principal sectors for possible further limitation of the access of socialist countries to advanced technology;

– possible disagreements between Western Europe and the USA when discussing the question of expanding the list of strategic commodities;

– the prospects for organisational changes in COCOM;

– American measures to exercise greater control over COCOM decisions and prevent 'leakage' of advanced technology to socialist countries via third countries (including neutral and developing countries).

The question of gathering intelligence information on the EEC is directly related not only to the timely provision of information to the authorities concerned, but also to the organisation and implementation of active measures.

If this work is to be carried on effectively, it is essential that the information obtained should be specially studied in Residencies from the point of view of active exploitation and that it should be directed to the appropriate subdivision of our Service which is concerned with preparing active measures. In view of the growing importance of work on the 'Common Market', it is also important to apply more initiative in this sector and to submit more often to the Centre specific and well-grounded proposals for carrying out comprehensive, large-scale operations, and to pay more attention to finding reliable channels for implementing them.

With regard to specific aspects of work on active measures, attention must be concentrated principally on the following questions:

1. Exposing and holding back the process of West European military/political integration:

– weakening the position and influence of reactionary forces who are in favour of building up a 'European Union' (including one founded on the West European Union) on an anti-Soviet and anti-socialist basis;

– aggravating existing disagreements between individual member-countries of the 'Common Market' over political and economic matters (the struggle for leadership of the EEC, relations between the large and small states, agricultural policy, currency and financial relations, the budget, etc);

– compromising the idea in European eyes of a 'European Union' as an attempt to limit the national sovereignty of the states of Western Europe; exposing plans for establishing a military/political 'directorate' of the larger states (France, the FRG, Britain, Italy) to administer the affairs of the small countries (Belgium, Greece, Denmark, Ireland).

* The Coordinating Committee for East–West Trade (made up of NATO members and Japan), which coordinates the embargo of defence-related technology to the Soviet Bloc.

2. Aggravating disagreements between the United States, Western Europe and Japan, weakening the USA's leading role and counteracting the development of political, commercial and economic links between the EEC and the PRC:

– exposing the incompatibility between the economic interests of individual West European countries and those of the United States, and between the EEC as an organisation and the USA; discrediting United States activity in international economic organisations (the OECD, the UN ECE, the IMF, the IBRD and others);

– inspiring mistrust and misgiving in governmental, political and social circles with regard to the adventurist policy of the American administration.

3. Helping to create conditions for adjusting relations between the CMEA and the EEC, expanding commercial and economic contacts, especially in the sale of hard-currency commodities to the USSR, and imports of the latest equipment and technology (especially in electronics and robot technology), and for granting the Soviet Union the necessary credits:

– implementing Active Measures in connection with the Food and Energy Programmes;

– countermeasures against the common credit policy of the West towards the USSR; the aggravation of disagreements within the 'Ten' in matters of credit policy;

– discrediting the activity of COCOM.

In order to deal successfully with the abovementioned tasks in the information-gathering field, and the implementation of active measures, it is essential to step up efforts to establish solid agent/operational positions in the principal agencies of the community, and in the first place in those agencies where the most important information about its activity is to be found: the establishments of the Council of Ministers and Commission of the EC; the committee of permanent representatives; the economic and social committee; the European Parliament; the member-countries' permanent representatives on the Council of Ministers; and the specialised committees and working groups within the community. In addition to the EEC headquarters in Brussels, many agencies of the 'Common Market', and institutions associated with them which are located in the territory of other states, are also of interest to us from the point of view of agent/operational penetration.

In this connection more work must be done on agent penetration of inter-mediate targets in the EEC, such as the EC Commission's information bureau, the permanent missions of the EC Council of Ministers in international organis-ations, European centres for training personnel to work in the community's establishments, diplomatic missions of the member countries, international economic organisations, large banks and their research departments, national and trans-national monopolies, associations and other organisations. Attention should also be given to studying and processing national agencies and institutions connected with the 'Common Market' – departments of EEC foreign, economic and finance ministries, research centres and firms.

The multinational character of the EEC, the existence of agencies and establishments connected with it in many states, the active participation of representatives of the 'Ten' in the work of the community and the EEC's wide range of international contacts all provide the objective prerequisites for intelligence work against the 'Common Market', both from the Residencies in member countries and from the territory of third countries which have commercial and economic relations with the organisation. The necessity for this has also been underlined by the exacerbation, of which we have become aware recently, in the international situation, the stronger counter-intelligence measures in the community's headquarters, the noticeable increase in the subversive activity of the EEC in relation to the socialist states, and other factors.

In this context, Residencies in EEC member countries and also in third countries where there are facilities for working on this target must make a careful examination of the state of intelligence activity in this sector, having at the same time determined the main lines of their future work in relation to the specific character of the region in question.

The work of studying and developing operations against the EEC must be organised on targeting lines. To this end, as agreed with the Centre, it will be expedient to clarify the main and intermediate EEC targets in the country of residence and allocate them to the Residency's operational personnel.

In working on the EEC greater use must be made of the practice of exchanging leads, and this presupposes the maintenance of closer contact between Residencies, and also informing the Centre in good time about visits to the USSR, via various channels, of foreign nationals of interest to the work on this target.

In order to improve their reporting and checking, Residencies in member countries must include in their annual reports a special section on the work done on the EEC target and make provision for specific measures with regard to the 'Common Market' in plans for their work in each forthcoming period.

Success can only be achieved in carrying out the set tasks involved in studying a target like the European Economic Community by adopting a comprehensive approach, comprising not just the efforts of individual case officers and Residencies, but of all lines of intelligence, with precise, coordinated action in the work of agencies abroad and the Centre itself.

ALEKSEEV
[GRUSHKO]
[First Deputy Head, FCD]

8

The Socialist International

OUTSIDE the Soviet Bloc the KGB devoted more of its time to the non-Communist left than to Communists. Relations with foreign Communist Parties were the jealously-guarded preserve of the International Department (ID) which, with few exceptions, forbade the KGB to recruit Party members as agents. The ID did, however, use the KGB to channel secret subsidies to most Western Communist Parties. While stationed at the Copenhagen Residency from 1973 to 1978, Oleg Gordievsky was able to witness this process at first hand. The Danish Communist Party was better regarded by the ID than any other in Scandinavia. As well as being loyal to Moscow, it appeared well organised and won a few seats in parliament. Each year the ID used the KGB to transmit to the Danish Party one million kroner (then worth almost £100,000, about 12 per cent of the Party budget) in four quarterly instalments. The money was handed over in person by the Copenhagen Resident to the Danish Party leader, who sometimes requested additional funds to finance election campaigns. As in other countries, the subsidies were known only to a small circle in the Party leadership.

The KGB was also sometimes called in by the ID to help deal with problems which arose in foreign Communist Parties. The main problem in the Danish Party during Gordievsky's time in Copenhagen was the heavy drinking and declining health of the Party leader, Knud Jespersen. In August 1977 the KGB Resident, Mikhail Petrovich Lyubimov, was asked to investigate. Lyubimov reported that Jespersen was terminally ill with cancer, and that, without his knowledge, the Central Committee of the Danish Party was discussing his replacement. A senior official of the ID, V. S. Shaposhnikov, and its desk officer for Denmark, V. S. Savko, then flew to Copenhagen to discuss the succession to Jespersen with Lyubimov and the Soviet ambassador. Shaposhnikov initially favoured the acting Chairman Ib Norlund, a Danish academic, to succeed Jespersen but was eventually persuaded by Lyubimov and the ambassador that Jorgen Jensen, a Communist of working-class origins little known in Moscow, would make a better Party leader. Late in 1977, after Jespersen's death from cancer in a Soviet clinic, he was succeeded by Jensen. The ID's influence on his election remains difficult to assess.

During the 1970s Western Socialist and Social-Democratic Parties moved higher in the Centre's order of priorities. At the beginning of the decade it was impressed by the cooperation between Socialist and Communist Parties in France, Italy, Finland and Japan. Elsewhere, though the Parties usually remained apart, Socialist collaboration with Communists in campaigns against the American presence in Vietnam, the Pinochet dictatorship in Chile, Apartheid in South Africa and other right-wing regimes, persuaded the Kremlin of the potential advantages of Socialist support against the 'Main Adversary' and its allied governments. At the Twenty-Fifth Soviet Party Congress in 1976, Leonid Brezhnev emphasised the importance of establishing closer ties with Western Socialist and Social-Democratic Parties. The theme was enthusiastically taken up by the head of the ID, Boris Ponomarev. 'Positive changes,' he declared, 'are taking place in the social-democratic movement over a wide range of international issues.'[1] He wrote in a major article timed to coincide with the triennial conference of the Socialist International in 1976: 'Constant and larger-scale cooperation between Communists, Socialists and Social-Democrats could become one of the decisive factors for peace and social progress'.[2]

At the 1976 conference the Socialist International underwent what its secretariat described as 'a major overhaul',[3] designed both to raise its profile and to increase its worldwide influence. Ponomarev and the ID greatly exaggerated the significance of the International, seeing it as a watered-down Socialist version of the old highly-centralised Comintern (Communist International) of which he had once been a functionary. A false analogy between the two was suggested by the ID's frequent use of the term 'Sotsintern', an abbreviation not used by the Socialist International itself. At its triennial conference in November 1976 the Socialist International elected as its Chairman the former West German Chancellor, Willy Brandt, whose *Ostpolitik* establishing the first formal ties with Eastern Europe had won him a degree of favour in the Kremlin. In the view of the International Department:

This was not a routine change of leadership, but a serious political step designed to make use of the international prestige, experience and ability of an outstanding leader of contemporary social-democracy in a bid to overcome the differences experienced by the Sotsintern, enhance its prestige and influence throughout the world, and lend its activity greater purposefulness and effectiveness.[4]

The ID's interest in what it called the 'Sotsintern' reflected first and foremost its own preoccupation with competing left-wing ideologies. Most KGB Residencies in Western Europe considered the ID's estimate of the Socialist International's importance greatly inflated. The International's London-based Secretariat had a staff of only twelve and seemed chiefly occupied with organising a triennial conference, twice-yearly council meetings, various special congresses, and the publication of a monthly magazine; it showed little capacity to influence the policy of member parties. General Kryuchkov, however, shared the ID's view of the Sotsintern's significance. In January 1977 a Centre circular to West European Residencies asked for intelligence on a wide range of issues associated with the Socialist International and its member parties. The invitation to the Chilean Communist Party to attend the 1977 Socialist International 'Conference on Future Perspectives for Chile' – the first invitation to a Communist Party since 1922 – was interpreted by both Ponomarev and Kryuchkov as further evidence of the potential for Communist–Socialist collaboration.[5] In August 1977 Kryuchkov issued under his own signature – a certain indication of its importance – a major directive on the Socialist International. Its leaders, he claimed, had been obliged to shift their foreign policy to the left, and now acknowledged 'the positive role of the Soviet Union in developing the process of détente'. As a result, the KGB had 'specific possibilities to exert influence, which will benefit us, on individual activists within the Socialist International'. But there were also pro-NATO elements within the International which Residencies should seek to 'neutralise' by active measures 'exposing, compromising and discrediting their rightist leaders'.

No 644/54   Top Secret
                                                                   Copy No. 2

To Residents (according to list)

Guidance for Work on the Sotsintern

The new correlation of forces on the international stage, the development of the process of détente and far-reaching changes in international circumstances have obliged the leaders of the Socialist International (SI) along with its constituent parties to take the appropriate corrective measures with regard to their political course and tactics.

The latest Congress of the Sotsintern (November 1976) on the whole endorsed the results of the Conference on Security and Cooperation in Europe (CSCE) and expressed its intention of promoting the implementation of the Final Act.

A resolution of the Congress dealing with international détente stated: 'It is possible and necessary to broaden, strengthen and consolidate détente on a wider scale'.

In general terms the Congress took up a constructive position on questions of disarmament. The resolution stated: 'Disarmament and the imposition of controls on armaments and arms deals is of vital importance for the whole world with regard to an escalation of the arms race and a worsening of the economic situation in most countries'.

The Congress spoke out in favour of a prompt conclusion to the talks between the USA and the Soviet Union with the aim of obtaining agreement on a qualitative and quantitative reduction of strategic arms, and underlined the great importance of the talks taking place in Vienna on the mutual reduction of arms and armed forces.

The Congress called for a halt in the spread of nuclear weapons and pointed to general disarmament as the really important goal.

In contradistinction to the period of the 'cold war' the leadership of the Socialist International now refrains from unilateral and over-simplified treatment of the foreign policies of the countries of the socialist community and acknowledges the positive role of the Soviet Union in developing the process of détente.

On the other hand, the Social-Democratic leaders of the important Western European countries which play a leading role in the Sotsintern adhere to their previous line regarding the need to consolidate NATO. They also play a part in the conversion of the EEC into a military-political alliance, and promoting in this connection a demagogic slogan 'Let the Europe of monopolies be transformed into a Europe of workers'. Emigré groupings – the so-called 'parties in exile' – maintain their positions with the support of rightist circles within the Socialist International.

The latest Congress of the Socialist International declared that 'Capitalism and Communism continue to represent the basic forms of oppression in present-day society' and that supposedly 'Socialism is the sole alternative to capitalism and Communism' in the form in which it is represented by Social-Democracy.

Thus the duality of the Social Democratic political stance remains its characteristic feature, just as the Social Democrats are unable to overcome the perennial problem of the gulf between words and deeds.

An analysis of the activities of the new leadership elected at the latest Congress of the Socialist International (BRANDT, CARLSSON)* allows us to

* Bernd Carlsson, Swedish secretary-general of the Socialist International.

conclude that it is making active efforts to develop its new programme. According to BRANDT's way of thinking such a programme must contribute to the modernization of the Socialist International and lead to a consolidation of its organizational structure, a further closing of the ranks in the Social Democratic movement and the dissemination of its ideas and influence throughout the world.

In particular, by widely promoting the theory of 'Democratic Socialism as a Third Way' (in contradistinction to Capitalism and Communism) for the development of Society, the Social Democratic leaders have put forward a 'Socialist Strategy for the Third World' and have launched a campaign to spread their influence in different sections of the national liberation movements in Asia, Africa and Latin America.

Developments within the international communist movement and in particular all that has been termed the 'Euro-communism' have been the objects of keen attention from the leaders of the Sotsintern.

On the subject of the evolution of a series of communist parties in Western Europe, the Social-Democratic leaders would first of all like to see signs of a rebirth of individual Communist Parties in the spirit of Social Democracy, and they are taking steps to prod these parties on to the road of reformism. The question of the normalisation or the development of collaboration with the communist and workers' parties was sidestepped in the Congress resolution. As is well known this question is the subject of deep differences of opinion within the international Social-Democratic movement. Nonetheless the Sotsintern has been compelled of late to refrain from imposing sanctions on those parties which in one form or another have embarked on the road of contacts or collaboration with the Communists.

In spite of this, the Social Democratic leaders are, as previously, following the line of setting off some Communist Parties against others in order to cause a split in the communist movement.

In the final analysis the efforts of the Sotsintern leadership have been directed towards transforming this organization into a body which will lead the fight of the Social Democratic movement in opposing the international Communist movement.

Thus, on the one hand the inherent anti-communist tendency of the Socialist International demands the increased attention of our service to its activities, and on the other hand positive changes which are taking place within the Socialist International provide us with specific possibilities to exert influence, which will benefit us, on individual activists within the Sotsintern and to weaken the results of those of its activities which are prejudicial to the USSR.

The problems enumerated above are being carefully studied at the Centre and in view of their importance it is desirable that Residents should outline their assessment and view of the situation within the Social-Democratic (Socialist) parties in their countries of residence; and they should also give their opinion about the direction which our work should follow with regard to the Sotsintern as a whole.

In the process of studying these problems it would be expedient to consider and evaluate the possibilities open to you for initiating active measures, the purpose of which would be to support and increase the operations of those leading activists and functionaries of the Social Democratic (Socialist) parties and associated organisations, who are speaking out in favour of widening and strengthening the process of détente, curbing the arms race, and in favour of international cooperation.

It would also be desirable to think up ways to neutralize negative aspects in the activities of the Social-Democratic (Socialist) parties in your country of residence and in the Sotsintern as a whole, by exposing, compromising and discrediting their rightist leaders, by pointing out the evils caused to the world-wide Social-Democratic movement by anti-communist and anti-Soviet activities, which are in contradiction to détente and only serve to strengthen reactionary forces.

The Centre would be interested to have ideas from Residencies on how we can exploit to our advantage:

– divergences between the parties of the Sotsintern on individual questions of ideology and tactics (differing approaches to the solution of economic problems, to capitalist monopolies, to the political concept of a 'United Europe', to cooperation with Communist Parties);

– rivalry between the leaders of the German Social-Democrats, the French and Austrian Socialist Parties, the Swedish Social Democratic Workers' Party and the British Labour Party for the leading role in the Socialist International;

– contradictions between the pronouncements and the actual policies of Social-Democracy;

– specific examples of selfish neo-colonialist policies by the social-democrats of the industrially developed countries towards Third World countries etc.

In the light of the foregoing you are asked:

1. To increase the production of reliable intelligence: on specific steps worked out and adopted in closed sessions of Social Democratic party leaders, at sessions of the Sotsintern Bureau, or at meetings of its 'missions' with the leaders of political organizations from the 'Third World' countries; disruptive activities by Social-Democratic parties against the international communist movement, or attempts to make use of 'Euro-communism' to shake the authority of the CPSU and cause a split in the Communist movement; disagreements between parties of the Sotsintern; the attitudes of the various groups of the national liberation movements towards its activities;

2. To report in general terms, using information available to the residency, on

the position of the Social-Democratic party in your country of residence, its influence in the internal and external political course of the country, the contacts and degree of cooperation between bourgeois parties and those of the Sotsintern, the relations with the local Communist Party, its attitude towards the most important international problems, and possible divergencies of view regarding all those problems between various groupings and individual leaders within the party;

3. To submit proposals for a wider and more purposeful exploitation of existing agent-operational resources with a view both to obtaining the necessary intelligence and to implement active measures. In particular, ideas should be submitted on the direction that further work with existing agents and confidential contacts from within the ranks of the Social-Democrats should take; information should be communicated to us which might open the way to us to recruit either as an agent or as a confidential contact other prominent, active figures in the movement, who we can use to penetrate its leading bodies and means of propaganda and information.

Please submit the material when it is received, but in any case not later than 15 October this year.

Answers to paragraph 3 of the present requirement should be addressed to the heads of operational departments.

ALYOSHIN
[KRYUCHKOV]

No 644/54
   '26' VIII 1977

T HE Helsinki conference organised by the Socialist International in April 1978 was regarded by the International Department as 'a milestone' in its history. It was the first devoted solely to disarmament, and the first also to invite an official Soviet delegation. Ponomarev, the delegation leader, attached great importance to his conference speech, later including it in a collection of his eighteen most significant speeches and articles over a forty-year period. He put all the blame for the arms race on 'the NATO countries, chiefly the USA', made a sideswipe at China (for following a policy 'based on the doctrine that another world war is inevitable'), and invited a Socialist International Delegation to Moscow for talks with Brezhnev.[6]

On 7 June 1978 the Centre sent telegrams to a number of Residencies, claiming that Ponomarev's proposal for a dialogue had thrown the International into confusion. The Swedish and Finnish Social-

Democratic Parties led a group welcoming the proposal. The British Labour Party headed another group opposed to any collective response by the Socialist International, and favoured leaving it to member parties to decide individually whether to begin a dialogue with the Soviet Union. Willy Brandt was said to be adopting a 'wait and see attitude'; his Swedish secretary-general, Bernd Carlsson, was alleged to favour Ponomarev's proposal but to be unable to take action without Brandt's approval. The telegram carried a surprisingly high priority. In Copenhagen, where Gordievsky was stationed at the time, the Residency was asked to convey its contents to the Danish Communist Party leadership. A Socialist International delegation, including Carlsson but omitting Brandt, eventually visited Moscow to hold talks with Brezhnev on 1 October 1979. Brezhnev proposed further talks. 'We appreciate the results achieved,' he told the delegation, 'and are prepared to go on developing this kind of relations.'[7]

The dialogue, however, was interrupted by the Soviet invasion of Afghanistan less than three months later, and dealt a further blow by the suppression of Polish Solidarity in 1981. 'Unfortunately,' said a Soviet analyst, 'the leaders of the Socialist International have been affected to a certain extent by the anti-Soviet and anti-Communist campaign launched by the United States.'[8] The London Residency, however, was ordered to remain in contact with the small Socialist International secretariat in London. Until 1983 both the ID representative in London and a KGB officer under diplomatic cover sought regular pretexts to call on the secretary-general. On one occasion they must have surprised him by calling on consecutive days. After the election of the Finn Pentti Vaananen to succeed Carlsson in 1983, however, it was over a year before a KGB officer arranged a meeting with him.

Moscow's favourite Socialist Party during the difficult early 1980s was the Greek Pasok, led by Andreas Papandreou.[9] Both the ID and the Centre saw Pasok's anti-American, anti-nuclear policies as a model for other West European parties to follow. They were delighted when Papandreou won the 1981 election and formed a government supported by the Greek Communist Party. Over the next few years Papandreou received more visits than any other West European leader from the Soviet ambassador, who sought to cultivate him by giving him advance notice of a number of Soviet political initiatives. Papandreou's refusal to join the rest of the European Community in condemning the crushing of Solidarity in 1981 and the Soviet shooting down of KAL 007 in 1983 were interpreted in Moscow as significant diplomatic successes. By the mid-1980s, however, the Centre was disillusioned with Papandreou. It regarded him as a careerist bourgeois nationalist, whose real intention, despite his anti-American rhetoric, was not to take Greece out of NATO but simply to secure more rent for leasing US bases.

№ 473/ПР/54

09.04.85

Резидентам
(по списку)

О работе по Социнтерну

Серьезное обострение международной обстановки и усиление военной опасности, вызванные резко возросшей агрессивностью политики империализма - и прежде всего американского, последовательный миролюбивый курс Советского Союза и развернувшееся особенно в странах Западной Европы широкое антивоенное движение поставили Социалистический интернационал (СИ) перед необходимостью выступить с собственной программой борьбы за мир и разоружение.

В наиболее полном виде такая программа была декларирована на состоявшемся в 1983 году ХУI конгрессе СИ, провозгласившем "самой основной" из задач социал-демократии - "обеспечить выживание человеческого рода". Но сформулирована эта задача как обращение к двум "сверхдержавам" - США и СССР.

Конгресс призвал СССР и США к достижению соглашений по проблемам прекращения гонки вооружений, практически повторив при этом многие конкретные предложения, неоднократно выдвигавшиеся ранее Советским Союзом: об ограничении и сокращении стратегических вооружений, о ядерном оружии в Европе, прекращении производства новых видов оружия массового уничтожения, запрещении химического и биологического оружия, демилитаризации морского дна и космоса, создании безъядерных зон и т.д.

Таким образом, апеллируя одновременно к США и СССР, Социнтерн представляет проблемы мира и войны как результат соперничества

Гордон 1974

During Gordievsky's three years as a PR line officer in London from 1982 to 1985, the Residency received regular telegrams from the Centre containing instructions for active measures designed to influence Socialist International policies on arms control and nuclear disarmament. On 22 February 1983, for example, the Residency was ordered to promote proposals for an SI congress in Australia in April or, if this failed to materialise, an alternative proposal by the Finnish Social-Democratic Party for a meeting of European Socialist leaders. The Centre was anxious that either the congress or the meeting should strengthen support within the International for nuclear-free zones as well as opposition to the NATO deployment of medium range missiles in Europe. A further telegram from the Centre on 30 March instructed the London Residency to employ active measures designed to secure Socialist International backing for a nuclear-free zone in the South Pacific and condemnation of French nuclear tests. On 13 July telegrams to a number of European Residencies announced that Scandinavian and Benelux Social Democratic parties were preparing a joint manifesto on defence policy. Residencies were instructed to exploit all 'reliable possibilities' to exert a 'favourable influence' on the policy document.[10]

In April 1985 the Centre issued its first major directive on the Socialist International for several years. The International, it reported, was divided between supporters of 'Atlantic solidarity' and those genuinely anxious to improve East–West relations. None the less Western Socialist and Social-Democratic Parties had 'considerable political weight and influence' which could be used to support 'a policy of détente'. Residencies were ordered to step up both intelligence collection and active measures against the Socialist International with the double aim of strengthening the Left and exposing 'the subversive activity of Washington and right-wing conservative forces against the Sotsintern and its leaders'. For these aims to be achieved, the KGB would need to make greater use of existing agents and 'confidential contacts' within Socialist parties and to recruit others.

Top Secret
Copy No 1
No 473/PR/54   No 247
09.04.85   To Residents (according to list)

Work on the Sotsintern

Serious exacerbation of the international situation and the intensifying threat of war, evoked by the sharp increase in the aggressiveness of imperialist – above all, American – policy, the consistent peace-promoting line adopted by the Soviet Union, and the broadly based anti-war movement developing especially in West European countries, have combined to confront the Socialist International with the necessity of putting forward its own programme to fight for peace and disarmament.

Such a programme was announced in its most complete form at the 16th SI Congress held in 1983, which declared that the 'most fundamental' task of social democracy was to 'ensure the survival of the human race'. This task was, however, formulated as an appeal to the two 'superpowers' – the USA and the USSR.

The Congress called on the USSR and the USA to reach agreement on the questions of stopping the arms race, virtually repeating many of the specific proposals more than once put forward previously by the Soviet Union: for limiting and reducing strategic weapons; on nuclear weapons in Europe; on stopping production of new kinds of weapons of mass destruction, banning chemical and biological weapons, demilitarisation of the sea-bed and space, and establishing nuclear-free zones, etc.

Thus, by appealing simultaneously to the USA and to the USSR, the Sotsintern is conceiving the problems of war and peace as the result of rivalry between the two powers. Thereby it side-steps the fact that their foreign policies are directly opposed and that there exist two tendencies in world politics, and strives to portray itself as virtually the only consistent champion of the universal cause of peace.

However, even this type of programme did not receive full support from the delegations of all parties represented at the Congress. As the Americans speed up the arms race and implementation of their missile plans in Europe, the disagreements between the parties in the Socialist International on the issues of war and peace are becoming more and more noticeable.

Even formerly active supporters of the well-known NATO 'twin-track decision', the West German social democrats, and also British Labour Party members, while continuing to demonstrate their loyalty to 'Atlantic solidarity', are increasingly filled with a sense of national responsibility and advocating the stepping up the SI's work in dealing with the fundamental problems of peace. In this they have the support of the social democrats of the countries of Northern Europe.

The so-called 'Romance group', containing the French, Italian and Portuguese socialists, is opposing the line taken by the leaders of these parties, known in SI circles as 'radicals'. The leadership of the former, which on many issues adheres to NATO positions, is blocking the 'radicals'' attempts to put forward initiatives on the part of the SI designed to improve relations between East and West.

The divergence of views among SI leaders and their waverings and inconsistency on the key questions of the present day are the result, in the first place, of the actual opportunist nature of the parties which belong to this organisation, and the presence in them of various groupings holding right-wing, centrist and left-wing views.

Many social democratic leaders are, as usual, taking an anti-communist stance. Some of them take an active part in campaigns organised by imperialist groups against the socialist countries and justify the arms race by referring to 'Atlantic solidarity'. Their attacks on communist parties and the countries representing real socialism are mounted under the flag of 'democratic social-ism', thereby misleading the broad masses of workers throughout the world.

External factors too affect the situation in the SI. The American administr-ation and the right-wing conservative governments in the other NATO coun-tries regard the activity of some leaders of the Socialist International as 'prejudicial to Western interests' and have recently been utilizing every opportu-nity, including involvement of their special services, in efforts to consolidate and strengthen the influence of right-wing, pro-American forces in this organis-ation, and exert increasing pressure on individual prominent figures in the social democratic movement. The sustained attack on the SI is being led by the so-called 'International Democratic Union' (IDU) formed in 1983 with the support of President Reagan – an alliance of Western right-wing conservative parties which calls on the social democrats to participate in 'joint opposition to the spread of Marxism'.

However, notwithstanding the disagreements mentioned inside the SI and pressure on it from without, contemporary social democracy continues to carry considerable political weight and influence. Objectively speaking, it makes a definite contribution to the cause of the struggle for peace and disarmament and a return to a policy of détente. Its representatives take part in various fora of supporters of peace and often adopt points of view close to, and sometimes even coinciding with those of the socialist countries.

All this opens up certain possibilities for exerting a positive influence on forming the views of the Sotsintern and the parties belonging to it, on important international issues, and above all on questions of war and peace, thus providing effective assistance in our party's struggle to improve the international situation and stop the arms race.

With this end in mind, you must do your utmost to step up work among the leaders, prominent officials and activists of social democratic and socialist parties in the countries where you are stationed, concentrating your efforts in the following principal sections:

1. In *gathering information* particular attention must be given to clarification of:

– the intentions and specific plans of the Sotsintern and of individual promi-nent figures in it to promote implementation of the measures announced at the 16th SI Congress and designed to check the nuclear arms race;

– the disagreements between the so-called 'radical' wing and the 'Romance group' regarding the role and place of the SI in the system of contemporary international relations, on the issue of the struggle for peace and specific manifestations of their rivalry for the leading role in the organisation;

– policy divergences of the USA and the SI concerning the countries of the socialist community, the activity of the 'radicals' directed towards achieving greater independence for Western Europe, and enhancing the role of the Sotsintern as 'intermediary and arbiter in regulating relations between East and West';

– operations of the American administration, right-wing conservative governments of the other NATO countries and their special services, and political organisations under their control (IDU etc) to consolidate pro-NATO forces inside SI and advance their representatives to leading posts in the organisation.

2. Under *active measures* carry out special operations designed to achieve the following:

– induce the leaders of the SI and the parties belonging to it to increase the effectiveness of their speeches about questions of restraining the arms race, especially in nuclear weapons, preventing the militarisation of space, in the interests of normalisation of the whole range of East–West relations, and returning to detente, and also instigating anti-militarist speeches and action on the part of the international social democrat movement;

– use secret channels and mass information media to convey documents and material to point out the discrepancy between the long-term interests of the USA and those of social democracy, and expose the subversive activity of Washington and right wing conservative forces against the Sotsintern and its leaders;

– oppose the participation of social-democrats in the activities of reactionary forces, directed against the socialist countries, through interference in their internal affairs;

– help to enhance the influence of left-wing and also of moderate groupings which adopt realistic attitudes, in the parties belonging to the SI, and promote advancement of their representatives to leading and influential posts in their parties.

3. *In order to achieve success in dealing with the above tasks relating to information-gathering and carrying out active measures:*

– take steps to make more effective use of and expand the existing operational facilities in the SI bureau, in the headquarters of social democratic and socialist parties in the countries of Western Europe;

– make special efforts to consolidate operational positions in the SI parties which are in power or form part of coalition governments of their countries, bearing in mind the tasks to be achieved not only in the Sotsintern, but also in relation to other issues of international politics;

– step up work in youth organisations of a social democrat persuasion which at times adopt more radical positions than the party, especially among the activists of such organisations who may be of interest in the future.

While operating in the directions mentioned, it is essential at the same time to continue to keep watch on the development of attitudes in the Sotsintern towards other important international questions, to counter the intentions of its leaders to strengthen the influence of social reformism on political developments in the countries of the 'Third World', and on the international communist and workers' movement.

Your ideas and suggestions for utilizing existing operational assets and creating additional ones for working on the Sotsintern, and on the possibility of carrying out active measures both with the resources of your residency and jointly with the Centre and other stations abroad should be set out in the prescribed order.

Please inform the Soviet Ambassador of the content of this instruction.

[illegible signature]

[The front page has the following MS note:
'Comrade Gornov, Feliks and PR Line operational personnel and return to me for briefing the Ambassador'

LAVROV [NIKITENKO]
17.4.85]

OLIVER SIMON   GORDON
19.4   19.4

THE Centre's interest in the Socialist International was undiminished at the beginning of the Gorbachev era. On the evening of 25 March 1985, the London Residency received an urgent telegram asking for British reactions to Gorbachev's meeting with the Consultative Committee of the International. The PR line had no time to contact its limited range of sources. Instead, as sometimes happened, it simply concocted a plausible reply without consulting any source at all.[11]

9

China

THE International Department sinologist, Yuri Tavrosky, aptly described Sino–Soviet relations during the thirty years after the foundation of the People's Republic of China (PRC) in 1949 as falling into two contrasting phases: first, the era of 'eternal friendship' between the world's two largest socialist states; followed from the early 1960s onwards by the era of 'eternal enmity'.[1] The 'Cultural Revolution' launched by Mao Zedong in 1966 made China a more difficult and dangerous country for KGB operations than anywhere else on earth. Soviet contact with Chinese officials was minimal and closely supervised. Recruiting them as agents or 'confidential contacts' became virtually impossible. The spymania and xenophobia of the Red Guards made it difficult for foreigners even to walk round Beijing unmolested. The winding down of the Cultural Revolution at the end of the decade did little to reassure Moscow. Instead, border clashes in Central Asia and at Damansky Island conjured up a nightmare vision of invasion by millions of Chinese armed with nuclear weapons. The dramatic state visit by President Richard Nixon to Beijing in 1972 left behind a more enduring fear of collusion between the People's Republic and the 'Main Adversary'. So long as Mao remained alive, the Kremlin saw no prospect of reconciliation with the PRC.

In the summer of 1976, with Mao's death correctly judged to be imminent, the Politburo set up a high-level commission to assess the future of Sino–Soviet relations. Chaired by the chief Party ideologist, Mikhail Suslov, the commission also included Andri Gromyko, the foreign minister, Dmitri Ustinov, the defence minister, Yuri Andropov, Chairman of the KGB, and Konstantin Chernenko, like Andropov a future General Secretary. Following Mao's death on 9 September, Soviet newspaper attacks on China were suspended until the policy of his successors had clarified itself. KGB Residencies around the world were instructed to report any sign of changed attitudes by Chinese officials to the Soviet Union, and to identify 'deep study' targets among them. To guide them in agent recruitment they were sent a lengthy brief 'On certain national-psychological characteristics of the Chinese, and their evaluation in the context of intelligence work'. Such psychological studies had become a speciality of the Centre. Two years earlier the FCD's main British expert, Mikhail Petrovich Lyubimov, assisted by Kim Philby, had completed a much lengthier classified dissertation entitled 'Special Traits of the British National Character and their Use in Operational Work.'

The brief on Chinese national psychology circulated to foreign Residencies omitted the swear words (in which the Russian language is rich) commonly used to describe the Chinese by Soviet diplomats and intelligence officers. But, even with expletives deleted, it made clear the Centre's loathing for the citizens of the PRC. They were, the brief reported, deeply imbued with an egocentric view of the world; became 'uncontrollable' when their pride was hurt; were 'distinguished by their hot temper, great excitability, and a tendency to sudden changes from one extreme to another'; possessed an innate ability to dissemble which made them 'a nation of actors'; had characters in which, in most cases, 'the negative qualities of perfidiousness, cruelty and anger are inherent'; were 'noted for their spitefulness'; and were indifferent to misfortune and misery in others. Though, for these and other reasons, the Chinese were difficult to recruit and run as agents, however, their very vices offered some operational advantages. Because of their concern with 'loss of face', for example, the Centre believed that 'the use of compromising material is a strong lever to make a Chinese collaborate'.

The FCD's attempt to define Chinese national character bore some resemblance to jaundiced Western stereotypes of the people of Beijing. But, curiously, it took little account of differences between the capital and the rest of China. Most Westerners find the people of South China far more lively and gregarious, as well as a good deal less inscrutable, than the population of the North.

Copy No 1

No 822/PR/62
13 September 1976

To Residents
On certain national-psychological
characteristics of the Chinese, and
their evaluation in the context
of intelligence work.

The increasing scale of intelligence work against China raises more and more the question of how best to set up personal contacts between officers and agents with persons of Chinese nationality. The establishment of personal contacts with the Chinese – citizens of the PRC – appears to be especially complex, as here we come across complicated personalities, who possess the common national psychology of the Chinese but have also been through an intensive ideological and psychological conditioning with the ideas of Mao Tse-tung and anti-Sovietism.*

Experience has shown that success in agent-operational work with persons of Chinese nationality depends to a large extent on the possession by intelligence personnel of a sound knowledge of their national-psychological peculiarities. A sound appreciation of the traits of the Chinese national character is essential for the study of potentially interesting sources of information, for progress towards a satisfactory recruitment, and for agent running.

This report discusses some of the more typical national-psychological characteristics of the Chinese. In making use of these peculiarities it is essential to approach each case individually. It is also essential to remember that Chinese émigrés living in capitalist countries, and those from Taiwan, can have very substantial psychological differences compared with the 'continental' Chinese.

I. *National character*

a. *Behaviour towards 'their own kind' and towards 'the foreign'*

The ethnic self-awareness of the Chinese came into being with the concept of Chinest superiority over the neighbouring 'barbaric' nations, who were supposedly only capable at best of embracing the cultural achievements of the Chinese. This egocentric picture of the world was based on certain objective circumstances – on a comparatively high level of science, technical knowledge, and the culture in China, and on its leading role in this area in ancient times and in the middle ages. This traditional idea of the ethnic superiority of the Chinese over all other peoples continued to exist in the minds of the Chinese right up to the present time. This, in particular, is one of the spiritual sources of the Peking leaders' nationalistic great power policies.

On the other hand a substantial impression was made on the Chinese mentality by the transformation of China in the 19th century into a semi-colony by the intrusion of the capitalist states and the subordination of the country's economy to the interests of imperialism. Irrefutable evidence of the superiority of foreigners in natural science, technology, military matters and so on, developed and strengthened the feeling amongst the Chinese of their own inadequacy and backwardness compared with European countries. In this way, the notion of the greatness of China in this period was overlaid by a feeling of

---

* Soviet transliteration from Chinese corresponds to the traditional English method rather than the modern Pin-Yin (Mao Tse-tung, not Mao Zedong; Teng Hsiao-ping, not Deng Xiaoping; Peking, not Beijing). On transcription systems from Chinese into English and Russian, see Raymond Huang, *Mandarin Pronunciation*, revised edition (Hong Kong, 1981).

inferiority and backwardness, which created amongst some of the Chinese a psychology of dislike and suspicion towards the foreign 'offender'.

The successes which the new China achieved in the first 10 years after the establishment of the PRC, with the direct support of the USSR and other socialist countries, revived and reinforced a feeling of self-confidence and the old traditional idea of the national superiority of the Chinese. A thesis began to appear in propaganda that 'the Chinese could do everything', the population was asked to act critically with regard to the experiences of foreigners, doubts were expressed about the recommendations of Soviet specialists, and so on.

On the basis of this notion of their own exclusivity, the Chinese have developed an exaggerated feeling of national pride which can be classed as the most pronounced characteristic of their national character. The testing of a Chinese nuclear weapon, victories in the border clashes with India (in 1962 and 1965); the pilgrimages to Peking observed in recent years of the leaders of many capitalist states, including the visits of US Presidents 'with outstretched hand' (as stated in the unofficial propaganda from Peking); the existence in 'the third world' of a definite number of countries sympathising with China; economic and technical assistance by the PRC to developing countries and the despatch abroad of Chinese specialists – all this and other facts, strengthened by propaganda, have created a deep impression on the population of the PRC and have helped towards the further consolidation of condescending and at time contemptuous attitudes by the Chinese towards other nations. Chinese officials frequently deal even with Englishmen, Frenchmen and Japanese as representatives of once powerful states who have now lost their influence and who are now acting in a secondary role in international affairs.

The nature of the Chinese attitude to the representatives of other nationalities must necessarily be considered in operational work – in building up leads to the Chinese, in studying them, in arriving at conclusions about the information obtained, in the choice of the recruiting officer, and so on. For example, it will be difficult to expect a Chinese to agree to be recruited by a 'not yet ripe for revolution' African or by a 'reactionary Indian'.

It is worth remembering that notwithstanding their exaggerated feeling of national pride, many Chinese are still suffering to a certain extent from a complex of 'national inferiority' remaining from the last century. Because of this one must in conversations with Chinese weigh up each phrase so as to avoid upsetting their national self-esteem and pride. Any propaganda regarding the achievements of one's own country, if it draws attention to the backwardness of China, in one or another sphere, will only create in a Chinese audience a feeling of antipathy to the speaker.

On the other hand the Chinese greatly value any signs in the foreigner of respect for his nation and of respectful behaviour to himself. Any person interested in their history, culture or art, who knows their customs, not to mention someone with knowledge of the spoken Chinese and especially of their written characters, will receive definite preference to those without these qualities. By way of appreciation of this knowledge and understanding of their traditions and customs the Chinese may forgive a foreigner many things.

b. *Attitude to the 'old' and 'young'*

The Confucian idea of the young respecting the elders is fairly solidly rooted in the minds of the Chinese and is frequently evident in almost unconditional obedience to the authority of 'an elder'. On the surface this is expressed by the acceptance in good faith of everything coming from 'an elder', and in the absence of criticism of anything decreed from above. From this point of view the paradoxical fact of the mockery by the Red Guards during the 'cultural revolution' of the teachers of the higher educational establishments, of party workers, representatives of the administration and so on, appears contradictory to the canons of Chinese thought. In actual fact this was a case where the authority of the elders was sacrificed to a blind obedience to the will of the more highly placed Mao Tse-tung.

It is most important to know that other powerful personalities besides Mao Tse-tung exist for the Chinese. For example, in the recent past these were the Minister of Defence and First Deputy to Mao Tse-tung in the Party hierarchy Lin Piao and Premier Chou En-lai. It is possible that the new Premier Hua kuo-feng will also become a high authority.

So far as foreigners are concerned, the Chinese respect influential political and public figures (even those with right wing views), personalities holding important posts in the commercial world, highly qualified specialists on Chinese matters, etc.

c. *Concepts of reputation and prestige*

The so-called anxiety about 'saving one's face' by any means is extremely typical for the Chinese. To admit openly one's shortcomings or mistakes represents to them a 'loss of face'; it means to do something unworthy in public, to lose the respect of the people around you, or, in the sphere of international relations, to lose one's authority in the eyes of world public opinion. That is why a Chinese can radically change his attitude to one point or another, but will not do this openly and honestly, and will not admit that the previous attitude was incorrect. In a political sense, good examples of this can be seen in the refusal to carry through the 'great leap forward' and the 'peoples communes' in 1958, without admitting the mistakes of such a course, and in the switching of their econimic connections with socialist countries to capitalist states while carrying on with criticism of the West, etc. The Maoists' struggle against dissidents in present day China makes it essential for them to force their opponents to admit their faults publicly because 'loss of face' to a public figure is tantamount to political death.

In all their actions the Chinese strive to appear worthy in the eyes of others. With the aim of 'saving face' they can agree to the most risky and foolhardy actions.

The Chinese cannot stand ridicule, especially from people who are not well known to them, and in situations where their self-esteem and pride are upset they can lost their self-control and become 'uncontrollable'. They are particularly sensitive to ridicule and insults from foreigners, because in these cases there is added to the personal insult the feeling of insult to their national self-esteem and pride.

Since the publication of compromising material about a Chinese (a PRC Embassy employee, for example) threatens him not only with unpleasant consequences but also with 'loss of face', the use of compromising material is a strong lever to make a Chinese collaborate. As experience has shown, 'compromising material' can in the case of a Chinese consist of: meetings with foreigners without special permission from his superiors; any critical statement about his leaders, intimate relations with a woman, especially one of the local women, visits to restaurants and dubious places of entertainment, acceptance of presents or commissions on signing trade contracts; an attempt to buy an expensive article and send it secretly to his relatives, and so on. In the event of a recruitment approach when compromising material is to be used, one must be very tactful, so that the Chinese will not get the impression that the case officer feels any contempt for him for 'losing face'.

The Chinese cannot stand orders and shouts from foreigners. They are distressed when told off or put to shame for their shortcomings, especially in the presence of others, and a direct statement of complaint is interpreted as showing a lack of confidence and a lack of respect. So when pointing out certain shortcomings in the work of a Chinese agent, one must do this in a tactful way, saying for example 'the agent saw no difficulties over fulfilment of the given task, but he simply had no time'. It is not ruled out that this sort of 'compliment' will make the Chinese agent eliminate his shortcomings at the next meeting, in order to 'save face'.

There are cases when a Chinese agent, misunderstanding the task set by the case officer, has as a result not carried it out, and in order 'not to lose face' invents all kinds of excuses which would allow him to preserve his dignity and respect in the case officer's eyes. In order to avoid this, it is advisable, when briefing a Chinese agent, to explain everything very carefully and to be satisfied that he has understood it all correctly. The case officer must keep in mind that owing to the difficulties of the Chinese language his Chinese agent cannot always catch the right meaning of what is said, but does not want to ask again (partly so that the case officer himself will 'not lose face'). It is therefore advisable to repeat important points several times.

II. *Psychological characteristic*

a. *Frame of mind*

When working with Chinese it is necessary to take into account the peculiarities of their frame of mind. The Chinese method of thinking is synthetic and specific. It can definitely be said that the bulk of the Chinese have not been taught to think in an abstract way.

The dogmatic approach to reality developed in Chinese metaphysicism. Metaphysics and dogmatism are specific characteristics both of Confucian thought, on which for centuries generations of Chinese have been educated, and of the 'ideas of Mao Tse-tung' now inculcated in the minds of the population. The Chinese thinkers considered all phenomena in nature and society from a metaphysical point of view, narrowly and as things isolated from one another. Many of the Chinese even now think in postulates, but if life does not confirm the truth of these postulates it does not embarrass them, because whereas the sayings of the sages are valid in perpetuity, deviation from them is only a temporary phenomenon. In exactly the same way the Chinese are able to treat, and do treat, the thoughts of Mao Tse-tung dogmatically.

The predominance of form over contents in the everyday consciousness of the Chinese, the need to 'save face', the long years of subjugation of the Chinese people and the harshness of Confucian precepts have all helped to form in their character duplicity, cunning, evasiveness, adaptability and time-serving. Endless campaigns of 'criticism', 'self-criticism', struggles with various deviations, and purges on all levels have developed these negative qualities to an even greater extent.

Suspicion and disbelief among the Chinese is increasing in the present conditions, because they have got used to the fact that people, things and events look different in the official propaganda to what they really are. This conclusion can be illustrated by Peking proclaiming that many leading party and government officials of the PRC are 'right-wing elements' and 'counter-revolutionaries', and by systematic disinformation of readers concerning the state of the economy of the country, the position of the working masses, etc.

Outward agreement accompanied by internal insubordination is yet another distinctive trait of the Chinese. Outwardly they agree with their interlocutor, wearing a mask of absolute obedience but what they are actually thinking in many cases remains an enigma. This frequently leads the other person astray. Owing to this 'outward agreement' the Chinese frequently succeed in wrapping foreigners round their little finger, both in political matters and in personal relations.

b. *Emotional characteristics and national feelings*

The Chinese are distinguished by their hot temper, great excitability, and a tendency to sudden changes from one extreme to another, for example from an apparent imperturbability, indifference, complacency and level-headedness to violent displays of joy, anger, indignation and protest. In partictular this is precisely the key to the understanding of the spontaneous, uncontrolled mass protests in China which have occurred in the past, as well as in the present, notwithstanding the fact that on the whole the Maoist regime has up till now controlled the situation in the country.

Moreover the Chinese have for centuries developed the ability to restrain themselves and hide their emotions from others behind a mask of cold tranquillity or a polite smile. By common consent, this is a nation of actors; this is why the Chinese, and in particular the representatives of the older generation, are able not only to hide their true feelings, but also to exhibit them very theatrically. A good example of 'theatrical' behaviour by the Chinese has been provided by the behaviour and speeches of the PRC delegates at the United Nations and at other international fora.

Mimicry and gestures often have a special meaning to them. If, for example, during a conversation a Chinese is looking not at the other person but to one side, this may mean that he regards either the other person or the very conversation as unpleasant. In the same way the Chinese can show complete disregard or even contempt for the other person.

In the case of most Chinese the negative qualities of perfidiousness, cruelty and anger are inherent, and were particularly evident at the time of the internal conflicts and anti-Soviet activities in the country (mockery of the party workers and elderly teachers by the Red Guards during the 'cultural revolution', the outrages on wives and children of Soviet diplomats in Peking, the taunting of wounded Soviet soldiers at Damansk). The Chinese are noted for their spitefulness, their unforgiveness, and vindictiveness, especially if they have been offended and as a result feel that they have 'lost face'. In such cases, according to the evidence of many sinologists, the Chinese will stubbornly and insistently, with great patience and self control, search out the appropriate method and time for revenge.

The low value set on the individual human being in old China, with its vast population, has given rise to an indifferent attitude on the part of the Chinese towards the fate of others around them and an indifference to people in trouble. The growing callousness and heartlessness of the Chinese has been aggravated by the endless propaganda campaigns appealing to them not to be scared by death, 'to obliterate your own "ego"' and not to care about the 'trifling' experiences of your near ones. This, however, does not mean that a highly-placed Chinese, for example, would reject medicines in short supply if they would save the life of his father, wife or son.

An inherent feeling of envy has also been noted among the Chinese, both in personal relationships and with regard to the economic, scientific and technical achievements of other countries; as well as efforts to take over the leading position in a collective and to be in authority over others.

Although a sense of humour is inherent to the Chinese, jokes are only permitted amongst persons well acquainted with each other. Not every kind of joke is acceptable in conversations between strangers or those who are not well acquainted, especially if persons with official connections are involved. In such cases it is more in place to make ironical jokes aimed at oneself. A joke of this kind will evoke a reaction from a Chinese, and will give one some idea of his sense of humour and of willingness to communicate.

III. *Traditions, manners, customs and habits*

Many centuries of tradition and customs, which reflect the stable social, cultural and domestic way of life of the Chinese, have to a certain extent been preserved to this day. Even the mass political movements such as the 'cultural revolution', the campaign of the 'struggle with the old four' (tradition, customs, manners and habits) 'as criticised by Confucius and Lin Piao', etc, which have been foisted on them by Mao Tse-tung, could not prevent this. All the Peking regime's efforts in this direction meet with stubborn resistance from the population.

Many sinologists, especially those of Chinese origin, have often remarked in their works on the characteristic ability of their compatriots to 'enjoy life, using very little', on their modesty, moderation, and adaptability, on their satisfaction with their fate in the framework of a guaranteed minimum, and on their belief that even without wealth one can be happy, the most important thing of all being to find happiness in oneself and to acquire the knowledge to enable one to organise one's life.

Since the mass of Chinese are not well to do, they treat money and people with wealth with respect. These characteristics need to be considered when paying our Chinese agents. The amount paid must be in direct relation to the results achieved by the agents. At the same time it is advisable to state specifically why the agent is being materially rewarded. Payment of a fixed and regular reward may have a bad effect, as the case officer paying out without regard to the results achieved will most probably be considered a squanderer and will lose the respect of the Chinese, who are renowned for their rationality and thrift. When paying out money to a Chinese agent one must remember the generally low standard of life in the PRC. Encouragement should be given by moderate payments, as any signs of overspending in the conditions of continuous control and mutual snooping amongst the Chinese, will invariably be noticed by the adversary's special services and can easily compromise the agent. One must also remember this when giving presents to the Chinese, because with the typical overcrowding of the Chinese population and the frequent housing of the employees of their establishments abroad in hostels, they all know exactly who has what.

Notwithstanding that Chinese cooking is well known for its excellence, as well as for the abundance of its dishes, the Chinese are moderate eaters, and especially moderate in the consumption of alcoholic drinks. In general, the Chinese belong to the category of light drinkers. Basing themselves on this very positive trait, the Maoist special services constantly instil in the minds of the representatives of the PRC abroad the idea that Soviet intelligence makes great use of excessive drinking as a means for recruiting their agents. Bearing this in mind, it is unlikely that in the case of the Chinese one can rely on strong drinks to 'loosen their tongues'; it is not likely to happen, as the mere mention of vodka will cause Chinese officials to show immediate fear, to refuse this form of entertainment, and to believe even more strongly in the correctness of the warnings they were given in Peking or in their Embassies.

In our view, it is more sensible to entertain the Chinese with high-class tea and fruit juices, and to offer cakes, sweets and sandwiches containing delicacies. Bearing in mind that the employees of PRC missions abroad eat very modestly, quite apart from the fact that their own produce is in short supply, such a move should give rise to a positive reaction from Chinese. Their alertness vis-à-vis the Soviet official will diminish, and they may even become quite well disposed if a quiet and easy conversation on everyday life can be opened up, without thrusting on them ideological arguments or an intrusive interest in their work. And of course a host can surpass all the expectations of a Chinese if he can 'unexpectedly' produce some Chinese produce (flower tea, arakhis, soya sauce, etc) or articles of Chinese manufacture (a calendar published in the PRC, pottery, an album with landscape views, or a Chinese picture, etc).

Before the 'cultural revolution' the Chinese liked presents, especially on birthdays, holidays (1 October – proclamation of the PRC, the New Year in the lunar calendar, or the Spring Holiday, Holiday of the Lanterns, Beginning of Summer, the Middle of Autumn) and used willingly to accept them from foreigners. But, at the present time, to make use of presents as a means of establishing and strengthening contacts is not always possible because PRC citizens more often than not refuse to accept even small souvenirs from foreigners. This situation is explained by the strict regulation of their lives and the system of spying on each other and control; it is difficult for a Chinese to explain the sudden appearance of a present, and the actual fact of receiving a present from a foreigner is itself regarded as evidence of serious compromise. In view of this, presents can only be given when the particular situation and position of the individual Chinese permits it. In such cases one must make a prior arrangement as to how the Chinese can explain to others the appearance of such gifts, or at least how he can hide them from view. It is quite obvious that large and expensive presents are out of the question in these circumstances.

In order to avoid making mistakes when dealing with the Chinese, it is worth knowing the rules of Chinese etiquette; their observance will make the Chinese feel well disposed to one, but their disregard will create hostility and animosity. For example, a Chinese will take offence at an over familiar greeting if it shows lack of respect. A greeting must be polite. One must not use rude and disrespectful expressions when addressing even strangers if they are of Chinese nationality. It is considered good manners to meet all Chinese visitors politely, and to see them to the door or gate on departure. It is considered tactless during a conversation to begin discussing business straight away. It is better to start the conversation on abstract subjects, such as the health of the visitor and members of his family, and to listen to a Chinese attentively and patiently without interruption.

The Chinese watch very jealously the behaviour of foreigners towards Chinese women. One cannot, for example, take a Chinese woman by the hand, or go arm in arm, or make dubious jokes, or offer compliments about her appearance, as this is not done in China. One can praise a Chinese woman for her business qualities or converse on a neutral subject (about the weather, about cooking or children). Taking into account the new way of life and the more prominent role of the Chinese woman compared with the past, one can now address her as 'comrade'.

In China a mixed marriage is considered a disgrace, not to mention a short-lived affaire between a Chinese woman and a foreigner. Nevertheless, before the beginning of the 'great leap forward' Chinese women were not particularly strict in adhering to this moral code in their relationships with foreigners, if the circumstances permitted. They showed preference for foreigners from some of the more 'revolutionary' countries (in Peking's view) such as Albania.

As far as Chinese men are concerned, there is evidence to show that absence abroad without their wives sometimes causes them to waive their principles and to enter into relationships with foreign women.

When working with Chinese one must also consider their characteristic of solid family ties and origins. Several of Mao Tse-tung's fellow countrymen from the province of Hunan are members of his entourage; and many of the Chinese officials holding important posts were from the same region as Lin Piao and Chou En-lai.

When a Chinese has been persuaded to collaborate, one must remember that he is suffering from a serious psychological blow, because he has agreed 'to work for a foreigner against his own people'. Therefore it is necessary to prove to him convincingly that his help will be utilised in the interests of the Chinese people and that our aim is to re-establish good relations between our two peoples. In connection with this, it is necessary to approach a Chinese very carefully (especially in the first stages of collaboration) when briefing him to obtain intelligence on his own compatriots.

Conclusion

As a result of analysing the national psychological characteristics of the population of the PRC, one is in a position to express some opinions regarding attempts to recruit people of Chinese nationality. The increasingly brutal anti-people and anti-socialist policy of the Peking leadership is creating in the country the growth of opposition attitudes and the appearance of individuals who under specific conditions would be prepared to collaborate with Soviet intelligence on ideological and political grounds. It is particularly from this category of individuals that the most useful agents could be obtained.

In efforts to recruit citizens of the PRC, a materially based approach can also be adopted, although in the present conditions it is difficult to interest a Chinese in material gain as they are not always able to make use of any money or valuable goods which they might obtain from intelligence work.

Definite positive results can be expected as well from the use of a moral and psychological basis for a recruitment attempt, although as a result of the extremely harsh police regime in the PRC, and the total surveillance by the special services of Chinese officials, including those in establishments abroad, the Chinese as a whole lead an ascetic form of life in order to avoid reprisals, and do not deviate from the prescribed rules of behaviour in the presence of compatriots. Nevertheless many cases are known where the Chinese have committed compromising acts. One of the tasks in working against the Chinese is to create the conditions in which they would be prepared to act contrary to the prescribed rules.

Another good and effective method can be by establishing a solid friendly relationship with a Chinese, based on respect for Chinese history, culture, and art, as well as for the individual under study. Such a relationship could in future acquire a confidential nature.

In conclusion, it is necessary to point out that this report has tried to show a stereotype Chinese – a citizen of the PRC, who may appear abroad as an employee of an Embassy or Trade Delegation, on the staff of a Military Attaché, or a Press correspondent, or in the capacity of a specialist or student. It is obvious that much depends on the age of the individual, his level of education, the position he holds, etc, and some modifications may be necessary to this sketch, since the appearance of one psychological tract or another might express itself differently in different persons. One cannot, for example, equate an elderly, well educated, versatile diplomat 'from the school of Chou En-lai', who is acquainted with European culture, with a young Maoist, one of the original Red Guards, who dogmatically follows 'the ideas of Mao Tse-tung'. However, one cannot consider the Chinese as absolutely 'inaccessible'; like the representatives of other nations, they are open to recruitment. As existing experience has shown one can carry out effective work with them.

SEVEROV
[GRUSHKO]

THOUGH Moscow welcomed the disgrace of the so-called 'Gang of Four' and the formal ending of the Cultural Revolution after Mao's death, it remained pessimistic about the prospects for reconciliation with Mao's successors. The Centre's list of intelligence requirements for 1977 concluded that 'the ruling circle in China remains as before, nationalistic, hegemonistic and anti-Soviet'. China, it admitted, was a 'conundrum'. The FCD wanted intelligence on power struggles within the Party leadership and the People's Liberation Army, and on policy changes in the post-Mao era. While it saw no prospect of major improvements in Sino–Soviet relations, it hoped 'for a gradual overhaul of Maoism and for a partial abstention from its more odious aspects', leading to 'a more sober approach' to China's dealings with the Soviet Union.

vk 1   Top Secret
No 551/PR   Copy No 1
14 March 1977

                                           To Residents (according to list)

   We are sending you a plan of requirements for the current year, with a list of the areas of interest to the Centre on the subject of China, both for you to take into account during your work; and also to guide you in the collection of intelligence on the internal situation and on Chinese external policies.

Attachment: as indicated in text, 8 pages, Top Secret, No. 891/PR/52

                             SEVEROV
                             [GRUSHKO]

891/PR/52   Top Secret

Plan of requirements on Chinese subjects for 1977

   In 1977 China entered a complicated internal political situation. The struggle amongst the top Chinese leadership continues, serious economic difficulties are discernible, the material position of the population is deteriorating and un unstable situation remains in many provinces. The practical steps taken by the new government in the internal and external political spheres testify to the fact that the ruling circle in China remains as before nationalistic, hegemonistic and anti-Soviet.

   The present Chinese leadership remains a serious and dangerous adversary of the Soviet Union. The provision of intelligence on Chinese matters remains as before one of the most pressing requirements in the work of Residencies. We ask you to keep the Centre regularly informed (depending on your possibilities) about the situation in China, about major developments in the sphere of Peking's foreign policy and also about the various aspects of mutual relations between the PRC and the country where you are based.

   I. After the death of Mao Tse-tung and the removal of the group of [Mao's

№ 891/ПР/52

План-задание по китайской тематике на 1977 год

В 1977 год Китай вступил в сложной внутриполитической обстановке. Продолжается борьба в высшем китайском руководстве, наблюдаются серьезные экономические трудности, ухудшилось материальное положение населения, остается нестабильным положение во многих провинциях. Практические шаги нового руководства в области внутренней и внешней политики свидетельствуют о том, что правящая верхушка Китая по-прежнему стоит на националистических, гегемонистских, антисоветских позициях.

Нынешнее китайское руководство остается для Советского Союза серьезным и опасным противником. Разведывательное освещение китайской проблематики по-прежнему является одной из наиболее актуальных задач в работе резидентур. Просим Вас, исходя из Ваших возможностей, регулярно информировать Центр о положении в Китае, важнейших событиях в области внешней политики Пекина, а также о различных аспектах двусторонних отношений страны Вашего пребывания с КНР.

I. После смерти МАО Цзэ-дуна и устранения группы ЦЗЯН Цин между ветеранами КПК и выдвиженцами "культурной революции" в руководстве КНР продолжается борьба по многим вопросам внутренней политики. Положение в руководящей верхушке остается нестабильным. Идет борьба за вакантные посты в Политбюро ЦК КПК и других партийных и государственных учреждениях. В процесс формирования нового руководящего ядра вовлечены различные силы - старые партийные и государственные руководители, высшие военачальники, лица, выдвинувшиеся в результате "культурной революции" при поддержке ЦЗЯН Цин и ее сторонников.

Наиболее актуальными в этой связи являются сведения по следующим вопросам:

- Соотношение сил и возможные изменения в составе высшего китайского руководства. Политическая характеристика высших

wife] Chiang Ch'ing the struggle continues between the veterans of the Chinese Communist Party (CCP) and the promoters of the cultural revolution within the Chinese leadership about many aspects of internal policy. The situation amongst the leading clique remains unstable. A struggle is going on for the vacant posts within the Politburo of the Central Committee (CC) of the CCP and in other party and state establishments. Various forces have been drawn into the process of producing a new leading nucleus – old party and state leaders, senior military commanders, figures who were elevated as a result of the 'cultural revolution' with the support of Chiang Ch'ing and her supporters.

In this connection the most pressing need is for information on the following questions:-

– The correlation of forces and possible changes in the make up of the top Chinese leadership. A political assessment of politicians who have now entered the leadership for the first time. The presence and nature of disagreements within the Politburo of the CC of the CCP. The relations between Hua kuo-feng, Yeh Chien-ying and Li Hsien-nien. The political future of the promoters of the 'cultural revolution' (Wu Teh, Ch'en Hsi-Lien, Chi Teng-Kuei, Wang Tung-hsing, Wu Kuei-hsien, Ni Chih-fu and others). The mutual relations between army representatives in the senior leadership of the country (Yeh Chien-ying, Ch'en Hsi-Lien, Li Te-sheng, Hsu Shih-yu, Su Chen-hua);

– Assessment of the consequences of another rehabilitation of TENG Hsiao-p'ing on the balance of power in the leadership, its effect on the internal and foreign policies of China, the attitude to this question of individual members of the Politburo. The probability of the filling of vacancies in the Politburo and in the state apparatus by supporters of Teng Hsiao-p'ing and also by those leaders who fell foul of repression during the years of the 'cultural revolution' (Hsu Hsiang-Ch'ien, Tan Chen-lin, Chen Yun, Li Ching-ch'uan);

– The structure, functions and leading figures of the CCP CC apparatus, and possible changes in it.

II. Incoming intelligence bears witness to the fact that during 1977 important organizational measures are to be expected in China on the basis of which assessments will be made of the purge of the group of Chiang Ch'ing and her supporters, nominations for empty posts in the party and state apparatus will be made, and the basic directions of internal and external policies of the country will be finally determined.

In connection with this the Centre is interested to obtain intelligence on the following questions:-

– The preparations of the Chinese leadership for the holding of a CC plenum, the 11th Congress of the CCP and the session of the VSNP* – (the timing for the holding of these meetings, the agenda and possible resolutions). The scale

* VSNP – All-China Assembly of People's Representatives.

of the purge of the supporters of the 'group of four'. Changes in the distribution of forces within the CCPCC and the state apparatus. The possibility of cadre workers who have received training in the USSR and countries of the Socialist camp acceding to leading posts; the possibility of a return of China to the policy line of the Eighth CCP Congress; the possibility of a review of some of the fundamental ideological and political standpoints of Mao Tse-tung.

III. The main force which is capable of exercising an immediate and decisive effect on the situation in the country is, as usual, the People's Liberation Army of China (PLA). Representatives of the military leadership hold top posts in the party and state hierarchy, they are keeping a watch on the situation and exerting an influence on the development of the situation in the majority of economic centres of the country. The elimination of the 'left' opens the way for the introduction of a widespread modernisation of China's armed forces and for a swifter growth of China's nuclear potential. At the same time, the army leadership is not united in its views. Amongst the commanders of military districts regionalism plays a role, while all the top military commanders belong to different internal army groupings which have developed as a result of historical developments.

Information on the following questions is of significant interest in this respect:–

– Changes in the composition of the leadership of the CC's Military Council, of the Ministry of Defence, of the general staff, of the main political directorate, of the commands of the various arms of service and of the military districts. Facts about the change of position of the most influential military leaders. The political posture of these military leaders, their links and attitude towards the USSR. The composition of different groupings within the army leadership, details about the manifestation of regional or local tendencies amongst the military. New tendencies in the development of military doctrine;

– The numerical strength and composition of the armed forces, their technical level, their deployment, the transfer of military units and formations. Facts about the production and quantity of nuclear weapons, the distribution of missile launchers and missile factories. Information about the development and production of new kinds of mass destruction weapons and means of delivery;

– Scientific research which has a military application;

– The role of the army in the country's political life, the part it plays in economic activity. The use of PLA units for suppressing the population. New developments in mutual relations between the army with the national militia. The scale of the purge in the army. The progress of the campaign for war-preparedness.

IV. The efforts of the Chinese leadership in the field of economic construction are directed at present towards the overcoming of economic difficulties and the solution of a tense situation in various branches of the economy. Work is under way to draw up a new outline for the 5th 5-year plan. In accordance with official announcements by Chinese leaders the basic direction for the development of the country's economy is to be the creation by 1985 of an independent, relatively integral system for industry and for the whole national economy, and by the end of the present century the wholesale modernisation of agriculture, industry, defence, science and technology. An increase in the external trading links of China with foreign countries is planned which is intended to obtain from abroad goods and technology which are essential for an accelerated development of the basic branches of industry, including those related to the build-up of nuclear missile potential.

As a result, intelligence is needed on the following questions:–

– The features of the economic policies of the Chinese leadership at the present stage; signs of a move away from Mao's line on economic development; possible changes in methods and principles of economic construction and in production management; the use of such concepts as material stimuli, profit, a return on capital, and profit and loss accounting. The contents of guidance material on economic questions, the unofficial statements of Chinese representatives on the questions of the country's economic development. The most pressing current questions facing the Chinese leadership in the economic field. The results of the Conference on Industry (due to be held in May 1977) and the results of other conferences on economic problems;

– The level of production in individual branches of industry and agriculture. The development of raw-material resources, the presence of strategic raw materials. Information about the state budget and military expenditure;

– The material situation of the workers. The system of supply of foodstuffs and manufactured goods;

– The orientation of China in its external economic links. The change of balance in external trade with different groups of countries, the significance of external economic links for Chinese development, any change in the geography of external trade, of the pattern of exports and imports. Information about big deals by the PRC with other countries. The possibility of an expansion of trade with Socialist countries;

– Trends in China's trading relations with countries of the 'Third World'. The volume, content and conditions for the provision of economic aid by the PRC to the developing countries. The use by China of external trade channels for obtaining from Western countries military technology, strategic goods, licences and so on.

V. In accordance with incoming intelligence the main efforts of the central leadership of China in its policy towards the provinces are directed towards the stabilisation of the situation, the suppression of the activity of the adherents of the group of Chiang Ch'ing and the stamping out of any signs of separatism and armed outbreaks. During 1977 it is planned to hold meetings of national representatives in the provinces, and to elect the leadership of new revolutionary committees, thereby completing the process of purging the supporters of the 'four' throughout the whole country.

The following questions are the most important in this connection:

– The situation in the leadership of the provincial party committees and revolutionary committees, the existence of fractional struggle. The names of the more promising leaders of the future. The appearance of tendencies towards separatism. The influence of local leaders on industry and agriculture. The contents of speeches by local leaders, and instructions from the Centre sent to the regions. Personnel changes among the leadership instigated by the party and administrative organs in the provinces;

– The attitude of the population towards the various official measures taken by the authorities. Indications and instances of social discontent, the possibility of an organised opposition emerging, the presence of underground organisations. The causes, the scale and the moving forces behind possible anti-governmental outbursts;

– The situation of the population in national autonomous regions, indications of anti-Han feeling and separatist tendencies.

VI. In the assessment of the majority of authoritative sources the forth-coming period will not see any basic changes in China's external policy. Some reduction of the PRC's activity in foreign affairs is to be expected in connection with a new stage of the power struggle amongst the top Peking leaders. Also it is not to be excluded that a number of new developments of a tactical nature may appear in the Chinese leadership's foreign policy.

Amongst the current subjects on which intelligence is required are the following:-

– Instructions given by the MFA and other foreign policy bodies in the PRC (the International Department of the CCPCC, the intelligence service, the Society for Friendship with Abroad) on questions of foreign policy; documents from governmental organisations of third countries containing analyses of the activities of the Chinese leadership in the sphere of foreign policy;

– Changes amongst the Chinese MFA leadership; the influence of staff changes on Chinese foreign policy; the activity of the Chinese representatives in the country where you are; specific examples of practical steps taken by the PRC directed towards the establishment of links with reactionary circles, the scale and spheres of this kind of co-operation;

– The course and results of the visits to the PRC of state and party officials from foreign countries. The results of official and unofficial trips by Chinese leaders to third countries;

– New developments in relations between the PRC and the USA, Japan, the EEC countries and 'Third World' states. Which countries' governments and political circles are most concerned to develop contacts with the PRC? In which regions and countries does Peking have the most durable position and influence?

– Facts about resistance to Chinese attempts to penetrate the countries of the 'Third World', examples of Peking's subversive activity. The most vulnerable areas in Chinese strategy with relation to countries of Asia, Africa and Latin America. New developments in mutual relations between the PRC and the organisation for the non-aligned countries, the Organisation of African Unity (OAU) and the Organisation of American States (OAS);

– Possible changes in the attitude of China towards the settlement of the Middle East crisis, the Palestinian question, the Cyprus problem, the Rhodesia and Angolan questions;

– The solution of the problem of the establishment of diplomatic relations between the PRC and the USA. The practical activity of the sides directed towards the solution of this question. The limits of co-operation between the PRC and the USA in the political, economic and military spheres. The attitude towards the development of links between the PRC and the USA in the various influential circles of Washington and among the Chinese leadership;

– Facts about the use by Peking for subversive purposes of colonies of Chinese émigrés, and of pro-Maoist parties and groups; the size and forms of the help given them by China. Attitude of the pro-Maoists to Peking policy (the utterances of the pro-Maoists leaders, documents of splinter parties and groups on the questions of Chinese internal and external policy).

VII. The political course followed by the Chinese leadership continues to contain all the former elements of anti-Sovietism. In the near future the Chinese leadership does not intend to relinquish anti-Sovietism as the pivot for all its activity. At the same time the departure from the political scene of Mao Tse-tung and of those closest to him creates the pre-requisites for a gradual overhaul of Maoism and for a partial rejection of its more odious aspects. All this, together with the manifestation of pragmatic tendencies, both in the PRC's internal and external policies, does not exclude in the future the possibility of a more sober approach by Peking towards international state relations with the Soviet Union.

In this connection the Centre is interested to obtain concrete intelligence and authoritative assessments on the following questions:–

– The plans and intentions of the Chinese leadership towards the USSR (in the political, ideological and military spheres). Possible tactical steps by Peking directed towards a partial normalisation or a further exacerbation of relations with the USSR. Information about signs of the preparation of provocation operations against the USSR;

– The prerequisites and conditions under which the Chinese leadership might move towards an improvement of relations with the Soviet Union. Character studies of the Chinese leaders who occupy the most flexible standpoints on the question of Soviet/Chinese relations. New developments in the approach of the Chinese leadership to solving the territorial dispute with the USSR. An assessment of the results of the next round of negotiations to settle the frontier issue;

– New developments in the anti-Soviet campaign in China (the course of preparations for war, the fundamental tendencies of both overt and covert propaganda). Concrete information about Peking's activity to undermine the international position of the USSR, concrete information about the resistance to the Soviet Union's line on détente, and about the split in the unity of the socialist community. Facts about the exploitation by the imperialists and other countries of Peking's anti-Sovietism in the interests of their own struggles with the USSR.

A MONG the topics on which the Centre had sought intelligence in its requirements for 1977 was the likelihood of a return to power by the disgraced former General Secretary, Deng Xiaoping. Deng's rehabilitation in August caused mixed feelings in the Centre. Though he was believed to be a pragmatist rather than an ideological fanatic, his past record suggested that he was also strongly anti-Soviet. The Centre concluded that Deng had two main foreign objectives: first, to gain concessions from the United States; second, to make a show of improving relations with the Soviet Union in order to blame Moscow for the lack of real progress. His economic modernisation programme, with its initially heavy dependence on Western technology, experts and capital, caused further distrust in Moscow.

In January 1978 Residents were informed by a circular from the Centre that the Deng regime was on 'a collision course with the USSR', and that the modernisation of Chinese armed forces with Western help presented 'a particular danger'.

Urgent intelligence operations against the PRC, however, were seriously hampered by 'the continuous intensification of the counter-intelligence measures in Peking'. It was therefore necessary to compensate for the weakness of intelligence collection within China itself by stepping up operations against Chinese targets abroad. The

Centre reported that some 'KGB residencies in third countries' had achieved 'positive' results. But 'lack of the essential agent apparatus' remained a severe problem. Residents were admonished for their lack of energy in Line K work and ordered to redouble their efforts.

vk 1   Top Secret
No 16/PR   Copy No 1
12 January 1978

To: Residents

Guidance on measures designed to improve the work against
China from third countries.

The Peking leadership is continuing to act in a hostile manner towards the Soviet Union on the international stage and, at the same time, is hotting up its anti-Soviet campaign inside the country. The recent 11th Congress of the Chinese Communist Party has again emphasised that the policy of struggle with the USSR remains the basic direction of the PRC's foreign policy. Of particular danger to the Soviet Union and the countries of the socialist community are the measures being taken by China aimed at modernising its armed forces, with the assistance of reactionary Western circles.

In these conditions, the foreign political intelligence service has an increasingly important role in gathering intelligence on the processes at work in China, the situation within the Chinese leadership, its specific intentions and plans concerning the Soviet Union, the basic directions of Chinese foreign policy, the present condition, and the possible future potential, of the Chinese armaments industry etc. The requirement for high-quality intelligence on China and the need for timely receipt of such material is increasing.

Great importance is attached to the work of the intelligence service, which is called upon to contribute to the fulfilment of the policy of our Party and of the Soviet Government with regard to China and also to exert appropriate influence on its governing circles and on the situation in the country.

Present conditions require that intelligence work on China is carried out in a particularly versatile and skilful manner so as not to give the Peking leadership a pretext for stirring up anti-Soviet feeling or for laying charges of interference in the internal affairs of the Chinese People's Republic. At the same time more active use must be made of certain new factors affecting operational conditions which have emerged as a result of changes taking place in China, notably the instability within the Chinese leadership, the appearance of uncertainty amongst cadre workers including officials of overseas missions of the Chinese People's

Republic and a certain softening of the hard line on contacts with officials from overseas institutions of the socialist countries.

The continuous intensification of the counter intelligence measures in Peking which is to a significant degree hampering recruitment work among the local population, has imposed on us the necessity for augmenting our Line K intelligence effort by working from positions in third countries.

For the last few years KGB residencies in third countries have carried out positive work in obtaining intelligence and mounting active measures operations against China, and acquiring new agents and confidential contacts.* There are positive examples of the use of foreign agents in work against Chinese citizens. Some experience has been gained in introducing agents who are citizens of third countries† into the People's Republic on either a long or short-term basis.

However neither the present position nor the results obtained from this work are adequate compared with the requirement imposed by the KGB leadership neither do they meet the requirements emanating from the present circumstances.

In recruitment work with Chinese, the use which is being made of agents from among local citizens and other categories of foreigners is unsatisfactory; purposeful work to acquire agents for carrying out the deep-study of targets, agent-recruiters and auxilliary agents is also unsatisfactory. A systematic study of Chinese targets and of those Chinese en poste abroad who might be recruited has not been carried out by residencies. The planting of our agents on Chinese has been inadequate, while technical methods of attack are only rarely used.

The future improvement of the level and efficiency of active measures on China is adversely affected by the lack of the essential agent apparatus. Residencies are not exploiting anything like all the facilities available to operational staff and agents.

In accordance with the instructions of our Service leadership which aim to eliminate the faults mentioned in work on the Line K target and with a view to improving this work in the future, we propose to:

– concentrate the efforts of the Residency on acquiring agents within target institutions in the PRC, from among Chinese citizens on assignments abroad (staff of embassies, missions to international organisations, press representatives and also civil servants in international organisations, experts, post-graduate students and students) – people who are capable of ensuring the supply of secret information on China during the period of their assignment abroad and after their return to the Chinese People's Republic; to regard Chinese missions overseas as essential targets for agent penetration;

– step up the effort to acquire agents and confidential contacts from among foreigners of the following categories:

* Some agents had been recruited in Hong Kong, Singapore and Taiwan.
† Overseas Chinese.

– Chinese émigrés who possess real potential for undertaking the deep study of Chinese missions and for returning to the People's Republic for permanent residence or short visits;

– Chinese citizens of Taiwan, including the staff of Taiwanese overseas missions, journalists, scholars, businessmen and students who are capable of obtaining intelligence on the People's Republic by virtue of their qualities or access; also those who are suitable for sending to the PRC, Taiwan or Hong Kong;

– Sinologists, journalists, representatives of industrial and trading companies, technical experts and scholars having business ties with China; students going to the People's Republic for study with possibilities for future employment in firms dealing with China and persons of other categories. In this connection it is essential to draw your attention to the need to acquire agents who can be used on the illegal front by providing the necessary legitimate cover facilities for illegals who are active on the Chinese target;

– members of pro-Maoist organisations who have kept up their contacts with Chinese;

– raise the level of work with existing Line K agents; investigate more thoroughly the potential of each agent; define ways and means for the most effective use of his services both short and long term; pay particular attention to a more active use of agent-cultivators for studying Chinese citizens en poste abroad and also create the prerequisites for infiltrating agents into China for long or short periods. Work should also be organised in such a way as to transfer to Line N those agents who may be of use in the future as illegals and special agents;

– in order to carry out the deep study of PRC targets it is essential to make provision for:

the exploitation of the contacts between Soviet case officers, agents and cooptees and the officials in Chinese missions and other categories of Chinese on overseas assignments;

the despatch abroad of qualified Soviet agents to work on Line K, their use in the capacity of deep study agents and recruiters and also for planting on the PRC's 'special services';

the creation of the prerequisites and the potential for the mounting of technical operations* in Chinese official and private premises and the use of OT [operational-technical] facilities for the solution of other problems related to Line K work;

* For example, by using eavesdropping devices.

the coordination of action in essential cases with Residencies of friends* (in conformity with existing agreements);

in the field of active measures against the Chinese target attention should be focussed on the preparation and execution of effective operations which might exert influence favourable to us on developments in China, or on the foreign policy of the Chinese People's Republic or on Chinese relations with the country where you are posted.

In the organisation and execution of operational measures relating to China it is essential to observe strictly the precepts of security and secrecy. Each operation must be prepared thoroughly and in detail; and an effective check of the reliability of agents, confidential contacts and candidates for recruitment must be carried out in order to avoid provocations either from the Chinese or from the special services of the imperialist powers.

When making assessments of the activities of the operational staff account must be taken of the extent to which they have participated in work against China and their specific contribution to solving the requirement problems on the Chinese target.

SEVEROV
[GRUSHKO]

D RAMATIC evidence of Sino–American rapprochement during the early months of 1979 further heightened the priority of Line K intelligence. On 1 January the United States and China commenced full diplomatic relations. From 29 January to 4 February Deng made a highly-publicised visit to America. Less than a fortnight after his return, Chinese forces invaded Vietnam, the Soviet Union's Asian ally, and waged for the next month the world's first war between socialist states.

The FCD's review of 1982–3 concluded that 'the strategic policy of the PRC is based on exploiting and, above all, intensifying the conflicts between the two world social systems', led, respectively, by the USA and the USSR. The FCD Plan for 1984 ordered active measures aimed at 'countering the military and political rapprochement between the PRC and the USA and other imperialist countries on an anti-Soviet basis'.[2] Among the active measures intended to worsen Chinese relations with the West of which Gordievsky had personal knowledge were those designed to disrupt Anglo–Chinese negotiations over the future of Hong Kong. By an agreement signed in December 1984 Britain and the PRC agreed that Hong Kong would return to full Chinese sovereignty after

---

* Other Soviet Bloc intelligence services.

the expiry of the British lease on the bulk of the colony in 1997; but that for the next half-century capitalism would continue in Hong Kong under the formula 'one country, two systems'. The KGB sought, without striking success, to disseminate through the media the 'thesis' that weak-kneed Britain had suffered a major humiliation at the hands of the Chinese. To the extent that this argument appealed to the media, it had little need of the KGB to promote it.

At the beginning of the Gorbachev era the KGB continued to find the PRC the most difficult of its major targets to penetrate. A review of operations against China by Directorate T (scientific and technological espionage), one of the FCD's most successful sections, in April 1985 disclosed persistent and serious 'shortcomings'. Of the intelligence collected by Residencies only one per cent concerned China, and its quality was judged 'low'. Residents were informed of these findings during May in a circular which berated them for 'a number of negligences' – chief among them their lack of Chinese contacts, which was described as 'a source of extreme anxiety'.

el.1   No 340
No 11781/X   Secret
07.05.85   Copy No 1

To Residents (according to list)

Work on China

A review was held in April this year by the heads of Service 'X' [FCD Directorate T] on the results of work on China carried out by the central apparatus and stations abroad in the first quarter of 1985. It was noted that notwithstanding certain progress achieved in stepping up work against the PRC, on the whole the standard of effectiveness of the work on the Chinese target done by the Residencies concerned is not meeting the requirements laid down by the heads of our Department for Service 'X'.

Serious shortcomings still persist in matters of organisation and planning of 'K'-Line intelligence activity [operations against China]. Existing plans are, in most instances, based on the use of the limited resources available and not on expanding them to establish positions for agents in Chinese targets.

As a result of a number of negligences, the qualitative and quantitative indices for stations' output of information remain low. The volume of information obtained on the subject of China amounts to less than 1% of the total volume and the material itself does not, in its content, meet the requirements set down for our Service.

The absence, in the majority of Residencies, not only of targets of cultivation for recruitment, but even of operational contact with a prospect of working against the PRC, is a source of extreme anxiety.

Poor use is being made in this respect of existing agents among both Soviet nationals and foreigners. Plans for making use of them on 'K'-line work are frequently not carried out.

Most officers at Residencies do not show the necessary persistence in obtaining footholds in local institutions and organisations which have information about the PRC and which send their officials to China.

In addition to the shortcomings mentioned, it has also been noticed that there is little involvement on the Centre's part in amending the Residencies' plans and making them more specific, a lack of proper checking to see that planned operational measures are carried out, an inadequate standard of training on line 'K' for officers preparing for DZK [long-term foreign postings] and a failure to make proper use of professional and Party influence on staff both in the Residencies and at the Centre.

The following are recommendations for 'X'-lines [scientific and technological intelligence] of Residencies in order to improve the effectiveness of all intelligence activity directed against the PRC:

– concentrate your efforts on solving one of the main intelligence tasks, namely recruiting Chinese nationals from among scientists, students, trainees, posted abroad, officials of international organisations and officials of PRC missions in third countries etc;

– pay more attention to working on local nationals with prospects of success in the role of spotters and recruiters among Chinese nationals;

– make more active use of the Residency's existing agent network for work on the Chinese target;

– utilize agents among our Soviet nationals more effectively and to greater purpose, not only for working on persons of Chinese nationality, but also on local nationals who have facilities for obtaining material on China;

– organize effective and objective cooperation with other lines at the Residency in order to concentrate your efforts on studying and cultivating specific sinological centres in your country of residence;

– take energetic steps to increase your output of material on Chinese questions (Guideline No 9143/X of 22.05.84);

– make use of existing facilities and find new ones for preparing and carrying out active measures against the PRC;

– raise the level of personal responsibility of operational personnel for carrying out the 'K' line tasks set for them;

In order to step up work against the PRC, it is to become the practice for operational personnel responsible for organising such work at Residencies and also the heads of Line 'X' at Residencies to give an account of themselves to the Party and to the heads of our Service.

We hope that 'X'-line operational personnel share the concern felt by the heads of our Service, as mentioned in this letter, over the present state of work on the PRC and will put the necessary effort into improving it and obtaining solid results.

DAVIDOV

[V. N. LAZIN]

[Head of British Department, FCD Directorate T]

10

New Thinking?

THE Centre's assessment of the West between 1985 and the abortive coup of 1991 showed striking elements of both continuity and change with the attitudes revealed by the documents in previous chapters. The 'New Thinking' of the Gorbachev era and the end of the Cold War softened some traditional conspiracy theories. The old suspicions, however, ran very deep. They continued to colour the thinking both of the Centre and of the International Department which helped to determine the KGB's main foreign priorities. In an interview with Christopher Andrew in Moscow in December 1990, Valentin Mikhailovich Falin, the head of the ID, claimed to have documentary proof that:

> from 1943, no later, in both London and Washington, the idea was already being weighed up of the possibility of terminating the coalition with the Soviet Union and reaching an accord with Nazi Germany, or with the Nazi Generals, on the question of waging a joint war against the Soviet Union.

Thanks to Soviet Intelligence, according to Falin, Stalin was 'in the know' about much that the USA and Britain thought they had concealed from him: 'Therefore when we talk about Stalin's distrust with regard to Churchill, at a certain stage towards those surrounding Roosevelt, not so much towards Roosevelt himself, we should pay attention to the fact that he based this mistrust on a very precise knowledge of specific facts.'

Falin still believes that this 'precise' intelligence demonstrated that the United States dropped the atomic bomb on Hiroshima and Nagasaki less to defeat Japan than to intimidate the Soviet Union:

> It was known to the [Soviet] leadership why the order was precisely given to drop that bomb a few hours before we declared war on Japan. And we knew precisely why, and what the United States wanted to obtain by this act. This was not so much the last act, or one of the

last acts, of the hot war as one of the striking events of the next war, which was already the Cold War.[1]

Similar conspiracy theories continued to colour the thinking of the Centre leadership as well as that of the ID. Kryuchkov's interpretation of the development of the Cold War remains strikingly similar to that of his mentor Yuri Andropov. In the early 1960s, he argues, Western intelligence services, after the failure of 'more dangerous forms of struggle', embarked on a programme of 'ideological subversion' aimed at 'emasculating the [USSR] and eroding its political and ideological foundations'.[2]

The East–West dialogue inaugurated by Gorbachev, however, caused the Centre to revise some of its traditional views. Kryuchkov gave his valedictory address as head of the FCD, entitled 'An Objective View of the World', at a conference in the Soviet Foreign Ministry in the summer of 1988. It was a remarkable mixture of the old and new thinking which bore witness to the extent of the changes in the FCD's assessment of the West since the most alarmist phase of Operation RYAN only five years earlier. In general, he took an optimistic view. Progress towards disarmament, in particular 'the removal of the threat of major military conflict', had become a 'fully realisable' goal. Kryuchkov also added a note of self-criticism about the KGB's – and his – traditional view of the West. In interpreting the business world in capitalist countries, he confessed, 'we have always been submerged in clichés and stereotypes . . . Unless we have an objective view of the world, seeing it unadorned and free of clichés and stereotyped ideas, all claims about the effectiveness of our foreign policy operations will be nothing but empty words.' Kryuchkov's address made clear, however, that the old suspicions and conspiracy theories still lurked at the back of his mind. Without mentioning Operation RYAN by name, he attempted a retrospective justification of it: 'Many of [the FCD's] former responsibilities have not been removed from the agenda. The principal one of these is not to overlook the immediate danger of nuclear conflict being unleashed.'

Kryuchkov also made a traditional attack on Western 'and above all American' intelligence services:

These have retained in full measure their role of a shock detachment of right-wing forces, one of the sharp instruments of the imperialist 'brake mechanism' on the road to improvement of the international position. It is no chance occurrence that in the West the wide-ranging campaign of spy mania and brutal provocation employed against Soviet institutions abroad has not lost its impetus.

In the first half of 1988 alone, he claimed, there had been over 900 'provocation operations' against Soviet missions and nationals.

Kryuchkov's decision to publish his speech in October 1988, however, was striking evidence of the new intellectual climate created by glasnost.

Mezhdunarodnaya Zhizn, October 1988

AN OBJECTIVE VIEW OF THE WORLD
Deputy Chairman of the KGB V. A. KRYUCHKOV

Our rapidly changing world with its immense variety and diversity and its manifold different aspects demands a profoundly scientific approach towards assessment of everything which is going on around us. Only a new kind of political thought and an objective, unprejudiced view of world development will enable us to keep in step with the times and not fall behind in attaining important practical results, and it appears that in this respect there is much that is new and useful in E. A. Shevardnadze's deeply interesting and substantial report.

All aspects of life of our Soviet society are involved in revolutionary renewal and its most important field is foreign policy. Perestroika and the vigorous line adopted in Soviet foreign policy have yielded their first concrete results. It is possible to state, without straining credibility, that disarmament, achievement of a non-nuclear world and removal of the threat of major military conflict are not just Utopian, but a fully realizable category of ideal.

Statesmen, public figures, but also ordinary people abroad are to-day reflecting on the processes taking place in our country. The 'enemy image', the image of the Soviet state as a 'totalitarian' 'half-civilized' society, is being eroded and our ideological and political opponents are recognizing the profound nature of our reforms and their beneficial effort on foreign policy.

The West's reaction is not unanimous. There are forces in both political, industrial and social circles which reckon that it is easier to deal with to-day's Soviet Union in solving international problems and those representing this point of view welcome the changes in our country and are watching them hopefully.

There are however also those who do not conceal their anxiety over the prospect of the USSR strengthening its influence and authority. Interviewed by the magazine *Newsweek* in October 1987, the head of the CIA, Webster, said straight out:

Hearing of what is going on in the Soviet Union, our politicians would like to know in the first place whether these changes are real . . . When we look into the matter, we find ourselves faced with a difficult question: if what is taking place is genuine in its nature, then do we wish Gorbachev to be attended by success?

Many among influential people in that quarter would answer this question in the negative.

There is significant inconsistency and discrepancy in regard to further steps towards disarmament. On the one hand, the Agreement on intermediate and shorter range missiles obviously marked a beginning in the process of laying the foundations for demilitarizing Soviet–American relations. On the other hand, right-wing circles in NATO countries are perceiving with alarm the increasing popularity and influence of the Soviet peace initiatives. They do not hide their uneasiness over the fact that this may lead to irreversible shifts in Western social consciousness in favour of the USSR. Hence the efforts to undermine confidence in the Soviet proposals on disarmament. It is claimed that 'perestroika' in the USSR will not lead to a change in the nature of its society or renunciation of aims which are hostile to the West. It is true that analysis has shown that this type of propaganda is encountering ever greater difficulties because our peace initiatives and the practical steps we have taken are capturing the minds of broad strata of the international community and becoming a real force.

Not so very long ago the question was raised as to whether it was worth making further efforts for disarmament with the present American administration? Time has confirmed the rightness of the policy adopted: there are solid results and something has been created which will have its own positive role to play in regard to the future president. There is a general feeling among the American public that they are tired of the high level of expenditure on armaments. Naturally, it is being asked whether the conservative cycle in American politics has come to an end? In our view there are clear signs of this.

Taking a sober view of the situation, we must not overlook the attempts of NATO countries to compensate for the elimination of medium and shorter range missiles and the considerable reductions projected in strategic offensive weapons. The world community must be alerted to these plans and not allow the West to circumvent us.

It is exceptionally important to see the world as it is, to assess our own position and our own deductions truthfully, objectively and self-critically, and strive to reinforce international security based on a strict balance of interests. A number of Party documents and material from the 19th Party Conference have provided us with a new methodology for looking at the world and new ideas for resolving the contradictions arising in world development.

In the past we often tended to adopt a mean in our view of the world, employing our own peculiar foreign policy 'yardstick'. We were not good at distinguishing between the social and political strata of contemporary capitalist society and the many shades and currents in the dispositions of political forces in a region or individual country. Our initiatives and the practical steps we took were often of a general nature, insufficiently differentiated and without specific aim, and we did not take into account the real position or the nuances in the attitudes of our opposite numbers abroad.

Finally, it is simpler and at first glance natural to take the majority view. But it is a much more complicated matter to perceive at the time a prospective minority emerging. Let us take the main problem – the problem of war and peace. When we engaged ourselves actively in disarmament, it seemed as though the whole of America, apart from a few judicious-minded people, would not support this move. But now it is evident that those who admit the possibility of conflict in which all available resources would be used are in the minority, and the majority are people who are confused by propaganda, and they are not thinking about war. We did not at once discern the potential of the anti-war movement, nor did we reach an objective assessment all at once of the potential of the 'greens'; indeed, we ourselves have not remained unaffected by their ideas.

We are not good at studying and getting to know people, and we pay little attention to developing contacts with politicians and other public figures abroad and our efforts to win their minds are slack and lacking in perseverance. Obviously, it is easier and simpler to make enemies than to win allies.

It is now essential to devote our maximum efforts to impartial study of representatives of the business world, above all in the developed capitalist countries, and here we have always been submerged in clichés and stereotypes and it now appears that in this vitally important matter for the Soviet State we must adopt an energetic role, with united efforts from all departments concerned with foreign policy and economics.

The processes of military integration in Western Europe reflect its aspiration towards greater independence in resolving military and political questions. It is time to consider seriously the political consequences entailed by uniting the internal markets of the countries of Western Europe in a single market in 1992. We must look reality in the face and admit that this will indeed ensure higher economic indices for these countries.

The world of to-day is a tissue of discrepancies. On the one hand, the process of polarization of political and economic forces continues with the principal centres of capitalism developing in the United States, Western Europe and Japan. On the other hand, intercommunication and mutual dependence are leading to a confusion of interests, giving rise to unprecedented diversity where demarcation and interaction displace and complement one another. This is a dialectic, but many of the nuances and trends in the process are unfortunately not discerned by us.

The facts of life convince us that success is only possible where large-scale policies are based on reality and precise reference points. The policy we announced more than two years ago of national reconciliation in Afghanistan enables us to look forward to the future with hope. In the long dark tunnel a shaft of light has appeared, showing ways of settling the Afghan problem which will be in line with the interests of the people of that country.

Unless we have an objective view of the world, seeing it unadorned and free of clichés and stereotyped ideas, all claims about the effectiveness of our foreign policy operations will be nothing but empty words.

One factor of no small importance in the international situation is the activity of the opponent's intelligence services, and above all the American intelligence community. These have retained in full measure their role of a shock detachment of right-wing forces, one of the sharp instruments of the imperialist 'brake mechanism' on the road to improvement of the international position. It is no chance occurrence that in the West the wide-ranging campaign of spy mania and brutal provocation employed against Soviet institutions abroad has not lost its impetus.

In a number of countries tension continues to be maintained as before around Soviet missions and in regard to Soviet nationals. In the first half of this year more than 900 provocation operations have been mounted against them, including anti-Soviet demonstrations, shooting, explosions, and so on. There were six attempted murders, three people were killed and three wounded.

The whole potential of the CIA and other intelligence services is aimed above all at agent penetration into key Soviet installations such as the Ministry of Defence, the KGB, the Ministry of Foreign Affairs and others. In the last three years the state security authorities have unmasked several dozen agents of foreign intelligence services who have done serious damage to our country, and cases of direct approaches with a view to recruiting Soviet citizens have become more frequent in recent years. Furthermore, these facts have been mentioned in the USA and in a number of other capitalist and developing countries.

With the coming of 'perestroika' in the USSR, the American intelligence service has been briefed, equally with pursuit of its traditional information-gathering tasks in the area of foreign policy and military strategy, to obtain information on the processes taking place in our country. It is interested in the mood of the population, its attitude to 'perestroika', the activity of unofficial organizations, especially among young people, and so on. At the centre of interest are international relations. In the opinion of important Western experts whose knowledge of our country is not to be denied, this is the area where the most serious trouble might develop for the Soviet State.

Generally speaking, the adversary's activity is not being reduced, and this means that practical measures must be taken in advance to increase the vigilance and the sense of responsibility and civic duty of Soviet citizens. Democratization and 'glasnost' are the motive force of 'perestroika' and we shall not win through without them. This, however, presupposes order and discipline and strict observance of the law. Now, when socialist pluralism of views is being encouraged at home, Soviet nationals abroad feel freer and less restricted. It is difficult for the intelligence services to 'catch' anyone making critical, so-called dissident statements regarding Soviet conditions and they are therefore endeavouring to find people with moral failings.

It is important that there should be an atmosphere of truthfulness and openness in our institutions abroad, in which those who work there are not afraid to talk openly about their mistakes and perhaps even about serious infringements. Much can be forgiven for the sake of truth, even if someone has committed a serious error.

The changes taking place in our country and their effect on the international situation have raised the question of 'perestroika' and other measures to improve the work of the state security authorities, especially the external services. The range of their responsibilities is being more precisely defined and also expanded. A more profound and sober approach is being developed in assessing the activity of the intelligence services and in cases where this is essential, their forms and methods of operation are being revised.

These are not simple problems and many of their former responsibilities have not been removed from the agenda. The principal one of these is not to overlook the immediate danger of nuclear conflict being unleashed. It is particularly important not to miss an enemy breakthrough in military technology, producing what are in principle new forms of weapon, enabling him to upset strategic parity and attain superiority over the USSR. Work is proceeding, for instance, in the USA on production of highly dangerous forms of weapon, and this is outside the generally known programme of the SDI.

Soviet security personnel are carrying on a complex and relentless struggle. We attach great importance to enhancing the role of the human factor and developing in our personnel the ability to understand and reason with new political categories. We are making a critical assessment and reviewing individual periods in the history of the state security authorities. Rigid observance of the law, an objective light shed on the past, and truth and nothing but the truth are to be the basis of training of present and future generations of security personnel.

I should like to emphasize that we value highly the team effort of the heads of the Ministry of Foreign Affairs to implement our Party's innovatory line in foreign policy. Energy, initiative, purposefulness and consistency in the pursuit of their aims are characteristic of Soviet diplomats. May I be allowed to wish the staff of the Foreign Ministry of the USSR fresh success on the course they are pursuing.

O NCE Chairman of the KGB, Kryuchkov's attitude to the West appeared to mellow as he embarked on an unprecedented public relations campaign. 'The KGB', he declared, 'should have an image not only in our country but worldwide which is consistent with the noble goals I believe we are pursuing in our work.'[3] Kryuchkov became the first KGB Chairman to court Western as well as Soviet public opinion in a series of press conferences and interviews.[4] In January 1989 he made a spectacular break with tradition by receiving the US Ambassador in his office. Early in 1990 the KGB opened a Public Relations Centre in Moscow. Later in the year it announced the election of the first Miss KGB, Katya Mayorova, who, according to a Soviet interviewer, wears a bullet-proof vest 'like a Pierre Cardin model' but is able to deliver a powerful karate kick 'to her enemy's head'.[5]

Kryuchkov did not, as his predecessors surely would have done, blame Western subversion for the disintegration of the Soviet Bloc in 1989. Instead, in a continuing attempt to gain international respectability for the KGB, he called for East–West intelligence collaboration 'in the drive against terrorism and drug trafficking'.[6] On one occasion he even referred to the CIA as 'colleagues': 'We understand their desire to learn as much as possible about us.'[7] But though warnings of the 'secret war' were frequently muted during Kryuchkov's public relations campaign, they did not disappear. It was, he declared in December 1989, primarily the operations of Western intelligence services which prevented 'the final burial of the Cold War'.[8]

As the Soviet Union's economic problems worsened and separatist movements strengthened during 1990, the Centre's traditional suspicions of the 'Main Adversary' and its allies revived. Unlike previous KGB chairmen, Kryuchkov did not claim that imperialist plots were the principal cause of Soviet ills. 'The main sources of our trouble, in the KGB's view,' he declared, 'are to be found inside the country.'[9] But he accused the CIA and other Western intelligence services of promoting 'anti-socialist' and separatist groups as part of their continuing 'secret war against the Soviet state'.[10] And he publicly revived the earlier KGB theory, set out in a top secret circular signed by Viktor Grushko in 1985, of a Western plot, 'akin to economic sabotage', to 'deliver impure and sometimes infected grain, as well as products with an above-average level of radioactivity or containing harmful chemical admixtures'.[11] In February 1991 Grushko, newly promoted as First Deputy Chairman of the KGB, denounced a plot by Western banks to undermine the rouble: a conspiracy theory which seduced the new Soviet Prime Minister, Valentin Pavlov.[12]

The fullest public version of the Centre's theory of a vast American plot to subvert the Soviet Union was set out in a remarkable speech in April 1991 to the conservative *Soyuz* (Union) group of People's Deputies by Nikolai Sergeevich Leonov, head of KGB assessments, formerly deputy head of the FCD responsible for operations in North and South America. In it he revealed, with unprecedented frankness, the assessment of American policy being given to 'the leadership of our country' by the KGB.

Sovetskaya Rossia, 26 April 1991

VULTURES SWOOPING OVER THE SOVIET UNION

Late last week the all-Union association of deputies, *Soyuz*, held a congress in Moscow. N. Leonov, head of the KGB assessment department, addressed it. We offer you an abridged version of his speech.

I have worked for over 25 years in intelligence, many of them in the assessment department. Believe me, our country will have many enemies, both the self-imposed provincial khans and foreign strategists who fear that if our great state, with its vast territory and unmatched resources, its large population and level of education, organises its life effectively, it will quickly develop into a truly great power.

The US does not need a great power, socialist or capitalist or monarchist, on the territory of the Soviet Union. During the Potsdam conference after the end of World War II, Americans advanced plans for dividing Germany into several states. They also suggested plans for dividing China in 1945. Now it is the turn of the Soviet Union. The US likes to operate on the weak and ailing.

I do not want to revive the enemy image; I am telling you the truth. Listen to Radio Liberty, financed by the US Congress, for just one day. Its programmes are brimming over with malice aimed at our united state; they are designed to incite our people to hate each other. Their programmes for Azerbaijan are setting local people against Armenians, while the adjacent studio is trying to do the same in Armenian. And the all-pervading tune is the incitement of hatred for Russians.

Read the articles and speeches of Zbigniew Brzezinsky, former national security adviser to the US President, and you will see that his goal is to eliminate the Soviet Union as a united state.

During his latest visit to Moscow, the Secretary of State James Baker hinted that the US recognise the USSR within the 1933 borders, when we established diplomatic relations. What does this mean? The matter concerns not only the Baltics, whose secession the US has always advocated. For many long years the US financed the 'embassies' of Lithuania, Latvia and Estonia in Washington. A return to the 1933 borders would mean a review of the Soviet–Finnish border, something which is being advocated in that country, too, a review of borders in the west of the Ukraine and Byelorussia and with Romania, a secession of a half of Sakhalin and the Kuriles. Actually, it is a programme for dissecting the Soviet Union.

Two groups of vultures, domestic and foreign ones, are swooping over the weakened Soviet Union. Moreover, they tend to get together. I want to tell you one simple truth. For a long time the official US representatives shirked the Baltics. They were afraid that an unwarranted contact with local governments would compromise their position of non-recognition of the unification of these republics with the Soviet Union. Today it is impossible to check the mass influx of Americans, including official representatives, into that region.

The situation has taken an alarming turn. One American citizen, a former Green Berets captain, instructed Sajudis [Lithuanian nationalist] groups who guard the building of the Supreme Soviet in Vilnius. He also taught them to make explosive devices and trained them in street fighting. The West is printing banknotes of the secessionist government and supplies it with communication, multiplication and other equipment.

The West is enamoured with our heralds of secessionism, who are given tit-bits in the form of highly-paid lectures and the highest possible royalties for articles and interviews. In return, they only have to denounce their homeland and call for its disintegration. Nobody in the West will pay you for your beautiful eyes. Calculating political touts will only pay for jobs which they order.

I would like to remind you that American Congressmen are not allowed to accept presents worth over 50 dollars, they must not allow their fare or hotel accommodation to be paid for, or take presents in any other form. This is an inalienable part of their ethics, and its violation can mean the loss of mandate. Under US laws any political or public organisation that has set itself the aim of breaking the integrity of the US in any form will be proclaimed unconstitutional and its fate will be settled in court. The Americans are encouraging us to do things which they prohibit at home.

In the past few years we have noticed that Western radio stations, newspapers and magazines have been giving more space and air time to former and current Soviet political and public figures. It is difficult to believe that the average American, Briton or German would be interested in the next verbal flight of our politicians. In this case their magazines and newspapers serve as a mirror to send rays of hatred into the eyes of our people. These interviews are taken in order to legalise payment to the few chosen and to pour oil on the flames of our internal discontent. We are the children of our homeland and should not invite foreigners to be our judges and patrons.

The KGB has been informing the leadership of the country about this in time and detail. We would not want a repetition of the tragic situation before the Great Patriotic War against Germany, when Soviet intelligence warned about the imminent attack of the Nazi Germany but Stalin rejected this information as wrong and even provocative. You know what this mistake cost us.

Any process of state unification is objectively akin to progress. Bismark, who united Germany 'by sword and fire' in the past century, created the foundations for the growth and prosperity of the state and the nation. The Italian King Victor Emmanuel and Garibaldi, acting each in his field, created a united state.

For this country to progress, we need a vast economic space, a common market, a stable monetary system and reliable law and order. Bourgeoisie has always sought these elements. Only people with feudal mentality called for disintegration, national alienation and isolation.

History will not forgive us for passivity and inaction. It will judge us by our actions and their consequences.

Aɴ even clearer indication of the influence of traditional conspiracy theories on the KGB's assessment of the 'Main Adversary' was contained in a speech by Kryuchkov to a closed session of the Supreme Soviet on 17 June 1991.[13] In order to justify the KGB's theory of a deep-laid plot by the CIA and other Western intelligence services to sabotage the Soviet economy, he quoted from a highly-classified KGB report sent to 'the country's top leadership' fourteen years before. The document was drawn up by the FCD at a time when it was headed by Kryuchkov, but considered so important that it carried the signature of Yuri Andropov, then KGB Chairman.

Novosti report

Chairman of the KGB Vladimir KRYUCHKOV said: '. . . Integration processes are taking place throughout the world. They are dictated by the times in which we live, and there is no other option. But in this country there is an active trend towards disintegration. Of course, the reasons for the current sorry state of affairs are primarily domestic. But it has to be mentioned that certain external forces are hard at work in this respect. Here I would like to make a small digression and draw your attention to a very interesting document that in 1977 was sent to the country's top leadership by the KGB external intelligence department [FCD]. It is now possible to reveal the contents of this document, since there is no possible danger to its source. It was stamped "of particular importance", and is dated January 24, 1977. It is addressed to the CPSU [Soviet Communist Party] Central Committee, and titled "On CIA plans to recruit agents among Soviet citizens".'

Kryuchkov then read the brief document out loud. It was signed by Yuri Andropov, and stated that:

'. . . today American intelligence is planning to recruit agents among Soviet citizens, train them and then advance them into administrative positions within Soviet politics, the economy and science. The CIA has drafted a programme to subject agents to individual instruction in espionage techniques and also intensive political and ideological brainwashing. In addition, one of the most important aspects of such training is instruction in management of the economy at the highest level. American intelligence plans, deliberately and regardless of cost, to search out people whose personal character and professional abilities make them likely to rise to administrative posts within the state bureaucracy, so that they can carry out the tasks assigned to them by their handlers. Also, the CIA intends that individual and isolated agents carrying out policies of sabotage in the economy and distortion of superiors' instructions will be coordinated from a single centre within the US intelligence system. The CIA believes that such deliberate action by agents will enable certain internal political difficulties to be created for the Soviet Union, retard development of its economy and channel its scientific research into dead-ends. Drawing up these plans, American intelligence believes that increasing contacts between the Soviet Union and the West create a favourable environment for them to be put into effect. According to statements by American intelligence personnel working directly with agents recruited among Soviet citizens, the current policy of the US special services will promote severe changes in various aspects of our society . . .'

Kryuchkov continued: 'Today also, in the era of the new political thinking, the West has no intention of ceasing such covert activities, which have already produced certain results.'

K RYUCHKOV was a conspirator as well as a conspiracy theorist. By the time he revived the FCD's fourteen-year-old warning of a vast and improbable CIA plot to sabotage the Soviet administration, economy and science, Kryuchkov was himself deeply involved in a plot against the Soviet President. On 19 August 1991 he was one of the prime movers of a plot to topple Gorbachev. Despite his addiction to conspiracy theory, Kryuchkov proved an incompetent conspirator. The coup ended with his own arrest on a charge of treason and a purge of the KGB old guard. So far from shoring up the Communist order, Kryuchkov had hastened its collapse.

Appendix A

The KGB Files and Archives

THE KGB's approach to documents and papers is extremely methodical. Everything is recorded on files which are maintained in accordance with a large number of strict bureaucratic rules drawn up by the Archives Department. In order to open a file, a case officer has first to obtain a special form (equivalent in size to an A4 sheet of paper) from the office safe. He then completes it as in the following example:

STATEMENT OF AUTHORISATION

I approve [space for signature of department chief]

I, senior authorised operational officer of the Second Department of Directorate K of the First Chief Directorate of the Committee of State Security of the USSR, Major IVANOV Pyotr Sidorovich, have taken the decision on 15 February 1985, on the grounds of operational requirements, to open an urgent cultivation file on 'MANFRED', N [blank space for file number], volume 1.

Signature: IVANOV

Agreed
   Signature: BELOZYOROV
   Section Chief, Second Department,
   Directorate K, FCD KGB USSR,
   Colonel BELOZYOROV

The document is then passed to the head of the second Department, Colonel Manannikov, who puts his signature after the words 'I approve' in the top left of the document, and adds the date. The file is now officially opened.

Next, the case officer, in this case Major P. S. Ivanov, visits the

Fifteenth (Archives) Department of the FCD, and hands over the completed 'Statement of Authorisation' to an official in the card index room. In return he is given two brown index cards, each measuring 12 × 9 cm. On one card he enters the subject of the file; on the other he writes the codename reflected for the file, in this case MANFRED. The second card has a box in the top right hand corner which contains the first three capital letters of the codename (MAN): a procedure which clearly distinguishes it from the first card which gives the real subject. The same basic data are on both cards: type of file (agent, agent cultivation, data file (usually on a target), working file, personal file, correspondence file, etc), the date on which the file was opened, the department responsible for it, and the name, position and office telephone number of the officer who opened it. An archives official then provides a number for the file (say 859674), enters it on the 'Statement of Authorisation', and hands the case officer a light blue loose-leaf binder on which he stamps the file number. The cover bears the following information:

Committee of State Security of the USSR
Agent Cultivation File

DAR* N859674 Volume 1 'MANFRED'

Opened: 15 Feb 1985 Closed:

Second Department, Directorate K, FCD KGB

The first page of the file becomes the Statement of Authorisation. Back in his office, Ivanov adds a number of forms to the loose-leaf folder. Typically, page 2 lists case officers concerned with the file; page 3 lists 'persons who are aware of the file', pages 4 to 10 consist of forms on which to list all those whose names appear in the file; pages 11 and 12 list payments to the target of cultivation; pages 13 to 18 list 'material held on file'. Documents which are subsequently added to the file are usually arranged in chronological order. When the file is 300 pages long, a new volume (in this instance DAR N859674, volume 2) is opened.

If MANFRED, the target of cultivation, is successfully recruited, two 'agent files' are normally opened on him: an operational file and a product file. The operational file contains all correspondence concerning the agent, case officers' reports on contacts with him, Centre documents analysing his work and making plans for him, the agent's receipt for sums paid to him and other material concerned with his running. If the agent is productive, his written and verbal reports, documents provided or copied by him, material from his sub-agents and other intelligence are filed in separate product files to avoid making the operational file too unwieldy.

* Russian acronym for 'Agent Cultivation File'.

All KGB illegals have several personal files, held by different departments of FCD Directorate S. The Third Department keeps a training file for each illegal; the geographical Department maintains an operational file; the Second Department maintains a file on the illegal's assumed identity and the bogus documentation required to support his 'legend' (cover story); the Financial Department keeps the file on the illegal's finances.

Other KGB officers have two personal files. The first, maintained by the FCD, Cadres Department, contains all documents dealing with his career inside the Soviet Union, medical and financial matters. When he serves abroad, his operational department keeps a file on him dealing exclusively with his work outside the Soviet Union.

The commonest FCD dossiers are the correspondence files with Residencies which are kept in the appropriate geographical department for about three years before being transferred to the archives. The most secret documents in each department are to be found in the 'Correspondence File of the Head of Department', kept by the head himself or by his deputy. Important papers on the running of each residency are similarly kept in an Organisational Correspondence File maintained by the head of the relevant geographical department (the Third in the case of Great Britain). All other documents on current matters are held in correspondence files run by the FCD officers responsible for them.

Before any file or volume of a multi-volume file is handed over to the archives a strict procedure is followed. An operational officer has to check the pagination and prepare an index (with page references) of all names mentioned in the file; beginning in the 1980s these names were also entered on computer. All pages in files transferred to the archives have holes punched in them and are then tagged together. Before the transfer, the bulk of each file is removed as far as possible – a process which traditionally involves cutting round brief notes with scissors and throwing the surplus blank paper away. Documents judged of no real importance are also removed, though in each case a record of the destruction or transfer is noted in the file. In addition to pages of varying size, files also commonly include enclosure envelopes containing, for example, personal letters from agents or rolls of film. Anthony Blunt's operational files, for example, contain a number of thank-you notes, still in their original envelopes, for the payments he was persuaded to accept three or four times a year during the Second World War. Once transferred to the archives, files are given archival numbers, beginning with the prefix ARCH., which are stamped on the front cover. The standard of file-keeping in the archives is very high. Temperature and humidity are carefully controlled.

By the early 1970s the quantity of files retained by the KGB was beginning to pose a storage problem. In 1972, however, the move of the

FCD out to Yasenevo, together with its records, created extra space in Dzerzhinsky Square. Despite the constant addition of more paper, further construction of new KGB office blocks in the city centre, all provided with extensive underground space, has kept pace with the demand. In addition to the main KGB archive, the FCD preserves its own archive at Yasenevo under the control of its Fifteenth Department.

The Archive Department at both the Centre and the FCD began slowly to photograph the old archives once the microfiche became available. Every year an exhortation is sent round all FCD departments emphasising the importance of photographing the most important papers from current files in order to ensure their survival in the event of war. The duplicates are transferred to a bunker – exact location not known, probably in Omsk (Western Siberia). Theoretically, this would enable the KGB to recreate its files after a nuclear Armageddon. Examining the current files and selecting papers for reproduction from the FCD's bulging cupboards and filing cabinets is immensely time-consuming for desk officers. The pages photographed are stamped as a record.

For many FCD officers the most frequent reason for consulting the archives either at Yasenevo or Dzerzhinsky Square is to trace an individual. The traditional method of beginning the trace is to fill in a form naming the individual concerned. In the case of a Westerner, the name has to be entered in both the Cyrillic and the Roman alphabet. A typical entry might read:

GRUBER, Ernst
son of GRUBER, Heinrich
born 15.10.1940 in Stettin, Germany
(now Szczecin, Poland)

The officer making the entry then has to enter the first three letters of the surname in both the Cyrillic and Roman forms in a box in the corner of the form. In the case of Gruber, he would complete the box thus:

Г	Р	У
G	R	U

Normally, the trace request is then signed by the head of section of the officer completing the form or by one of his deputies.

A non-urgent request for a trace during Gordievsky's career in the FCD normally took about three days. The reply from the archives takes one of two forms. Either the form is returned to the officer who completed it with the note on the reverse side: 'No traces in the archives'. Or, if traces exist, the references are given on the form; for example:

File N54357. Arch. 078341, volume 4,
pp. 75, 92–9, 134–6
File N63119, Arch. 084961, volume 8, pp. 108–12;
volume 9, pp. 31–3

By the mid-1980s trace references like these, originally kept in a huge card index, had been transferred to computer. But delays in responding to trace requests continued.

After handing in the form with the list of trace references, the requisitioning FCD officer is provided with an order giving him access to the Archives Reading Room. Reading Second Chief (Counter-Intelligence) Directorate and other non-FCD files necessitates a trip to the main KGB archives at the Centre. Junior officers welcome such outings since they give them the opportunity to spend the rest of the day in central Moscow. Second Chief Directorate officers, however, do not normally come to Yasenevo to consult FCD files. On occasion, FCD files are sent to them.

Occasionally an individual file may carry a note restricting access to it, for example: 'To be read only with the permission of head of Eighth Department, Second Chief Directorate'. In such a case, the FCD officer would visit the head of the appropriate section in the Second Chief Directorate. The latter might make a check with his superiors by telephone before clearing the file. Strictly speaking, the requisitioning officer is required only to identify himself as, for example, an operational officer of the Third Department at the First Chief Directorate. Only the most mistrustful Second Chief Directorate officer would telephone the Third Department to make sure that the requisitioning officer was who he said he was, and that his request to see Second Chief Directorate papers was connected with official business.

An index is maintained inside the cover of each file to record the identity of each reader of the file, the date of consultation, and with whose permission. The numbers of the pages supposedly read are also recorded. In practice, this does not prevent an officer from reading the entire file if he wishes to do so. He may also make notes on it in his official notebook.

A further important source of documents on KGB foreign operations is the FCD Memory Room which commemorates the FCD's main heroes and achievements. In 1979–80 Gordievsky was responsible for preparing an in-house history of operations in the countries of the Third Department (Britain, Ireland, Scandinavia, Australasia and Malta) to celebrate the sixtieth anniversary of the FCD. His sources included a number of important files in the research section attached to the Memory Room, then headed by Georgi Aleksandrovich Sokolov, previously a section chief in Directorate S. Among these files were short histories of the main residencies written by some of their senior officers for the fiftieth anniversary of the FCD ten years earlier. There were also a number of documents on the Cambridge Five, including a summary of the career of John Cairncross, the last of the Five to be publicly identified.

Appendix B

Residency Records and Communications with the Centre

For security reasons, Residencies, unlike the Centre, keep no classified files or archives. Their records consist solely of notes made by individual KGB officers in their official 'working notebooks' (*rabochaya tetrad*) and of a few key documents retained by senior officers for limited periods. At the end of the working day each officer stores his notebooks and papers in a working satchel (*papka*) slightly larger than a briefcase, applies a piece of plasticine to the end of the zip, and presses on it his own individual seal, usually kept on his key ring. The satchel is then placed in the Residency safe until the next working day begins at 8.30 a.m.

When a telegram arrives from the Centre, a KGB cipher clerk deciphers it and takes it to the Resident who writes on it the pseudonyms of those officers to whom it is to be shown. (Gordievsky's pseudonym was 'Gornov'). Occasionally the Resident orders a telegram to be read by all officers of the Line concerned. The cipher clerk then takes the telegram from officer to officer, allowing each only a limited time to digest its contents. In theory, only the head of each Residency Line is allowed to take notes on its contents in a special 'telegram notebook' which he keeps in his satchel. In practice, during Gordievsky's career in the KGB, notes were also taken by PR Line officers. KR Line officers were more likely to stick to the rules.

A page from the official KGB notebook in which Oleg Gordievsky took notes, of varying length, on telegrams from the Centre received by the London Residency.

Correspondence from the Centre arrives by diplomatic bag on 35 mm. film, and is read on a microfilm reader. Residencies sometimes print out paper copies of incoming despatches and write instructions on them. Both film and photocopies are normally destroyed after two or three months, and certificates of destruction forward to the Centre. There are periodic security inspections at Residencies by teams from the KGB Eighth Chief Directorate (Ciphers and Communications). In an emergency Referentura staff are supposed to be able to burn all classified documents within forty minutes. They are supplied with oxygen cylinders and special containers designed for rapid combustion.

Residencies send their own communications to the Centre by telegram and 35 mm. film in diplomatic bags. There are regular complaints from the Centre at the excessive use of telegrams and poor drafting by Residencies.

vz-2   Top Secret
No 10/1ss   Copy No 1
6 January 1977

To: Residents
and Heads of Representations

Measures to Improve the Regulation of Cipher Traffic

The results of the analysis which has been conducted on the cipher traffic between Residencies and Representations with the Centre during recent times bears witness to the extent of very real infringements of the established regulations. In many cases the communications of the Residencies and representations about various questions have been transmitted by cipher whereas, without prejudicing the matter in hand, they could have been sent by bag. This leads to an unjustifiable increase in the volume of cipher traffic and an overloading of the cipher service apparatus, causing delays in the processing of the cipher telegrams.

This situation has also not been helped by the insufficiently high quality of telegram drafting in Residencies and Representations (verbosity, the inclusion of inessential detail, the distortion of names and other inexactitudes). For this reason many cipher telegrams containing intelligence have to undergo a thorough revision and re-drafting before they can be sent to the authorities [Instantsiya] and interested departments, all of which stretches the time before they reach addressees. The inclusion in one telegram of intelligence about different subjects produces the same results.

The transmission of the most urgent intelligence is also held up by the unwarranted use by Residencies and Representations of the telegraphic precedences URGENT and EXTRAORDINARY inasmuch as in the Centre a large number of telegrams with these precedences can build up awaiting decoding; amongst these are some which are really urgent and whose decoding will not brook delay.

In connection with the above, it is proposed that you should:–

1. Not allow the use of cipher traffic for sending intelligence to the Centre which could just as well come by bag.

2. Ensure the high quality of the drafting of the telegrams so as to reduce to the minimum the time needed for their processing in the Centre and onward transmission to addressees.

3. Check that, unless there are strong grounds, information on different subjects or relating to the competence of different sub-sections should not be included in one and the same telegram.

4. Be guided by the following in deciding telegraphic precedences:–

    a. the precedence 'EXTRAORDINARY' [*vnyeocheryednaya*] may be used as a rule in the following cases:–

       – on receipt of information about an impending military attack against the territory of the USSR or about a serious provocation against the Soviet Union or its leaders.

       – on receipt of important information connected with top level visits to the USSR or of trips of Soviet Party or Government delegations abroad, when there is only a limited amount of time available before the start of a meeting or negotiations.

       – attacks on the Soviet Embassy or another Soviet establishment abroad;

       – major natural catastrophes endangering the security of Soviet citizens or affecting the stability of circumstances in a country with serious repercussions for the interests of the USSR;

       – crisis situations (a change of regime by revolutionary means or a coup d'état or an outbreak of armed conflict) in a particular country, if it may have a vital effect on the interests of the USSR.

       – threats of arrest or detainment of a case officer, illegal or agent;

       – the disappearance of a holder of secret information from among Soviet citizens.

       – other exceptional circumstances depending on the discretion of the Resident or Representative.

b. The precedence 'URGENT' [*srochnaya*] is used to communicate by cipher information on the following subjects:-

– military action between states or the presence of unmistakable signs of preparations for war;

– the preparation or carrying out of terrorist acts against states or political leaders friendly towards the USSR or acts against the major states;

– the contents of conversations of Soviet representatives with leaders of foreign states, of major political parties, of Parliaments and also with the organs of state security on questions of cooperation with the USSR;

– assessments of major political campaigns linked with the elections of heads of state or with the renewal of Parliaments in the world's leading countries.

– operational measures the fulfilment of which carry deadlines;

– transit arrangements for the special contingent [illegals], meetings and DLB operations with illegals.

– other important and urgent matters.

ALYOSHIN
[KRYUCHKOV]

T HE major problems, however, lay at the Centre. The sheer quantity and complexity of KGB regulations designed to protect the security of its records and communications are partly self-defeating.[1] Residencies are required to fill in too many forms, to obey too many instructions and to follow too many bureaucratic procedures. As a result they tend to take short cuts, some of which have helped to make this volume possible.

Notes

Unless otherwise indicated, the source of information about the KGB in the Introduction and commentary on the documents is Oleg Gordievsky.

Abbreviations used in the Notes:

KGB Christopher Andrew and Oleg Gordievsky, *KGB: The Inside Story of Its Foreign Operations from Lenin to Gorbachev* (London: Hodder & Stoughton, 1990)

SWB BBC, Summary of World Broadcasts

Introduction, pp. xiii–xiv

1. *Sovetskaya Molodezh*, 27 Feb. 1991. US Foreign Broadcast Information Service, FBIS-SOV-91-054, 20 March 1991.
2. 'Who's Who', 10 Aug. 1990, *SWB*, SU/0842, B/1, 14 Aug. 1990.
3. Interview in *New Times*, 1989, no. 32.
4. Gordievsky.
5. *SWB*, SU/0496, B/2, 30 June 1989.
6. *Izvestia*, 9 Feb. 1991.
7. Gordievsky.
8. *Izvestia*, 9 Feb. 1991.
9. ibid.
10. Gordievsky.

1 The KGB's Global Priorities, pp. 1–16

1. *KGB*, pp. 387, 423–4.
2. See below, chapter 4.
3. See below, chapter 9.
4. See below, pp. 40–8.
5. On S & T collection see *KGB*, pp. 521–3; Philip Hanson, *Soviet Industrial Espionage: Some New Information* (London: R11A, 1987).
6. See below, chapters 5, 6.
7. Arkady N. Shevchenko, *Breaking with Moscow* (New York: Ballantine Books, 1985), p. 138.
8. B. N. Ponomarev, *Selected Speeches and Writings* (Oxford: Pergamon Press, 1981), pp. 353, 367.

9. Shevchenko, *Breaking with Moscow*, p. 292.
10. Ponomarev, *Selected Speeches and Writings*, pp. 352–68 (quotation from p. 364).
11. See below, chapter 2.

2 Agent Recruitment, pp. 23–49

1. See above, p. 21.
2. *KGB*, pp. 437–43.
3. *KGB*, pp. 475–8.
4. *KGB*, pp. 363, 375–6, 511.

3 Illegals, pp. 52–64

1. *KGB*, pp. 156–60.
2. Louise Bernikov, *Abel* (New York: Ballantine Books, 1982), ch. 2.
3. Notes by Valeri Agranovsky on interviews with Molody, published in *Znamya*, September 1988.
4. *KGB*, p. 413.
5. See below, chapter 9.
6. Friedrich Thelen, 'Post-Cold War Spies: Cloak and Stagger?', *European Affairs*, April–May 1991.

4 Operation RYAN, pp. 67–81

1. For a more detailed analysis of RYAN, see *KGB*, pp. 487–507.
2. Maclean gave a copy of the memorandum to George Blake. George Blake, *No Other Choice* (London: Jonathan Cape, 1990), pp. 269–70.
3. Michael MccGwire, *Perestroika and Soviet National Security* (Washington: Brookings Institution, 1991), p. 115.
4. ibid. p. 116; *Pravda*, 17 June 1983.

5 The 'Main Adversary': The United States, pp. 91–102

1. See above, p. 10
2. Vadimov [Kirpichenko] to London Residency, tel. no. 5101/R, 22 Jan. 1983 (noted by Gordievsky), and subsequent active measures telegrams to London.
3. The text of the forgery appears in *Soviet Active Measures. Hearings before the Permanent Select Committee on Intelligence, House of Representatives. Ninety-Seventh Congress, Second Session, July 13, 14, 1982* (Washington: US Government Printing Office, 1982), pp. 95–7.
4. ibid.
5. See above, p. 10.

6. Alekseev [Grushko] to London Residency, tel. no. 56460/A, 9 Sept. 1982 (noted by Gordievsky).
7. See above, p. 10.
8. Silin [Titov] to London Residency, tel. no. 56047/A, 1982 (noted by Gordievsky).
9. Silin [Titov] to London Residency, tel. no. 56432/A, 7 Sept. 1982 (noted by Gordievsky).
10. Silin [Titov] to London Residency, tel. no. 56685/A, 12 Oct. 1982 (noted by Gordievsky).
11. *KGB*, pp. 529–30.

6 *The Main Ally of the 'Main Adversary': The United Kingdom, pp. 137, 138*

1. Centre to London Residency, tel. no. 56597/A, 29 Sept. 1982.
2. Silin [Titov] to London Residency, no. 57186/A, 20 Dec. 1982.

7 *The European Community, pp. 142–61*

1. Cited in subsequent directives on the EEC, no. 1666, 8 July 1976. See below, p. 146.
2. Hugh Arbuthnot and Geoffrey Edwards (eds), *A Common Man's Guide to the Common Market* (London: Macmillan, 1979), p. 169. We are grateful to Dr Edwards for further information.
3. See below, chapter 9.

8 *The Socialist International, pp. 171–83*

1. *World Marxist Review*, 1976, no. 5.
2. *Kommunist*, November 1976.
3. 'The Socialist International', background brief by the Socialist International Secretariat, April 1991.
4. Nikolai Sibilev, *The Socialist International* (Moscow: Progress Publishers, 1984), p. 272. Progress Publishers' foreign editions were selected in consultation with the ID.
5. ibid. p. 133.
6. Ponomarev, *Selected Speeches and Writings*, pp. 268–86.
7. Sibilev, *Socialist International*, p. 251.
8. ibid. pp. 139–40.
9. Pasok (the Panhellenic Socialist Movement), then a consultative member of the Socialist International, later became a full member.
10. Centre to London Residency, tel. no. 1144/A, 22 Feb. 1983; Silin [Titov] to London Residency, tel. no. 59239/A, 30 March 1983; Silin [Titov] to London Residency, tel. no. 60100/A, 13 July 1983. Gordievsky noted all three telegrams.

11. Cf above, p. 129.

9 *China, pp. 184–207*

1. *USSR – China in a Changing World: Soviet Sinologists on the History and Prospects of Soviet–Chinese Relations* (Moscow: Novosti, 1989), p. 74.
2. See above, p. 20.

10 *New Thinking? pp. 212–21*

1. Interview with Valentin Falin by Christopher Andrew, Moscow, 12 Dec. 1990.
2. *Izvestia*, 27 Oct. 1989.
3. *SWB*, SU/0496, B/1, 30 June 1989.
4. Richard Popplewell, 'Themes in the Rhetoric of KGB Chairmen from Andropov to Kryuchkov', *Intelligence and National Security*, vol. VI (1991), no. 3.
5. 'Miss KGB and the Images of the Past', *Washington Post*, 31 Oct. 1990.
6. *KGB*, pp. 533–4.
7. *SWB*, SU/0894, A1/3, 13 Oct. 1990.
8. *New Times*, 1989, no. 52.
9. *SWB*, SU/0955, C4/3ff, 24 Dec. 1990.
10. *SWB*, SU/0946, B/1, 13 Dec. 1990.
11. ibid. cf. above, pp. 102–6.
12. *Independent*, 13 Feb. 1991. Grushko interview on BBC2 'Newsnight'.
13. An abridged version of the speech was published in *Sovetskaya Rossia* on 27 June 1991, and subsequently circulated by Novosti Press Agency.

Appendix B Residency Records and Communications with the Centre, p. 233

1. cf. the comments by Mikhail Lyubimov, formerly the KGB's main British expert, in *Literaturnaya Gazeta*, 29 May 1991.